Problems of Old Testament Theology
in the Twentieth Century

Henning Graf Reventlow

Problems of
Old Testament Theology
in the
Twentieth Century

SCM PRESS LTD

Translated by John Bowden from the German
Hauptprobleme der alttestamentlichen Theologie im 20.
Jahrhundert,
Erträge der Forschung 173,
published by Wissenschaftliche Buchgesellschaft, Darmstadt 1982.

British Library Cataloguing-in-Publication Data available

334 02232 0
First published 1985
by SCM Press Ltd
26-30 Tottenham Road, London N1

Phototypeset by Input Typesetting Ltd
and printed in Great Britain by
Richard Clay (The Chaucer Press) Ltd
Bungay, Suffolk

Contents

Preface

What is the theological significance of the Old Testament? The question is one of immense complexity. Building on the results of Old Testament exegesis and introductory studies, the history of Israel and the history of religion generally, which have become increasingly complicated in their methods and approaches, 'Old Testament theology', the discipline concerned with the question, has over recent decades become a field almost too vast to survey. This account seeks to outline the most important themes in the main lines of development of the discussion which has taken place above all since the end of the First World War. In this way I hope that it will help the reader to become oriented in this central area of Old Testament research. I have attached particular importance to bibliographical information, and it has been my concern to list as far as possible all the publications which have made a substantial contribution to a particular problem. However, I have discussed only works which have been accessible to me. I am grateful to Drs Nijendijk of Utrecht for procuring some Dutch studies, and a series of assistants, all of whom I cannot mention by name, have helped me to get hold of literature. In particular I am grateful to Bochum University library and its staff, who have arranged for me to have the loan of countless books from far away.

This work could never have been produced without the commitment of my assistants over the time when it was being prepared. I am particularly grateful to Dr Gudrun Müller and Frau Christine Engelsing, who have constantly kept working carefully over the typescript, and to Frau Ute Portmann, who produced it so conscientiously. I am grateful to Dr John Bowden for his congenial translation and to my assistant Friedbert Fellert for his careful reading of the proofs.

For the sequel to this book, see the postscript.

Abbreviations

AELKZ	*Allgemeine evangelisch-lutherische Kirchenzeitung*
AnBib	Analecta biblica
Antic	*Anticipation*
Anton	*Antonianum*
ASTI	*Annual of the Swedish Theological Institute*
AT	*Année théologique*
ATANT	Abhandlungen zur Theologie des Alten und Neuen Testaments
ATD	Das Alte Testament Deutsch
ATR	*Anglican Theological Review*
AUSS	*Andrews University Seminary Studies*
AVTRW	Aufsätze und Vorträge zur Theologie und Religionswissenschaft
AzT	Arbeiten zur Theologie
BA	*Biblical Archaeologist*
BBB	Bonner biblische Beiträge
Beitr.päd.Arb.	Beiträge pädagogischer Arbeit
BETL	Bibliotheca Ephemeridum Theologicarum Lovaniensium
BEvTh	Beiträge zur evangelischen Theologie
BFCT	Beiträge zur Förderung christlicher Theologie
BHT	Beiträge zur historischen Theologie
BiBe	Biblische Beiträge
BibOr	*Biblica et Orientalia*
BiKi	*Bibel und Kirche*
BiLe	*Bibel und Leben*
BiLi	*Bibel und Liturgie*
BiOr	Bibliotheca Orientalis
BiTod	*Bible Today*
BJRL	*Bulletin of the John Rylands Library*
BK	Biblischer Kommentar

Bl.	*Blackfriars*
BPTF	Bijdragen van de philosophische en theologische faculteiten der nederlandsche Jezuiten
BR	*Biblical Research*
BS	Bibliotheca sacra
BTB	Bibliotheque de théologie. 3. Théologie biblique
BThSt	Biblisch-theologische Studien
BWANT	Beiträge zur Wissenschaft vom Alten und Neuen Testament
BZ	*Biblische Zeitschrift*
BZAW	Beihefte zur Zeitschrift für die alttestamentliche Wissenschaft
Cath (M)	*Catholica*
CB.OT	Coniectanea biblica – Old Testament series
CBQ	*Catholic Biblical Quarterly*
CBQ.MS	Catholic Biblical Quarterly. Monograph series
CFl	Concilium Florentinum
CJT	*Canadian Journal of Theology*
CMech	Collectanea Mechliniensia
Conc	*Concilium*
Cont	*Continuum*
CQR	*Church Quarterly Review*
CThM	*Calwer theologische Monographien*
CTM	*Concordia Theological Monthly*
CuW	*Christentum und Wissenschaft*
CW	*Christliche Welt*
DB.S	*Dictionnaire de la Bible. Supplément*
DE	*Deutsch-evangelische Monatsblätter für den gesamten deutschen Protestantismus*
DtPfrBl	*Deutsches Pfarrerblatt*
DT	*Deutsche Theologie*
DTT	*Dansk theologisk tidsskrift*
dtv	Deutscher Taschenbuchverlag
EHS.T	Europäische Hochschulschriften. Reihe 23: Theologie
EK	Evangelische Kommentare
ELKZ	*Evangelisch-lutherische Kirchenzeitung*
epd	*Evangelische Pressedienst*
ER	*Ecumenical Review*
ErJb	*Eranos-Jahrbuch*
ET	English translation

ETL	*Ephemerides Theologicae Lovanienses*
ETR	*Études théologiques et religieuses*
EvErz	*Evangelische Erziehung*
EvQ	*Evangelical Quarterly*
EvTh	*Evangelische Theologie*
ExBib	*Exempla biblica*
ExpT	*Expository Times*
FGLP	Forschungen zur Geschichte und Lehre des Protestantismus
FRLANT	Forschungen zur Religion und Literatur des Alten und Neuen Testaments
FUI	*Friede über Israel*
FV	*Foi et vie*
GBT	Ghana Bulletin of Theology
GS	Gesammelte Studien
GTB	Gütersloher Taschenbücher
GTT	*Gereformeerd theologisch tijdschrift*
GuV	R.Bultmann, *Glauben und Verstehen*
HAT	Handbuch zum Alten Testament
HBT	Horizons in Biblical Theology
HeB	*Homiletica et biblica*
HK	Handkommentar zum Alten Testament
HNT	Handbuch zum Neuen Testament
HO	Handbuch der Orientalistik
HTh Suppl	*History and Theory.* Supplement
HTR	*Harvard Theological Review*
HTTL	*Herders theologisches Taschenlexikon*
HUCA	*Hebrew Union College Annual*
HWDA	*Handwörterbuch des deutschen Aberglaubens*
HWP	*Historisches Wörterbuch der Philosophie*
IDB	Interpreter's Dictionary of the Bible
IEJ	*Israel Exploration Journal*
Imm	*Immanuel*
Int	*Interpretation*
IRM	*International Review of Missions*
JAAR	*Journal of the American Academy of Religion*
JBC	*Jerome Biblical Commentary*
JBL	*Journal of Biblical Literature*
JBR	*Journal of Bible and Religion*
JR	*Journal of Religion*
JSOT	*Journal for the Study of the Old Testament*

JSS	*Journal of Semitic Studies*
JTS	*Journal of Theological Studies*
KatBl	*Katechetische Blätter*
KBRS	*Kirchenblatt für die reformierte Schweiz*
KD/CD	Karl Barth, *Kirchliche Dogmatik/Church Dogmatics*
KeTh	*Kerk en theologie*
KiZ	*Kirche in der Zeit*
KKTS	*Konfessionskundliche und kontrovers-theologische Studien*
KS	Kleine Schriften
KuD	*Kerygma und Dogma*
KuM	*Kerygma und Mythos*
LM	*Lutherische Monatshefte*
LQHR	*London Quarterly and Holborn Review*
MKP	*Monatsschrift für kirchliche Praxis*
MPT	Monatsschrift für Pastoraltheologie
MySal	*Mysterium Salutis*
NedThT	*Nederlands(ch)e theologisch tijdschrift*
NF	Neue Folge
NGTT	*Nederduitse gereformeerde teologiese tydskrif*
NKZ	*Neue Kirchliche Zeitschrift*
NRF	*Nouvelle revue française*
NRT	*Nouvelle revue théologique*
NS	New Series
NT	New Testament
NThT	*Nieuw theologisch tijdschrift*
NTS	*New Testament Studies*
NTT	*Norsk Teologisk Tidsskrift*
NV	*Nova et Vetera*
NZST	*Neue Zeitschrift für systematische Theologie*
ÖF.S	Ökumenische Forschungen – Soteriologische Abteilung
Or	*Orientalia*
Orient	*Orientierung*
OS	Oudtestamentische studien
OT	Old Testament
OTL	Old Testament Library
PBl	Pastoralblätter für Homiletik, Katechetik und Seelsorge
PBL	Praktisches Bibellexikon

PEQ	Palestine Exploration Quarterly
Prot.	*Protestantesimo*
PRS	Perspectives in Religious Studies
PSB	*Princeton Seminary Bulletin*
PT	Pastoraltheologie
RB	*Revue Biblique*
RCI	*Rivista del clero italiano*
RelLife	*Religion in Life*
REvBib	*Revista Biblica*
RExp	*Review and Expositor*
RGG	*Die Religion in Geschichte und Gegenwart*
RHPR	*Revue d'histoire et de philosophie religieuses*
RivBib	*Rivista biblica*
RSPT	*Revue des sciences philosophiques et théologiques*
RSR	*Recherches de science religieuse*
RThom	*Revue thomiste*
RTP	*Revue de théologie et de philosophie*
SacDot	*Sacra dottrina*
SacPag	*Sacra pagina*
Saec	*Saeculum*
SANT	Studien zum Alten und Neuen Testament
SBEsp	Semana biblica espanola
SBL.DS	Society of Biblical Literature. Dissertation Series
SBS	Stuttgarter Bibelstudien
SBT	Studies in Biblical Theology
SBW	Studien der Bibliothek Warburg
ScC	*Scuola cattolica*
ScEc	*Sciences ecclésiastiques*
ScEs	*Science et esprit*
Script	*Scriptorium*
SEÅ	Svensk exegetisk Årsbok
SelTeol	Selecciones de teologia
SFF	Studien zur Friedensforschung
SGV	Sammlung gemeinverständlicher Vorträge und Schriften
SJT	*Scottish Journal of Theology*
SKG.G	Schriften der Königsberger Gelehrten Gesellschaft – Geisteswissenschaftliche Klasse
SM	*Sacramentum Mundi*

SPAW.PH	Sitzungsberichte der preussischen Akademie der Wissenschaften – Philosophisch-historische Klasse
SPK	*Schriften zur Pädagogik und Katechetik*
StGen	*Studium generale*
StMiss	*Studia missionalia*
StTh	*Studia theologica*
STU	*Schweizerische theologische Umschau*
StZ	*Stimme der Zeit*
SVT	Supplements to Vetus Testamentum
SvTK	*Svensk teologisk Kvartalskrift*
TA	Theologische Arbeiten
TAik	Teologinen aikakauskirja
TB	Theologische Bücherei
TBT	Theologische Bibliothek Töpelmann
TD	Textus et documenta
TDNT	*Theological Dictionary of the New Testament*
TDOT	*Theological Dictionary of the Old Testament*
TEH	Theologische Existenz heute
TG	*Tijdschrift voor geschiedenis*
THAT	*Theologisches Handwörterbuch zum Alten Testament*, ed. E.Jenni and C.Westermann
ThBl	*Theologische Blätter*
ThD	*Theology Digest*
ThG	*Theologie der Gegenwart*
ThMil	*Theologia militans*
ThPh	*Theologie und Philosophie*
ThT	*Theologisch tijdschrift*
ThTh	*Themen der Theologie*
ThTo	*Theology Today*
TLZ	*Theologische Literaturzeitung*
TP	*Theologia practica*
TQS	*Theologische Quartalschrift*
TR	*Theologische Rundschau*
TRE	*Theologische Realenzyklopädie*
TS	Theologische Studien, ed.K.Barth et al.
TT	*Teologisk tidskrift*
TTh	*Tijdschrift voor theologie*
TTK	*Tidsskrift for teologi og kirke*
TTS	Trierer theologische Studien
TTZ	*Trierer Theologische Zeitschrift*

TWAT	*Theologisches Wörterbuch zum Alten Testament*
TWNT	*Theologisches Wörterbuch zum Neuen Testament*
TynB	*Tyndale Bulletin*
TZ	*Theologische Zeitschrift*
USQR	*Union Seminary Quarterly Review*
UTB	Uni-Taschenbücher
UUÅ	*Uppsala Universitets Årsskrift*
VBW	Vorträge der Bibliothek Warburg
VC	*Verbum Caro*
VD	*Verbum Domini*
VF	*Verkündigung und Forschung*
VT	Vetus Testamentum
WdF	Wege der Forschung
WSCFB	World Student Christian Federation Books
WiWei	*Wissenschaft und Weisheit*
WMANT	Wissenschaftliche Monographien zum Alten und Neuen Testament
WPKG	*Wissenschaft und Praxis in Kirche und Gesellschaft*
WTJ	*Westminster Theological Journal*
WuD	*Wort und Dienst*
WuT	*Wort und Tat*
WuW	*Wort und Wahrheit*
WZ	*Wissenschaftliche Zeitschrift*
WZ(J).GS	*Wissenschaftliche Zeitschrift der Friedrich-Schiller-Universität*, Jena, Gesellschafts- und sprachwissenschaftliche Reihe
ZAW	*Zeitschrift für die alttestamentliche Wissenschaft*
ZDMG	*Zeitschrift der deutschen morgenländischen Gesellschaft*
ZdZ	*Zeichen der Zeit*
ZKT	*Zeitschrift für katholische Theologie*
ZNW	*Zeitschrift für die neutestamentliche Wissenschaft*
ZPK	*Zeitschrift für Protestantismus und Kirche*
ZST	*Zeitschrift für systematische Theologie*
ZTK	*Zeitschrift für Theologie und Kirche*
ZWT	*Zeitschrift für wissenschaftliche Theologie*
ZZ	*Zwischen den Zeiten*

I

Earlier History and the New Beginning
after the First World War

Summary accounts:

Baker, D.L., *Two Testaments, One Bible*, Leicester 1976; Betz, O., 'Biblical Theology, History of', *IDB* 1, 432-7; Clements, R.E., *A Century of Old Testament Study*, Guildford and London ²1983, 144-71; Dentan, R.C., *Preface to Old Testament Theology*, New York (1950) ²1963; Dirksen, P.B., 'Die mogelijkheid van een theologie van het Oude Testament', *NedTT* 36, 1982, 279-90; Fritsch, C.T., 'Biblical Typology I: New Trends in Old Testament Theology', *BS* 103, 1946, 293-305; Goldingay, J., *Approaches to Old Testament Interpretation*, Leicester 1981; Grollenberg, L., 'Het "begleidend schrijven". Bij het debat over de zin van het Oude Testament', *TTh* 2, 1962, 316-49; Hahn, H.F., *The Old Testament in Modern Research*, Philadelphia and London (1954) ³1970, 226-49; Harrington, W., *The Path of Biblical Theology*, Dublin 1973; Hasel, G.F., *Old Testament Theology. Basic Issues in the Current Debate*, Grand Rapids (1972) ²1975; Hessler, R., '*De Theologiae Biblicae Veteris Testamenti Problemate*', *Anton* 25, 1950, 407-24; id., 'Zum theologischen Bemühen um das Alte Testament', *WiWei* 15, 1952, 33-50; Hulst, A.R., *Hoe moeten wij het Oude Testament uitlegen?*, Wageningen 1941; Jacob, E., 'La théologie de l'Ancien Testament. Etat présent et perspectives d'avenir', *ETL* 44, 1968, 420-32; Köhler, L. 'Alttestamentliche Theologie (Literaturbericht)', *TR* NF 7, 1935, 255-76; NF 8, 1936, 55-69, 247-84; Koole, J.L. 'Ontwikkelingen op het gebied van de oudtestamentische theologie', *GTT* 67, 1967, 18-26; Kraeling, E.G., *The Old Testament since the Reformation*, London 1955; Kraus, H.J., *Die biblische Theologie. Ihre Geschichte und Problematik*, Neukirchen 1970 (cf. also the review by O.Merk, *TR* NF 37, 1972, 80-8); id., *Geschichte der historisch-kritischen Erforschung des Alten Testaments*, Neukirchen (1956) ³1982; Martin-Achard, R., 'Les voies de la théologie de l'Ancien Testament', *RTP* 9, 1959, 217-26; Minissale, A., 'La "Teologia" dell'Antico Testamento', *RCI* 60, 1979, 179-86; Porteous, N.W., 'Old Testament Theology', in H.H.Rowley (ed.), *The Old Testament and Modern Study*, Oxford 1951, reprinted 1961, 311-45 (cf. also *LQHR* 184, 1959, 27-31); id., 'Towards a Theology of the Old Testament', *SJT* 1, 1948, 136-49 = id., *Living the Mystery*, Oxford 1967, 7-19; Preuss, H.D., *Das Alte Testament in Christlicher Predigt*, Stuttgart 1984; Rendtorff, R., 'I principali problemi di una teologia dell'Antico Testamento', *Prot.* 35, 1980, 193-206; Reventlow, H.Graf, 'Grundfragen der alttestamentlichen Theologie im Lichte der neueren deutschen Forschung', *TZ* 17, 1961, 81-98; id., 'Basic Problems in Old Testament Theology', *JSOT* 11, 1979, 2-22; Robinson, H.W., 'The Theology of the Old Testament', in H.W.Robinson (ed.), *Record and Revelation*, Oxford 1938, 303-48; Rost, L., 'Zur Theologie des Alten Testaments: Eine Übersicht', *CuW* 10, 1934, 121-4; Schmidt, Werner H., ' "Theologie des Alten Testaments" vor und nach Gerhard von Rad', *VuF* 17, 1972, 1-25; Smart, J.D., 'The Death and Rebirth of Old Testament Theology', *JR* 23, 1943, 1-11, 125-36 = id., *The Interpretation of Scripture*, Philadelphia 1961, 232ff.; Saebø, M., 'Hermeneutiske grunnsporsmål. Fra kampen om en evangelisk forstaelse av det Gamle Testamente', *TTK* 28, 1957, 18-30, 71-93; id., 'Hvem var Israels teologer? Om structureringen av "den gammeltestamentlige teologi"', *SEÅ* 41-42, 1976-7, 189-205 = *Ordene og Ordet*, Oslo 1979, 25-41; Soggin, A., 'Den gammaltestamentliga teologin efter G. von Rad', *SEÅ* 47, 1982, 7-20 = 'Teologia dell'Antico Testamento oggi. Dopo Gerhard von Rad', *Prot.* 39, 1984, 1-17; Würthwein, E., 'Zur Theologie des Alten Testaments', *TR* NF 36, 1971, 185-208; Zimmerli, W., 'Biblische Theologie. I. Altes Testament', *TRE* VI, 426-55.

1. The Beginnings

The beginnings of the history of Old Testament theology as a specific discipline in theology go back to the end of the eighteenth century. A 'biblical theology' had already begun to develop in the period of Lutheran orthodoxy and Reformed federal theology (Johannes

Cocceius) as an independent area of activity extending beyond the traditional role of the Bible in dogmatics, which had been the provision of proof texts (*dicta probantia*) for individual dogmatic precepts (cf. Kraus, *Biblische Theologie*, 17-24). In Pietism this was resolutely opposed to 'scholastic' dogmatics; Anton Friedrich Büsching presented an alternative programme to this in the form of a 'biblical theology' as a 'biblical-dogmatic' discipline (cf. G. Ebeling, 'The Meaning of Biblical Theology', *JTS* NS 6, 1956, 210-225 = *On the Authority of the Bible. Some Recent Studies by L. Hodgson... G. Ebeling...*, London 1960, 49-67, = *Word and Faith*, Philadelphia and London 1963, reissued 1984, 79-97) in his *Gedanken von der Beschaffenheit und dem Vorzug der biblisch-dogmatischen Theologie vor der alten und neuen scholastischen*, 1756 (cf. also id., *Dissertatio exhibens epitomen theologiae e solis litteris sacris concinnatae*, Lemgoviae 1757; the requirement itself occurs first in a funeral oration of 1669 for the Württemberg court preacher Christoph Zeller, who is said to have made it in a lecture in 1652). The system of a 'biblical dogmatics' arranged according to topics, though occasionally also already incorporating historical perspectives, is also retained in the works cited below representing a 'biblical theology' from the time of Pietism (cf. Kraus, *Biblische Theologie*, 24-51). Thus the whole period is as yet without a direct bearing on modern problems.

Modern scholarship is unanimous that 'biblical theology' as an independent discipline begins with Johann Philipp Gabler's famous 1787 Altdorf inaugural lecture *Oratio de justo discrimine theologiae biblicae et dogmaticae regundisque recte utriusque finibus* (Altdorfii 1787; reprinted in id., *Opuscula Academica II*, Ulmae 1831, 179-94; German translations in O. Merk, *Biblische Theologie in ihrer Anfangszeit*, Marburg 1972, 273-82, and in *Das Problem der Theologie des Neuen Testaments*, ed. G. Strecker (WdF 367), Darmstadt 1975, 32-44. There is an extract in W. G. Kümmel, *The New Testament. A History of the Interpretation of its Problems*, Nashville 1972 and London 1973, 98-100. For Gabler, in addition to Merk, op. cit., see also R. Smend, 'J. Ph. Gablers Begründung der Biblischen Theologie', *EvTh* 22, 1962, 345-57). At the same time Gabler also laid the foundation for the discussion of all the problems which still occupy the discipline to the present day.

Gabler was the first to define biblical theology as being in principle a historical discipline and in so doing differentiated it from dogma: '*Est vera theologia biblica e genere historica, tradens, quid scriptores sacri de rebus divinis senserint; theologia contra dogmatica e genere didactico, docens, quid theologus quisque... ratione super rebus divinis philosophetur.*' In distinguishing between the doctrinal views of the writers of sacred scripture and the rational 'philosophy' of contemporary dogmatic theologians, this formulation is redolent of the atmosphere of the Enlightenment; its sole concern is with universal truths, so that 'biblical theology remained a preparation for dogmatics' (R.Smend Sr, *Lehrbuch der alttestamentlichen Religionsgeschichte*, Freiburg im Breisgau [1893], ²1899, 3). Nevertheless it contains the principle of a division of history into periods and thus the nucleus of the idea of development (for which Hume laid the foundations). In the nineteenth century this was to be the predominant way of presenting the themes (cf. Kraus, *Biblische Theologie*, 52-6). The subsequent history of the discipline was to be governed essentially by the juxtaposition and contrast of the two principles of a historical and a systematic discipline; this already presents us with the one great axis around which the whole complex of problems revolves.

This historical perspective very soon led to the separation of the theology of the Old Testament and the theology of the New Testament into two subsidiary disciplines.

> This first came about under the common denominator of a biblical theology: Georg Lorenz Bauer, *Biblische Theologie des Alten und Neuen Testaments*, Leipzig 1796-1802; W.M.L. de Wette, *Biblische Dogmatik des Alten und Neuen Testaments*, Berlin ³1831 (for Bauer cf. Merk, op.cit.; for de Wette, R.Smend, *Wilhelm Martin Leberecht de Wettes Arbeit am Alten und am Neuen Testament*, Basle 1958, esp. 73ff.), and most recently Daniel von Cölln, *Biblische Theologie*, posthumously published Leipzig 1836, but with the two Testaments discussed separately, in succession, and then soon in the form of separate works on a *Theology of the Old (or New) Testament*.

An even more significant sign was that the idea of development became increasingly influential during the course of the nineteenth century. Already von Cölln produced a work in which, in the view of E.Riehm (*Alttestamentliche Theologie*, Halle 1889, 17) 'there is the first significant attempt at a really historical and genetic account of the development of the history of the religion of the Old Testament.' Riehm himself defined the methodological aim of his account in the following terms (proving to be typical of the view dominant in the first half of the nineteenth century): '1. The nearest and most direct object of the investigation is not the revelation of God itself but the religion of the Old Testament... 2. The investigation and presentation must be historical and genetic' (op.cit., 8f.). There is a similar definition in the work of G.F.Oehler (*Theologie des Alten Testaments*, Stuttgart [I, 1873; II, 1874] ²1882, 7 [³1891; cf. already id., *Prolegomena zur Theologie des Alten Testaments*, Stuttgart 1845]), essentially one of a conservative group of scholars: 'The theology of the Old Testament, the first main division of biblical theology, is the historical and genetic account of the religion which is contained in the canonical writings of the Old Testament.' Although here there is still a faint reminiscence of the former unity of biblical theology, in reality it has long since fallen to pieces.

Although in many cases it was maintained down to the twentieth century, the traditional designation of such works as *Theology of the Old Testament* (cf. B.Stade, *Biblische Theologie des Alten Testaments* I, Tübingen 1905; II, ed. A.Bertholet, Tübingen 1911; E.Kautzsch, *Biblische Theologie des Alten Testaments*, Tübingen 1911) had long been superseded in terms of content; what they provided was in fact simply an account of Israelite and Judaean religion in the various successive stages of its development. In the case of Stade this became immediately clear from the sub-titles of the individual volumes: I, *Die Religion Israels und die Entstehung des Judentums*; II, *Die jüdische Religion von der Zeit Esras bis zum Zeitalter Christi* (The Religion of Israel and the Origin of Judaism; The Jewish Religion from the Time of Ezra to the Age of Christ). It was therefore only logical that K.Marti should also change the title of the new edition of the work by A. Kayser (*Die Theologie des Alten Testaments in ihrer geschichtlichen Entwicklung dargestellt*, Strassburg 1886, ²1892), for which he had taken over responsibility, from the third edition on (*Geschichte der israelitischen Religion*, 5. Auflage von August Kaysers *Theologie des Alten Testaments*, Strassburg 1907).

The shift in the theme from biblical (Old Testament) theology to the history of Israelite and Judaean religion had already been intimated in the first half of the nineteenth century. In addition to von Cölln, mention should be made here of Wilhelm Vatke (*Die biblische Theologie wissenschaftlich dargestellt*. I: *Die Religion des Alten Testaments*, Berlin 1835 [cf. L.Perlitt, *Vatke und Wellhausen*, BZAW 94, Berlin 1965; Kraus, *Biblische Theologie*, 93-6]) and Bruno Bauer (*Die Religion des Alten Testaments*, I, II, Bremen

1838/39), both of whom were influenced by the philosophy of Hegel. However, this influence was to disappear in the following period. Other outlines with an orientation on the history of ideas, like those of Ewald's pupils F.Hitzig (*Vorlesungen über biblische Theologie und messianische Weissagungen des Alten Testaments*, ed. J.J.Kneucker, Karlsruhe 1880) and A.Dillmann (*Handbuch der alttestamentlichen Theologie*, ed. R.Kittel, Leipzig 1895), were not to have a future. Future developments were characterized rather by a move from any conscious philosophy of history in the name of historical positivism and evolutionism. Works of this kind are: A.Kuenen, *De godsdienst van Israel*, Haarlem 1869f.; J.Wellhausen, *Prolegomena zur Geschichte Israels*, Berlin ⁵1905, which originally appeared under the title *Geschichte Israels* I, Berlin 1878 = ET *Prolegomena to the History of Ancient Israel*, Edinburgh 1885, reissued Cleveland, Ohio 1957; and K.Budde, *Die Religion des Volkes Israel bis zur Verbannung*, Giessen ³1912. In his much noted lecture 'Über die Aufgaben der biblischen Theologie des Alten Testaments' (*ZTK* 3, 1893, 31-51 = id., *Akademische Reden und Abhandlungen*, Giessen 1907, 77-96), B.Stade, an ally of J.Wellhausen, describes the working programme of the discipline as being purely historical, and attacks any relationship with dogmatics of the kind that he has to criticize in the work e.g. of Oehler. The influence of the Graf-Kuenen-Wellhausen school and its view of the stages of development in Israelite and Jewish religion reached its climax about the turn of the century and could be seen in the structure of the works by Stade and Kautzsch as also in Hermann Schultz, *Alttestamentliche Theologie* (Brunswick ⁵1896 = ET Edinburgh 1892) – a well-known work at that time – which only gradually adopted Wellhausen's view. However, with his theological interests (shaped by A.Ritschl), Schultz occupies a special position (cf. also Kraus, *Biblische Theologie*, 114-8). R.Smend Sr wrote a *Lehrbuch der alttestamentlichen Religionsgeschichte* (above 4) from the perspective of the Wellhausen school and thus brought this development to a provisional conclusion. (R.Kittel also wrote on *Die Religion des Volkes Israel*, Leipzig 1921 = ET *The Religion of the People of Israel*, New York 1925; G.Hölscher, *Geschichte der israelitischen und jüdischen Religion*, Giessen 1922, is a late phenomenon.)

However; the real conversation partner in the discussion within the movement for an Old Testament theology which revived after the First World War was not Wellhausen and his school but the so-called 'history-of-religions school', which in the case of the Old

Testament is connected particularly with the name of H.Gunkel (cf. J.Hempel, 'Religionsgeschichtliche Schule', *RGG*[3] V, 991-4 [and bibliography] and more recently H.Paulsen, 'Traditionsgeschichtliche Methode und religionsgeschichtliche Schule', *ZTK* 75, 1978, 20-55, who stresses above all the lack of clarity in its method).

For Gunkel see W.Baumgartner, 'Zum 100. Geburtstag von Hermann Gunkel', *Congress Volume Bonn 1962*, SVT IX, Leiden 1963, 1-18; K. von Rabenau, 'Hermann Gunkel', in *Tendenzen der Theologie im 20.Jahrhundert*, ed. H.-J.Schultz, Stuttgart/Berlin/Olten/Freiburg im Breisgau 1966, 80-7; W.Klatt, 'Die Eigentümlichkeit der israelitischen Religion in der Sicht von Hermann Gunkel', *EvTh* 28, 1968, 153-60; id., *Hermann Gunkel*, FRLANT 100, Göttingen 1969; F.Bovon, 'Hermann Gunkel, historien de la religion et exégète des genres littéraires, in id. (ed.), *Exegesis*, Neuchâtel 1975, 86-97; H.P.Müller, 'Hermann Gunkel (1862-1932)', in M.Greschat (ed.), *Theologen des Protestantismus im 19. und 20. Jahrhundert* I/II, Stuttgart 1978, 241-55; P.Gibert, *Une Théorie de la légende: Hermann Gunkel (1862-1932) et les légendes de la Bible*, Paris 1979; R.Smend, 'Hermann Gunkel', in H.G.Gundel et al.(eds.), *Giessener Gelehrte in der ersten Hälfte des 20. Jahrhunderts*, Marburg 1982, 345-56.

For this school, the decisive factor, alongside the results of literary criticism and the idea of development, was the influence of Herder.

Gunkel's concern can be seen most clearly from his article 'Ziele und Methoden der Erklärung des Alten Testaments' (*MKP* 4, 1904, 521-40 = id., *Reden und Aufsätze*, Göttingen 1913, 11-29, from which I quote). Gunkel (following Schleiermacher, though he does not give his name) sees the essential aim of all exegesis as the understanding of the writer – not his words ('words are the means of expression of thoughts and feelings'), but in the last resort not even his thoughts or feelings either ('thoughts and feelings are the expression of the soul stirred to life'), but his personality. 'So the living person, in its willing and thinking, in the manifold nature of all its spiritual being, is the real object of all exegesis.' For: 'The soul of man, the mysterious inner life,... is what is really precious.'

Although Gunkel stresses that he and his friends are second to none in their estimation of exact sciences, for him, 'exegesis in the supreme sense is... more an art than a science'; exegetical labours must be accompanied by 'the power of vision, noble fantasy', or, as Gunkel can also say, the inspiration of the artist (quotations 12-15).

As with all literature, it is also true in the interpretation of the Bible that the commentator must have a quite personal relationship to the work. 'The commentator who seeks to comment on a religious book without at the same time being a religious man' would be like an unmusical historian of music, and it is certain 'that the one for whom religion is a phenomenon of only pathological interest will not be in any position to understand its history either' (16f.).

Nevertheless, Gunkel warns the interpreter of the Bible against supposing that 'he can shift his modern problems on to the text and expect an answer to our questions in it' (15). For the aim of scholarly exegesis is not edification but knowledge: '...thus scholarly exposition of the Bible, too, can only regard historical knowledge as its real aim.' It must be stressed 'that theological exegesis is concerned with the *knowledge* of religion and not with anything else' (25f.). To the neuromantics which stresses empathy and the nearness of the interpreter to his partner, the writer (cf. 13: 'so he presses himself on this alien life and tries to grasp it: reveal yourself, spirit, I implore you!'), is added historicism, which stresses the historical gap between them (E. Troeltsch was the systematic thinker of the history-of-religions school, cf. below).

That is true to a special degree of the Old Testament. Gunkel stresses that the faith of the Old Testament is by no means obviously our own: 'We feel akin to the prophets and the psalmists in piety but not exactly the same as them'(17). 'How many exegetical disputes are resolved, how many "concepts" or lines of thought in biblical theology become clear once we have seen the distinctive nature of Israel as a people, which is so different from ours'(20). In particular, ancient Israel was 'great in lively awareness but unpractised in logical thought' (ibid.). The distance in time and patterns of thought between the Old Testament and ourselves, together with the distance between the Old Testament and the New, prohibits us from using the Old Testament like the New as a source of Christian teaching: it is no longer possible to claim it for Christianity, as happens in traditional dogma. However, in this connection the decisive thing is that 'doctrine is not the heart and soul of religion, but piety...'(25). On the one hand, the understanding of scripture must be historical (25); on the other, the minister or teacher can expect from an Old Testament commentary 'the presentation of the religious content of the Old Testament in the full light of knowledge'(29).

Now for Gunkel, historical exegesis also means an explanation of the sources from their historical context (and in this he shares the views of his generation of scholars which was oriented on the history of religions). Therefore he finds important not only the comparison of the Old Testament with material from the ancient Near East, which by then was incomparably richer than that available to Wellhausen, but also the 'basic conviction... that the life of humanity is not a matter of whim and chance, but that eternal ordinances prevail in it'(25f.). However, the idea of development expressed here comes to a halt before an interpretation in terms of Christian faith; science and faith are areas which must methodologically be kept strictly apart.

As Gunkel himself bears witness ('Die Richtungen der alttesta-mentlichen Forschung', *CW* 36, 1922, [64-7] 66; also in Klatt, *Gunkel*, 26f.), the history-of-religions school nevertheless understood itself as 'a thoroughly theological movement' (cf. also H.Gunkel. 'Was will die religionsgeschichtliche Bewegung?', *DE* 5, 1914, 385-97). It was opposed both to a purely philological and historical biblical exegesis and to the sort of traditional dogmatic 'biblical theology', bound to the canon, which was still influential in the 1880s. Instead of this it sought to understand and present the biblical religion of the two Testaments in the historical context it shared with other religions. In this way Gunkel indirectly thought that he was also serving the interests of the church whose faithful son he felt himself to be (cf. Klatt, *Gunkel*, 28, and the quotation in n.48).

We also find that an explicit theology of experience in the first lecture of W.Robertson Smith's *The Old Testament in the Jewish Church*, Edinburgh (1881) ²1892, 1-20, which is clearly dependent on Schleiermacher's hermeneutics ('...the Bible is a book of Experimental Religion, in which the converse of God with His people is depicted in all its stages up to... the person of Jesus Christ'; it is our task to steep ourselves in the experience of the psalmists, prophets and apostles in whose hearts God makes himself known, 8), can be undergirded by a strong awareness that precisely at this point it is being faithful to the Reformation understanding of scripture, since according to Robertson Smith, for Luther the Bible was 'the record of God's words and deeds of love to the saints of old, and of the answer of their inmost heart to God' (9f.). The study of those parts of the Bible which are not edifying, but are of purely historical or archaeological interest, is also worthwhile in this connection, since it enables the reader 'to put [himself] in the position of the men to whose heart God first spoke'(13).

Gunkel's remarks set out many themes which were still to play a major role in subsequent discussion. It is important to recognize that the views of the history-of-religions school exercised a significant influence far beyond the circle of its immediate members, and even among those who regarded it critically. Not a few of its ideas, e.g. the great stress on personality, corresponded to the general cultural situation of the time (here one might recall the view of the prophets in B.Duhm and G.Hölscher), and in other respects it contributed towards shaping opinions.

The new beginnings which led to a revival of the theological task of Old Testament scholarship after the First World War started from exegetes who were not far removed from the history-of-religions school in their thought. The impetus towards this was provided by a lecture given by R. Kittel at a conference of Old Testament scholars preceding the First Conference of German Orientalists in Leipzig in 1921: 'Die Zukunft der Alttestamentlichen Wissenschaft' (*ZAW* 39, 1921, 84-99). Here, encouraged by the clear assent of his audience (cf. Marti, 'Die Tagung der alttestamentlichen Forscher in Leipzig am 19.Sept.1921', ibid., 111), he formulated the task of Old Testament scholarship which in his view had hitherto been neglected. It was a task which fell to the discipline 'in the context of the theological faculty'(95). However, Kittel did not describe this task as theology but as 'the working out of specifically *religious material* in Old Testament religion, i.e. that element in our discipline which is particularly closely related to theology' (ibid.). For him it is quite natural to think of Old Testament study as a branch of the study of religion. However, what he ultimately requires of the study of religion generally is that it should progress from being a mere description in terms of the history and psychology of religion so that it becomes 'a systematic account of the nature and essence of religion and its *truth*, i.e. in terms of the philosophy of religion or dogmatics. In the end of the day it must want to find the foundation of the mystery of its divine power. That alone is the true study of religion.' It then follows for Old Testament religion 'that it is the culmination of all the old religions' (96). The purity of the idea of God, God as moral will, the idea of personality and universalism are the characteristics which move Kittel not only to regard Old Testament religion as 'the flower of all the religions of antiquity' but to say of it that it has 'come so close to religion as such' that one must also assert 'its truth-content and its abiding value, for all the weaknesses in individual details' (97). This brings us further into 'the sphere of the systematic study of religion and the philosophy of religion' and must raise the question of the position of Old Testament religion within all religions in the overall plan of God's ordering of the world.

Kittel's language and thought-world are those of Idealism (see, similarly, F.C.Porter, 'Crucial Problems in Biblical Theology', *JR* 1, 1921, [78-81] 79, who presents his high estimation of the 'special character' of Old Testament religion in the question: 'The tendency towards the ethical, the inward, the spiritual – where did it start? How did it work?'). However, one can sense the concern to work through to a new evaluation of the Old Testament, even if it has not yet found adequate expression. The difference from Gunkel is only one of degree. However, Kittel's call proved to be a pioneering move towards the revival of theological reflection within Old Testament research, thanks to his personal reputation.

The contribution of W.Staerk ('Religionsgeschichte und Religionsphilosophie in ihrer Bedeutung für die biblische Theologie des Alten Testaments', *ZTK* NF 4, 1923, 289-300) keeps to the same idealistic categories. Referring back to F.Brunstäd (and behind him to Kant and Hegel) he calls for a transition from a historical and factual account of Old Testament religion to a consideration of its validity, which he describes as a phenomenological construction of its characteristics (289f.). As 'the fulfilment of the dawn in history of the intimation of the unconditioned-personal, the transcendent world which is the world within' (298), the spiritual and moral religion of personality founded by the prophetic personality of Moses (296f.) is 'a turning point in the history of religion' (296). By being incorporated into the regularity of history in terms of the Idealistic concept of purpose (here Staerk follows Kant), this can be demonstrated to be 'an expression of the *revelatio specialis* in the whole of the *revelatio generalis*' (299). According to Staerk that means 'assigning a place in systematic theology to the religion of the Old Testament' (289). From the perspective of this position the author (in contrast to Gabler) regards 'the biblical theology of the Old Testament as part of systematic theology; *this is what it was originally and this is what it must remain...*' (290, cf. 299f.).

However, Idealist philosophy was not to have a future; nor was nineteenth-century-style conservatism, which enjoyed an Indian summer in the work of E.König's old age (*Theologie des Alten Testaments*, Stuttgart 1923).

This work does not represent a new beginning; it is more of a curiosity (cf. Dentan, *Preface*, 63). In rejecting all spiritualistic interpretation and insisting on the grammatical historical method (15f.), König follows critical scholarship, but accuses the customary history-of-religions perspective of toning down the special character of Israelite religion (4) and gives an apologia for the reliability of the historical traditions of the Old Testament (6ff.).

C.Steuernagel's contribution to the Marti Festschrift (BZAW 41, Giessen 1925, 266-73), 'Alttestamentliche Theologie und alttesta-mentliche Religionsgeschichte', breathes a different atmosphere. There is good reason for seeing in this article the real renaissance of Old Testament theology (Dentan, *Preface*, 63), since here for the first time there is an attempt to mark the discipline off from the history of religion. However, on closer consideration it does not really represent a departure from the history-of-religions perspec-tive; rather, as well as giving a genetic account of the overall development of Israelite religion within the history of Israel, Steuer-nagel is concerned to present another, systematic account in which individual lines of development in particular complexes of themes are put side by side. However: 'Both disciplines have the same subject-matter – Israelite religion, including the religion of earlier Judaism – ,the same sources and the same method: the historical method' (272). This lays the foundation for the programme of a descriptive and systematic presentation of the theology of the Old Testament (Hasel, 42ff.: 'cross-section-method'). In the case of Steuernagel this function is clearly auxiliary: it is meant to offer the 'philosopher of religion', the dogmatic theologian, a systematic survey of the Old Testament material which he needs in a suitable form. This almost amounts to taking up again the old task of 'biblical theology' as seen by Gabler; however, Steuernagel protects himself against two deficiencies in the old method of *loci*: the lack of an adequate perspective in terms of development and the need to arrange the material in accordance with a pattern taken over from dogmatics. 'It is in fact only the inadequacy of the *loci* method, which can rightly be held against it' (267).

To a large degree, then, the programme for a theology of the Old Testament is primarily a reaction to the evolutionist pattern of nineteenth-century accounts, rather than to the historical or history-of-religions perspective as such. The arguments over how best to divide up a theology of the Old Testament constructed on a thematic basis and understood essentially in descriptive terms (Part II below) remain in this area, while the question of the binding character of the subject-matter of an Old Testament theology understood only in idealistic and aesthetic terms (Gunkel) or by postulating a private sphere, whether in faith or within the practice of the church, to be maintained alongside historical theology, now came to the fore after having been concealed for a long time behind the demand for historical objectivity, which was long taken for granted.

However, to describe these developments it is necessary to set the course of discussion of Old Testament theology against the background of more far-reaching developments in the sphere of theology and public opinion, which were decisive in determining an understanding of the tasks of the discipline.

2. The programme of a 'pneumatic exegesis'

Baumgärtel, F., 'Pneumatische Exegese', *CuW* 2, 1926, 237-47; id., *Der Theologiestudent und die Bibel*, Gütersloh 1929; Behm, J., *Pneumatische Exegese?*, Schwerin 1926; Frick, H., *Wissenschaftliches und pneumatisches Verständnis der Bibel*, Tübingen 1927; Girgensohn, K., 'Geschichtliche und übergeschichtliche Schriftauslegung', *AELKZ* 55, 1922, 626-9, 642-5, 658-61, 674-8; id., 'Die Grenzgebiete der systematischen Theologie', *Greifswalder Reformgedanken zum theologischen Studium. J. Hausleiter und V. Schultze... zum 70. Geburtstage dargebracht von ihrer Fakultät*, Munich 1922, 73-96; id., *Die Inspiration der heiligen Schrift*, Dresden ²1926; Guisan, R., 'Y-a-t-il deux exégèses?', *RTP* 22, 1934, 207-21; Jelke, R., 'Historisch-kritische und theologisch-dogmatische Schriftauslegung', in id. (ed.), *Das Erbe Martin Luthers und die gegenwärtige theologische Forschung. Festschrift L. Ihmels*, Leipzig 1928, 215-35; Lindblom, J., 'Exegetisk och pneumatisk bibelutläggning', *SvTK* 4, 1928, 26-51; id., 'Vad betyder en "theologisk exeges" av Gamla testamentet?', *SvTK* 10, 1934, 249-59; id., 'Das Problem einer theologischen Exegese des Alten Testaments', in *Zur Neugestaltung des theologischen Studiums*, Göttingen 1935, 61-9; Macholz, E., 'Pneumatische Exegese – eine berechtigte theologische Forderung', *PBL* 69, 1926-27, 705-24; Oepke, A., *Geschichtliche und übergeschichtliche Schriftauslegung*, Gütersloh (1931) ²1947; id., review of J. Behm, see above, *TLZ* 51, 1926, 420-2; Procksch, O., 'Über pneumatische Exegese', *CuW* 1, 1925, 145-58; id., 'Die Geschichte als Glaubensinhalt', *NKZ* 36, 1925, 458-99; id., 'Ziele und Grenzen der Exegese', ibid., 715-30; Schmidt, S., *'De Protestantium exegese "pneumatica"'*, *VD* 27, 1947, 12-22, 65-73; Seeberg, R., 'Zur Frage nach dem Sinn und Recht einer pneumatischen Schriftauslegung', *ZST* 4, 1926, 3-59; id, 'Zum Problem der pneumatischen Exegese', *Festschrift E.Sellin*, Leipzig 1927, 127-37; Traub, F., 'Wort Gottes und pneumatische Schriftauslegung', *ZTK* 35, 1927, 83-111; cf. also H.E.Weber, *Historisch-kritische Schriftforschung und Bibelglaube*, Gütersloh ²1914.

In 1919 Karl Barth's commentary on Romans was published. In the preface to the first edition he announced his revolutionary hermeneutical programme: 'The historical-critical method of Biblical investigation has its rightful place; it is concerned with the preparation of the intelligence – and this can never be superfluous. But, were I driven to choose between it and the venerable doctrine of Inspiration, I should without hesitation adopt the latter, which has a broader, deeper, more important justification. The doctrine of Inspiration is concerned with the labour of apprehending, without which no technical equipment, however complete, is of any use whatever. Fortunately, I am not compelled to choose between the two. Nevertheless my whole energy of interpreting has been expended in an endeavour to see through and beyond history into the spirit of the Bible, which is the Eternal Spirit' (Karl Barth, *The Epistle to the Romans* [¹1919] = ET Oxford 1933, 1). In the preface to the second edition he explained his standpoint in more detail; he stressed that he recognized historical criticism, but was discontented with what he found there and had to press on to real *understanding* and *explanation*. Only at that stage, as is evident from the example of the Reformers' interpretation of the Bible, could there be a conversation between the inner dialectic of the *subject-matter* expressed in the text and the reader (Preface to the Second Edition [1923], ibid., 6ff.). In this sense he thinks that 'The critical historian needs to be more critical' (ibid., 8; the ET does not quite reproduce the German original: '*Kritischer* müssten mir die Historisch-Kritischen sein!').

Barth's demands can be understood against an intellectual background of historicism which had taken as a programme the view that historical method and knowledge are objective and value-free (especially in Max Weber, cf. 'Die "Objektivität" sozialwissenschaftlicher und sozialpolitischer Erkenntnis', in *Gesammelte Aufsätze zur Wissenschaftslehre*, Tübingen ³1968, 146-214; id., 'Der Sinn der "Wertfreiheit" der soziologischen und ökonomischen Wissenschaften', ibid., 489-540; id., *Methodologische Schriften*, ed. J.Winckelmann, Frankfurt 1968. For historicism cf. esp. E.Troeltsch, *Der Historismus und seine Probleme*, Gesammelte Schriften III, Tübingen 1922, reprinted Aalen 1961). The demand for historical objectivity had also made itself felt in biblical exegesis; we have already come across its effect in the sphere of the 'theology of the Old Testament'. Ernst Troeltsch explicitly extended the sphere within which the historical method - or in this case the history-of-religions approach – was valid to the sphere of theology and formulated as a demand what had already largely become established practice: not only should Christian and Jewish history be subjected completely to this method but they should also be understood expressly in terms of universal history, 'by noting the way in which Christianity is woven into universal history and involving oneself in the task of investigating it and evaluating it only in terms of the wider movements of history as a whole' ('Über historische und dogmatische Methode in der Theologie', *Studien des rheinischen Predigervereins, 1898* = id., *Gesammelte Schriften* II, Tübingen 1913, reprinted Aalen 1962, 729-53 = *Theologie als Wissenschaft*, ed.G.Sauter, TB 43, Munich 1971, [105-27] 113). Central to this method is the all-prevailing law of analogy: 'Correspondence with normal, usual, or often-attested procedures and circumstances as we know them is the sign that we may take as probable the events which criticism recognizes really to have taken place or which it can allow... But this omnipotence of analogy implies that in principle all historical events are of the same kind...'(Sauter, 108).

As we see in Troeltsch, this idea of analogy has a deliberate anthropocentric orientation; it is based on the assumption that 'human spirit and its historical activities have a common and similar character' (ibid.). Behind this perspective is evidently the hermeneutical view of W.Dilthey (and already Schleiermacher – cf. Troeltsch, 'Rückblick auf ein halbes Jahrhundert der theologischen Wissenschaft', *ZWT* NF 16, 1908, 97-135 = id., *Gesammelte Schriften* II, 193-226 = Sauter [73-104] 102f.). Of course there is no intention of sacrificing all value judgments to the 'levelling out of analogy', but this means (idealistically) only being able to arrive at a value judgment from an overall view of history (cf.115). The counterpart to this view is the 'dogmatic method' (the 'Catholic' view as opposed to the new 'Protestant' one, 119). The basis for this is provided by a special supernatural sphere which is to be investigated 'in accordance with particular methods grounded in inner experiences and the humble subjection of reason to well-tried methods' (117).

Troeltsch acutely recognized a basic dualism in this alternative; in his view this led not only to two spheres of history (secular history and salvation history), but also to dualistic concepts of God and man (118). The reaction to historicism in biblical exegesis which began immediately after the First World War (one early forerunner is J.Köberle, 'Heilsgeschichtliche Betrachtungsweise des Alten Testaments', *NKZ* 17, 1906, 200-22; cf. further below 57.) betrays such a dualism at least in methodological terms. That is particularly true of the programme for a so-called 'pneumatic' exegesis of scripture which is especially associated with the name of Karl Girgensohn (1875-1925; see the self-portrait in *Die Religionswissenschaft in Selbstdarstellungen*, ed. E.Stange, Leipzig 1926, 41-76). The ready hearing which his demands found at the time can be explained in the same way as the welcome given to the young Barth. Any theologian committed to the church could note a painful discrepancy between the results of historical-critical exegesis of the Bible and the religious practices of the community, which were based on the Bible. On the one hand there was a desire not to give up the academic approach, which could only be carried through by means of historical criticism (in fact Barth points this out in his preface to *Romans* and often repeated it); on the other hand there was deep dissatisfaction over the provisional character of the results of exegesis carried on in this way, as was manifested in commentaries whose orientation on the whole tended to be purely philological. In critical-historical interpretation of the Bible Girgensohn noted above all the distance between the observer and his subject-matter, and the relativity which results from setting the text in a specific historical context in history (*AELKZ* 1922, 643; *Inspiration*, 12). Moreover here man with his autonomous standards becomes 'judge of what should be part of the truth of scripture and what should not' (*Inspiration*, 14). The situation becomes quite different 'where in scripture at some point I hear not only a historical human word about God but the voice of the living God' (ibid., 16). When that happens, the historical distance between the word of scripture and its present reader disappears, and the timeless word of God makes direct contact with the person to whom it is addressed (it is heard in an attitude of meditative prayer, 21). However, Girgensohn is far from wanting to abandon the historical-critical method in favour of this 'pneumatic' exegesis, which largely corresponds to the way in which the Bible is handled in religious circles and in the church (*AELKZ* 1922, 643f.). He thinks that he can combine the two and see them as 'stages in the understanding of scripture' (*Inspiration*, 23): 'But normally the historical and psychological interpretation of the word of scripture and profound, timeless, normative pneumatic exegesis are two perspectives which complement each other in a very happy way; they can help each other if they see the deep unity of the sense of scripture from two different sides and can bind it all into a whole' (*Inspiration*, 27). In this connection Girgensohn would not want to see the either-or of community piety or university theology as the last word (*AELKZ* 1922, 644f.); he thus arrives at a two-stage understanding of scripture in which both historical research and the immediacy and binding character of the eternal Word of God are to be given their due.

Girgensohn found a series of successors, some of whom shared his programme and some of whom also questioned it. It was criticized not only for its dualism, which made a complete separation between the understanding of the Bible by scholars and that by the faithful, but above all for the metaphysics underlying the system. This becomes very clear when e.g. J.Behm distinguishes between historical exegesis and the metahistorical application of its results to the present, or when Oepke distinguishes between historical and supra-historical exegesis of scripture. While Oepke thought that a two-level approach had to be attempted, as one-level solutions were not satisfactory (*Schriftauslegung*, 24), he criticized the timelessness of pneumatic exegesis (27). Underlying Girgensohn's comment that 'At its deepest and best, pneumatic exegesis is timeless and identical at all times' (*Inspiration*, 52) is both an idealistic conception of man and a metaphysical image of God.

It is only against the background of the debate about the 'pneumatic' interpretation of scripture that we can place O.Eissfeldt's proposal that a distinction should be made between the history of Israelite and Jewish religion and Old Testament theology, between a historical and a theological approach ('Israelitisch-jüdische Religionsgeschichte und alttestamentliche Theologie', *ZAW* 44, 1926, 1-12 = id., *Kleine Schriften* I, Tübingen 1962, 105-14) in its right setting. It tends to get completely lost in the usual accounts of the history of Old Testament theology. Here Eissfeldt explicitly refers to Girgensohn and Procksch (*KS* I, 106f.), and to approaches in dialectical theology. For Eissfeldt, too, the historical approach on the one hand and the theological approach on the other clearly belong on two different planes. 'They correspond to two different kinds of functions of our spirit, knowing and believing' (109). The historical approach investigates what happened and is concerned with the history of Israelite and Jewish religion. Consideration of the New Testament has to be left out of account in this context; members of different Christian confessions and even non-Christian scholars can work together here (112). On the other hand Old Testament theology is concerned with the 'description of the revelation of God which has become faith in the Old Testament and becomes faith ever anew' (113). It cannot take the form of an account of history: 'For faith is not concerned with the past but with what is present and timeless; and revelation transcends the category of time' (ibid.).

Here again we have the distinction between time-conditioned history and timeless revelation, between historical research and personal belief. However, Eissfeldt did not develop a specific programme showing the character of a theology of the Old Testament which was thus separate from the history of religion.

In this form his proposal was not approved by his professional colleagues and remained in isolation. However, the underlying dichotomy in it, between faith and knowledge, between history and revelation, remained a fundamental problem for Old Testament theology. Adherents could still be found for the approach embarked on by Gabler, which made a strict distinction between the historical-descriptive task of exegesis (with a possible 'theology of the Old Testament' as its culmination) and an 'evaluation' (in Steuernagel's sense) made in dogmatics or proclamation.

Thus Lindblom (in *Zur Neugestaltung*, 65) tells the defenders of 'pneumatic exegesis': 'all that is not a task for scholars, but a matter of practical proclamation'; or, the historical and the dogmatic approaches must be clearly distinguished (67). The Old Testament scholar has fulfilled his task as an exegete when he has 'given the dogmatic theologian and the philosopher of religion reliable material which they can then use for their particular ends' (67f.).

This was later the attitude of the liberal school in the USA, where after the war the demand for a 'biblical theology' also found a considerable hearing (cf. my *Problems of Biblical Theology*, ch.I). The dilemma, which has its roots in the hermeneutical tradition of the discipline, has by no means been resolved, even today.

3. Dialectical theology

I have already quoted Barth's prefaces to *Romans* (above 14). The developed theology of the early Barth as it gradually emerged during the following years leading up to the publication of his *Christliche Dogmatik im Entwurf* (*Die Lehre vom Worte Gottes. Prolegomena zur christlichen Dogmatik*, Munich 1927) also affected discussion of the Old Testament.

For Barth's understanding of scripture cf. G.Eichholz, 'Der Ansatz Karl Barths in der Hermeneutik', in *Antwort. Karl Barth zum 70. Geburtstag*, Zürich 1956, 52-68; R.Smend, 'Nachkritische Schriftauslegung', in *Parrhesia. Karl Barth zum 80. Geburtstag*, Zürich 1966, 215-37; F.-W.Marquardt, 'Exegese und Dogmatik in Karl Barths Theologie', in *Kirchliche Dogmatik. Registerband*, Zurich 1970, 649-76 (not in the English equivalent); H.Seebass, *Biblische Hermeneutik*, UTB 199, Stuttgart 1974, 89-111, though these are principally concerned with the *Church Dogmatics*.

Barth's lecture 'Das Schriftprinzip der reformierten Kirche' (*ZZ* 3, 1925, 215-45) was particularly influential and at the same time is the best summary of the understanding of scripture in early Barth. Here we find the well-known dogmatic principle that the Bible is the Word of God (217ff.). True, human beings have spoken in the Bible, but also, 'refracted in the prism of their word, God himself' (220). For this Barth refers to Calvin's 'scandalous, yet unavoidably circular argument according to which the Bible is *recognized* to be God's Word by the fact that it *is* God's Word' (239). Its testimony to itself is the work of the Holy Spirit (243). However, over against the dualism of 'pneumatic exegesis' Barth strictly maintains the historicity of the word of God, preserving the Reformation insight into the 'in, with and under'. 'Any attempt to demonstrate the Word of God *directly* in the Bible is pseudo-science'; 'Knowledge of the Bible as the Word of God is an event, a breakthrough, which takes place again and again. The barrier which has to be broken through is the historical *conditioning* of the biblical testimony which must be recognized without remainder' (226f.). Barth also stresses the canon (cf. E.Thurneysen, 'Schrift und Offenbarung', *ZZ* 2, 1924, 3-30 =

Anfänge der dialektischen Theologie II, ed. J.Moltmann, Munich 1963, 247-76); its establishment by the church is an 'absolute datum', namely the confirmation that God's Word has already designated these writings God's Word (221). It follows from this (3.) that there cannot be a fundamental difference betwen the various parts of the canon, between the Old Testament and the New. Granted, these differences can be recognized in historical terms, but they are relative when set against the unity of revelation (222f.). This again brings up the theme of 'biblical theology'; the influence of Barth's position in this question of the unity of the Testaments was to prove very significant later.

The position of K.H.Miskotte ('Das Problem der theologischen Exegese', *Theologische Aufsätze. Festschrift K. Barth*, Munich 1936, 51-77 [an abbreviated version of 'Opmerkingen over theologische exegese', in *De openbaring der verborgenheid*, Baarn 1933, 65-99]) is similar. Here too there is very strong stress on the necessity of historical-critical and 'phenomenological' exegesis (an exegesis *kata sarka*, 58); alongside this stands 'theological' exegesis (exegesis *kata pneuma*). There is no way from one to the other (61). With Barth, Miskotte sees the foundation of theological exegesis in the dogmatic statement 'Scripture is the Word of God' (63f.). 'It cannot be seized by any method or through any intellectual brilliance' (66), and consists in subjecting itself to the claim of Holy Scripture as Word and to its authority (67). 'The "contemporaneity" is a miracle; the "repetition" granted by the spirit *cannot* be repeated from *our* side' (67). The identification of Scripture and the Word of God at the same time produces the *unity* of Scripture, which is a unity of the text and the Spirit and not historical continuity (64f.; cf. the following section). – For Miskotte see also my *Problems of Biblical Theology, II*, 5.

A last important feature of Barth's biblical hermeneutics is his christological interpretation of the Old Testament. As Barth only put forward his doctrine of the incarnation in 1938, in *KD/CD* I.2, where he was much more restrained about Christ in the Old Testament (14.2, 'The Time of Expectation', 77-111 = ET 70-101; cf. also H.D.Hummel, 'Christological Interpretation of the Old Testament', *Dialog* 2, 1963, 108-17), the main influence was exercised by his much more speculative comments in the *Prolegomena* (section 15, 'Weissagung und Erfüllung', 230-54) on 'history and primal history'. According to these, 'only revelation in Jesus Christ is the primal historical event' (230). History as such is not revelation (although revelation is history, 230); however, revelation can be found in history, though only by being heard as the word of God in person by the one who asks (234). Only in the specific element of 'primal history' (in the revelation in Christ) is history, interpreted by God's word, revelation (and not by being a historical event as such). This is the point of contact for Barth's particular form of speculation on time: as the content of the primal history is the Logos from whom all creation originally derives and receives its meaning (cf. John 1.3,14), all history in which God is believed in and confessed as the Word becoming and being made incarnate – Barth calls it the prophetic history, as history in history – is related to primal history; it surrounds it as a circle surrounds its centre (237-9).

Begrich,J./Doerne, M., *Das Alte Testament in der christlichen Predigt*, Dresden 1936; Birkeland, H., 'Israelitisk-jødisk religionshistorie og gammeltestamentlig bibelteologie', *NTT* 37, 1936, 1-19; Bonhoeffer, D., *Schöpfung und Fall. Theologische Auslegung von Genesis 1-3*, Munich 1933 ([2]1937, reprinted 1968) = ET *Creation and Fall. A Theological Interpretation of Genesis 1-3*, London 1959 (for Bonhoeffer cf. also M.Kuske, *Das Alte Testament als Buch von Christus. Dietrich Bonhoeffers Wertung und Auslegung des Alten Testaments*, Berlin and Göttingen 1971; M.Hohmann, *Die Korrelation von Altem und Neuem Bund*, TA 37, Berlin 1978, 74-110. For contemporary criticism of Bonhoeffer cf. F.Baumgärtel, *Die Kirche ist Eine – die alttestamentlich-jüdische Kirche und die Kirche Jesu Christi*, Bamberg 1936); E.Brunner, 'Die Bedeutung des Alten Testaments für den christlichen Glauben', *ZZ* 8, 1930, 30-48, = ET 'The Significance of the Old Testament for our Faith', in B.W.Anderson (ed.), *The Old Testament and Christian Faith*, Philadelphia and London 1964, 243-64; id., *Die Unentbehrlichkeit des Alten Testaments für die missionierende Kirche*, Stuttgart 1934; Brunner, E. and Köhler, L. et al., discussion on original sin, *KBRS* 41, 1926 [LK, 27, 105f.; EB, 113-16; LK, 31, 121; Marti, P., 32, 125-7; Kühni, F., 35, 137f.; EB, 36, 141f.; Hauri, P., 37, 145f.; Marti, P., 38, 155; Künzler, K. 43,174f.]; Brunner, E., 'Der Sündenfall und die alttestamentliche Wissenschaft', *CW* 40, 1926, 994-8; de Diétrich, S., *Rediscovering the Bible*, Toronto 1942; id., *Le renouveau biblique*, Neuchâtel-Paris 1945, [2]1949, = *Wiederentdeckung des Bibel*, Zurich 1948; *God's Unfolding*

Purpose, Philadelphia 1960; Echternach, F., 'Wie behandeln wir das Alte Testament?', *PBl* 78, 1935/36, 385-93; Eichrodt, W., 'Zur Frage der theologischen Exegese des Alten Testaments', *ThBl* 17, 1938, 73-87; Elliger, K., 'Das Christuszeugnis des Alten Testaments', *ZST* 14, 1937, 377-92; id., 'Warum gehören Altes und Neues Testament zusammen?', *DtPfrBl* 40, 1936, 777f.; Feldges, F., 'Die Frage des alttestamentlichen Christuszeugnisses. Zum Angriff von Gerhard von Rad auf Wilhelm Vischer', *ThBl* 15, 1936, 25-30; Gressmann, H., 'Paradies und Sünde', *CW* 40, 1926, 842-6; id., Die Bibel als Wort Gottes', ibid., 1050-3; Haag, H., 'Vom Eigenwert des Alten Testaments', *TQS* 160, 1980, (2-16) 9ff.; Heim, K., 'Die Christusoffenbarung im Alten Testament', *WuT* 10, 1934, 257-69; Hellbarth, H., *Abrahams Lüge*, TEH 42, Munich 1936; id., 'Die Auslegung des Alten Testaments als theologische Disziplin', *ThBl* 16, 1937, 128-43; id., 'Christus das Telos des Gesetzes', *EvTh* 3, 1936, 331-46; id., *Der verheissene König Israels. Das Christuszeugnis des Hosea*, EvTh Beiheft 1, Munich 1935; id., *Das Bild Gottes*, TEH 64, Munich 1939; Hermann, R., *Deutung und Umdeutung der Schrift. Ein Beitrag zur Frage der Auslegung*, ThMil 12, Leipzig 1937 = id., 'Bibel und Hermeneutik', *Gesammelte und nachgelassene Werke* III, Göttingen 1971, 38-83; Herntrich, V., 'Theologische Auslegung des Alten Testaments? Zum Gespräch mit Wilhelm Vischer', *PT* 32, 1936, 119-31, 177-89, offprint Göttingen [2]1938; Hummel, H.D., *Dialog* 1963, above 20; Köhler, L., 'Christus im Alten und im Neuen Testament', *TZ* 9, 1953, 241-59; Leo, P., 'Die theologische Exegese des Alten Testaments', *PT* 34, 1938, 66-84; Lindblom, J., *Zur Neugestaltung*, above 13; Machholz, A.W., 'Die heimliche Deutung der Schrift', *EvTh* 3, 1936, 3-21; von Rad, G., 'Das Christuszeugnis des Alten Testaments. Eine Auseinandersetzung mit Wilhelm Vischers gleichnamigem Buch', *ThBl* 14, 1935, 249-54; id., *'Sensus Scripturae duplex?* Eine Erwiderung', *ThBl* 15, 1936, 30-4; Schlatter, A./Schmidt, G./Stoll, C., *Das Alte Testament als Buch der Kirche*, Munich [3]1934; Schlier, O., *Das Christuszeugnis des Alten Testaments*, Heidelberg 1936; Schreiner, H., *Das Alte Testament in der Verkündigung*, Schwerin 1937; Sellin, E., *Das Alte Testament im christlichen Gottesdienst und Unterricht*, Gütersloh 1936; Staerk, W., 'Der Christ und sein Altes Testament', *Furche* 20, 1934, 423-34; Strathmann, H., 'Zum Ringen um das christliche Verständnis des Alten Testaments', *ThBl* 15, 1936, 257-60; Vischer, W., 'Das Alte

Testament als Gottes Wort', *ZZ* 5, 1927, 379-95; id., 'Das Alte
Testament und die Verkündigung', *ThBl* 10, 1931, 1-12; id., *Die
Bedeutung des Alten Testaments für das christliche Leben*, TS 3,
Zurich 1938, [2]1947; id., *Das Christuszeugnis des Alten Testaments*,
I, *Das Gesetz*, Zurich 1934 ([3]1936) = ET *The Witness of the
Old Testament to Christ*, London 1949 (cf. the discussions by
W.Eichrodt, *ThG* 29, 1935, 123-5; O.Procksch, *ThBl* 26, 1935,
326-8); II, *Die früheren Propheten*, Zürich 1942, [2]1946 (no ET);
id., *Esther*, TEH 28, Munich 1937 (English *EvQ* 11, 1939, 3-21);
id., *Das Kerygma des Alten Testaments*, Zürich 1955 (French
1955); Vogel, H., 'Wie predigen wir über das Alte Testament?',
EvTh 2, 1935, 339-60; Würthwein, E., 'Bemerkungen zu Wilhelm
Vischer, *Das Christuszeugnis des Alten Testaments*', *DT* 3, 1936,
259-73; Zimmerli, W., 'Vom Auslegen des Alten Testaments in
der Kirche', *VF* 1941, 7-22.

The claim of dialectical theology that in both parts of the Bible the
hearer (reader) has a direct encounter with the Word of God set off
a much more enduring discussion in the world of Old Testament
scholarship than that over 'pneumatic' exegesis; the foundations of
the latter were weaker and it was now crumbling away. Along with
the contemporaneous Luther renaissance the new development
represented a return to the Reformation understanding of scripture,
but with the claim that in so doing it was fully integrating the insights
and methods of historical-critical scholarship. The possibility for
this was accorded by the fact that the Reformation had already
stressed the literal sense of Holy Scripture in contrast to the fourfold
interpretation of Scripture in the early church and the Middle Ages.
However, this reference back to the Reformation principle of
Scripture in dialectical theology also brought with it the danger of
repeating the hermeneutical weakness of the Reformation and not
reflecting adequately in methodological terms on the relationship
between exegesis and dogmatics (for Luther cf. G.Ebeling, 'The
Meaning of Biblical Theology' [above 3], 73 = ET 214/53/82).

The representatives of liberal exegesis were in no way inclined to
accept the dogmatic understanding of Scripture in dialectic theology
without discussion. A vigorous debate, in which a number of Swiss
pastors belonging to both camps also took part, was held in the
columns of the *KBRS*, intended for a wider readership, in 1926. The
protagonists were the exegete L.Köhler and the dogmatic theologian
E.Brunner, and they discussed the interpretation of the narrative

of the 'Fall' in Gen.3. Köhler had stressed that this narrative was not to be understood in dogmatic terms but as an aetiological myth; it was not relevant for understanding sin right through the Old Testament and had only become the starting point for the church's doctrine of 'original' sin as a result of the Pauline Adam-Christ speculation. As a result of the critics' dismissal of the myth of the Fall 'Paul's whole doctrine of salvation was shattered' and 'the Reformation doctrine of original sin destroyed'. For it was clear 'that no Old Testament scholar of standing today would dream of arguing for the historicity of the Fall' (106). Brunner retorted that if Paul was a novice, he would prefer to sit at table among novices, with Paul at their head. The myth of the Fall was not to be understood historically but eschatologically and teleologically; it answered the question of man's present-day historical existence, characterized by emancipation beyond the limits appointed by his God. Jesus always presupposes the doctrine of the primal state. Brunner ends by observing 'that in this region, in which Gen.3. and Rom.5 move, the "Old Testament scholar of note" has nothing to look for in that capacity' (116). The discussion continued in *CW* 1926 between Brunner and H.Gressmann, a prominent representative of the history-of-religions school. Here it is worth noting that Brunner sees Köhler and Gressmann as representatives of 'normative Old Testament scholarship' (994). Gressmann sees himself as the defender of 'absolute objectivity'; exegesis has the task of '*ascertaining the facts* as they really happened from the written works which have been handed down to us or working out the thoughts of the author of the time' (1050). However, Gressmann's thought really has just as many presuppositions; for him the expulsion from Paradise is 'a powerful step forward', since through his knowledge man has become Lord of the earth, even if he has attained this knowledge through guilt (846). Gressmann also denies that he is deliberately opposed to the principle of Christian faith that the Bible is the Word of God. 'On the contrary, I too believe that I hear the Word of God in the Bible, and I am convinced that this confession also holds for any modern Old Testament theologian.' 'For the objectivity of the historian in no way excludes *subjective value judgments*' (1051). Still, a fruitful conversation between the two views is hindered by the fact that both think in dualistic terms, each on a different level: for Brunner (as for Barth) the story of the Fall is primal history as opposed to history: 'The Reformers were... aware that this was something which could not be incorporated into our historical reality, that it was another genus of event' (997). Gressmann in turn cannot acknowledge that the biblical revelation is exclusive: 'Since God is a living reality for me, I must think of him as a universal factor... Anyone who sets limits to his revelation denies his absolute power. Now if there is no absoluteness of religion, there is of course also no absoluteness of Christianity' (1051f. Gressmann explained this statement thoroughly in a brief postscript [1275], saying that he was not denying the absoluteness of Christianity since for him Christianity was *the* religion'; however, because of the absoluteness of religion he had to find a partial revelation of God in all religions). The discussion between these partners was not very fruitful; there is no way of reconciling a science which refers to the principle of presuppositionless exegesis and has an idealistic basis with a systematic theology appealing to the dogmatic principle that the Bible is the Word of God.

However, there were also exegetes who went over completely to the camp of dialectical theology. The best known of them is without doubt Wilhelm Vischer (cf. esp. Baker, *Two Testaments*, above 1, 211-28; also my 'Der Konflikt zwischen Exegese und Dogmatik. Wilhelm Vischers Ringen um den "Christus im Alten Testament"', in *Textgemäss, Festschrift E.Würthwein*, Göttingen 1979, 110-22, and e.g. K.Schwarzwäller, 'Das Verhältnis Altes Testament – Neues Testament im Lichte der gegenwärtigen Bestimmungen', *EvTh* 29, 1969, [281-307] 281-5). It should be stressed that during his life Vischer emphasized the need for historical-critical exegesis. However, while retaining a correct critical method, he wanted to advance to an exegesis which was 'theological' in the full sense of the word. For Vischer, who in this respect was fascinated by Barth, 'theological' here meant strictly christocentric. The second basic principle of his hermeneutics was that the Bible is the Word of God, or more exactly, as his central concern was with the Old Testament, that the Old Testament is the Word of God. Here, however, Vischer found himself in a conflict which could not be resolved, between the recognition of the 'servant form of revelation' which he took over from the Reformation and above all from J.G.Hamann, i.e. of the utterly human character of scripture, which therefore can only be investigated by means of historical-critical exegesis (he in no way wants to obliterate the historic character of the Old Testament, *ThBl* 1931, 8), and a christology conceived on metaphysical lines which seeks to read a timeless and pre-existent Christ into every relevant section of the Old Testament. With reference to the

Johannine Logos christology (*ThBl* 1931, 6f., *The Witness of the Old Testament*, I, 34 n.51 = ET 28f.n.1), Vischer first goes through the Pentateuch ('The Law') and then through the historical books ('The Former Prophets') looking for a hidden christological significance. Here his methodological weakness is that he does not reflect enough (he thinks that he is simply listening to the Word of God and delivering himself over to the freedom of the Holy Spirit, I, 37 = ET 32f.) on his form of allegorical interpretation (sometimes, not always; more cautious attempts at interpretation should not be overlooked, like the mark of Cain as the sign of the cross, Gen.4.15, in its relationship to the cross of Christ: 'In both cases the sign symbolizes the same most holy paradox – that he who as a murder falls under the judgment of God is neverthelesss upheld by the grace of God' [I, 94 = ET, 75], or the typological interpretation of the figure of Melchizedek, I, 161ff. = ET 132f.): thus Abraham offers his son Isaac believing in the resurrection of the dead; the sacrifice of the ram looks towards the sacrifice of the Son (Rom.8.32: I, 174ff. = ET 141ff.); the tabernacle of God in Ex. 35-40 is to be connected with the body of Christ which according to John 1.14 'tabernacled among us' (cf. also John 2.19: I, 256ff. = ET 210ff.); the red heifer in Num.19 is a reference to the sacrifice of Christ (I, 277f. = ET 226f.)

Vischer's method earned him sharp criticism from most of his professional colleagues. Despite his profession that he wanted to take the historicity of revelation seriously, he had fallen victim to the metaphysical christological view which was characteristic of early dialectical theology (for the charge of a 'docetic christology' cf. von Rad, *ThBl* 1935, 251).

But even H.Hellbarth, who went beyond Vischer in his assertion that the results of critical scholarship are not a presupposition for the christological exegesis of the Old Testament, which is, rather, established by the church's confession and cannot be proved but only outlined (cf. *ThBl* 1937), presented an interpretation of Hosea which only at the end turned into a christological exegesis and otherwise was completely historical and critical (1935). Here we can see what is ultimately an obscurity of method.

In the discussion with Vischer, the young von Rad gave a careful hint at his later programme: one must 'be attentive to this course of Israel's history and have the courage to grasp the individual documents, with all their uniqueness and historical limitations'

(*ThBl* 1935, 252). It is a matter of 'venturing an interpretation which enters into the faith of the witness concerned' (*ThBl* 1936, 33). Nevertheless, he too retains the reference to Jesus Christ which the Christian claim to the Old Testament must make (cf. also in A.Alt/ J.Begrich/G.von Rad, *Führung zum Christentum durch das Alte Testament. Drei Vorträge*, Leipzig 1934, esp. 68ff.). In his much-noted contribution to the discussion with Vischer, V.Herntrich referred above all to the salvation-historical difference between the time of the Old Testament and the time of the New (new edition, 16f.), and to the word which is given to us in history (23) but which does not do away with the unity of the two Testaments (31). However, this unity is not an identity (32). He makes the important proposal that there should be a trinitarian instead of an exclusively christological understanding of the Old Testament (ibid.).

At the beginning of the Second World War, when circumstances largely prevented the production of books, dialectical theology had already passed its peak. However, its effects on Old Testament theology emerged even later, and in the Anglo-Saxon sphere theological concern with the Bible only really developed at this time. One can see how it was reflected over large areas of Western European Protestantism from popular works, oriented on praxis, like S. de Diétrich's *Rediscovering the Bible*, which was published by the World Student Christian Federation. The notion that the Bible is the Word of God here becomes the concept underlying the whole understanding of the Bible and also serves as a leading idea in carrying out organized Bible study (*Wiederentdeckung des Bibel* [above 21], 69ff.)

The answer given by dialectical theology to the theological problem of the Old Testament also continued to be fraught with weaknesses of method. The basic problem was that it began from dogmatic positions which emerged in response to the approach to the Bible oriented purely on the history of religion, and which were concerned to meet the practical needs of the church (von Rad, *ThBl* 1935, 249, complains 'that the connection between the communities and Old Testament scholarship has been almost completely broken for more than a generation'), but could not cope hermeneutically with the problem of history. As will emerge in due course, this question has yet to receive a final answer, even today.

4. The ideological fight against the Old Testament and its consequences

Abramowski, R., 'Vom Streit um das Alte Testament', *TR* NF 9, 1937, 65-93 (survey of literature); Andersen, F./ Bartels, A./ Katzer, E./ Wolzogen, H.P.Frhr von, *Deutschchristentum auf rein evangelischer Grundlage*, Leipzig 1917; Chamberlain, H.S., *Die Grundlagen des neunzehnten Jahrhunderts* (1899), Munich [15]1932; Delitzsch, F., *Die grosse Täuschung*, I and II, Stuttgart 1920-21 ([13-14]1921, cf. the review by E.Sellin, *ThG* 15, 1921, 93f.); Dinter, A., *197 Thesen zur Vollendung der Reformation*, Leipzig 1926 (cf. also id., *Die Sünde wider das Blut. Ein Zeitroman*, Leipzig 1921); Fritzsch, T., *Der falsche Gott. Beweismaterial gegen Jahwe*, Leipzig (1911) [10]1933; Kuptsch, J., *Mit Hitler zur Volksgemeinschaft und zum Dritten Reich, mit Christus zur Glaubengemeinschaft und zur dritten Kirche*, Heiligenbeil 1934; de Lagarde, P., *Die Religion der Zukunft: Gesamtausgabe letzter Hand*, Göttingen 1891, 217-47; Ludendorff, E. and M., *Das grosse Entsetzen – die Bibel nicht Gottes Wort*, Munich 1936; Niedlich, J.K., *Jahwe oder Jesus?*, Leipzig 1925; Rosenberg, A., *Der Mythos des 20.Jahrhunderts*, Munich (1930) [3]1932; von Wendrin, F., *Die Entdeckung des Paradieses*, Brunswick 1924.

Baumgärtel, F., *Die Bedeutung des Alten Testaments für den Christen*, Schwerin 1925; id., 'Das Alte Testament', in *Die Nation vor Gott*, ed. W.Künneth and H.Schreiner, Berlin [4]1934, 97-114; Begrich, J., *Antisemitisches im Alten Testament*, Jena 1931; Eichrodt, W., *Das Alte Testament und der christliche Glaube*, Stuttgart/Basel 1936; Engelke, F., *Christentum, deutsch*, Hamburg 1933; Hempel, J., *Altes Testament und völkische Frage*, Göttingen [2]1932; id., *Fort mit dem Alten Testament?*, Giessen 1932; Herntrich, V., *Völkische Religiosität und Altes Testament*, Gütersloh 1933; Hertzberg, H.W., *Der Deutsche und das Alte Testament*, Giessen 1934; Kegel, M., *Das Alte Testament ein Freund oder Feind unseres Volkes?*, Breslau 1934; König, E., *Friedrich Delitzschs 'Die grosse Täuschung' kritisch beleuchtet*, Gütersloh 1921; id., *Wie weit hat Delitzsch recht?*, Gütersloh 1921; Meinhold, J., *Das Alte Testament und evangelisches Christentum*, Giessen 1931; Nielen, J., *Die religiöse Bedeutung des Alten Testaments für den katholischen Christen*, Paderborn [2]1935; Schlier,O., *Das Christuszeugnis*, above 22; Schuster, H., *Das Alte Testament heute*, Frankfurt am Main 1935; Sellin, E., *Abschaffung des Alten Testaments?*, Berlin 1932; id., *Das Alte Testament und die evangelische Kirche der Gegenwart*, Leipzig 1921; Traub, F., 'Die Kirche und das AT', *ZTK* 16, 1935, 175-89; Vischer, W., 'Gott und Volk in der Bibel', *EvTh* 1, 1934, 24-48; Volz, P., *Der Kampf um das Alte Testament*, Stuttgart 1932 (²1933). Nicholaisen, C., *Die Auseinandersetzung um das Alte Testament im Kirchenkampf 1933–1945*, Theological Dissertation, Hamburg 1966/7, surveys the whole development and literature.

Theological work on the Old Testament was unexpectedly stimulated from yet another side, by the battle waged against the Old Testament by nationalistic popular groups for antisemitic ideological reasons. Their aim was to do away with the Old Testament as part of the Christian Bible and to brand it as a 'Jewish book'. National Socialist ideology took up this programme on its way to the 'final solution' of the Jewish question; but it is important to recognize that its roots lie as far back as the nineteenth century and that the hostility to the Old Testament before and after the First World War was shared by broad strata of the German people.

At the beginning of this movement we have the significant figure of P. de Lagarde, the polymath steeped in Fichtean idealism (cf. W.Holsten, *RGG*³ IV, 200f. [with bibliography]; H.W.Schütte, *Lagarde und Fichte*, Gütersloh 1965; id., 'Theologie als Religionsgeschichte. Das Reformprogramm Paul de Lagardes', *NZST* 8, 1966, 111-20). In his programmatic writing of 1878, *Die Religion der Zukunft* (The Religion of the Future), he called for a new German national religion composed of authentic Christianity and the noble elements of the German soul, but purified of all un-German vices. The Old Testament (though in fact Lagarde made a significant contribution to philology) had no place in this religion, for Christianity, which arose in the sphere of the multi-national Roman world empire and drew on many sources, was doomed to decline above all because of the Jewish elements incorporated into it (231). The 95 principles, in *Deutschchristentum auf reinevangelischer Grundlage* (F.Andersen et al.), produced for the jubilee of the Reformation in 1917, which can be seen as a kind of foundation document for the German Christian movement (cf. K.Hutten, 'Deutsch-christliche Bewegungen', *RGG*³ II, [104-7] 104) made similar demands: a final separation of Christianity from the legacy of Judaism in the form of the Old Testament in order to free it for a connection with Germanhood. Here German nationalism from the euphoric period of the founding of the empire was mixed up with the history-of-religions view (which has not died out even today, above all among New Testament scholars) that Christianity as a religion is new in principle, stamped much more strongly by the sphere of Hellenistic and Roman religion than by the Old Testament (cf. e.g. K.Holl, 'Urchristentum und Religionsgeschichte', *ZST* 2, 1924, 387-430 = id., *Gesammelte Aufsätze zur Kirchengeschichte*, Tübingen 1928 [reprinted Darmstadt 1964], 1-32).

H.S.Chamberlain's *Die Grundlagen des XIX.Jahrhunderts* (The Foundations of the Nineteenth Century) was another book that proved influential in the context of the nationalist movement (cf. H.Hohlwein, *RGG*[3] VI, 1424-32 [with bibliography]). The author describes its basic notion as being the idea of the superiority of the Nordic race (Preface to Fourteenth Edition, I, 15). Here we already find most of the themes which were to recur in subsequent discussion of the Old Testament, whether in crude polemical or more exalted scholarly forms: the theory that the Christian religion essentially arose from two roots: 'Jewish historical-chronistic faith and Indo-European symbolic and metaphysical mythology'(608).

However, only Indo-European faith is true religion, since everywhere, except in the Semitic sphere, 'religion is permeated with the mysterious'(429). Judged by the criterion of the Romantic and Idealist view of religion (cf. also 240f. and passim), the religion of the Old Testament and Judaism clearly falls short: in fact the Jews of the Old Testament and of the present are a people 'whose religion is thoroughly stunted'(239). Thus the Jews are crass materialists (as is evident from their constant tendency to idolatry, 250). Their relationship to their God was a political one from the beginning (256) and their belief has a purely historical orientation (631). The Old Testament is therefore 'a purely historical work' (253). Whereas Aryan belief arrived at worship of the supreme being as a result of the fine regularity which it sensed in the whole of Nature, the one-sided dependence of Israelite belief on the will of God – the Jewish Yahweh can only be regarded as the embodiment of arbitrariness (264) – gives its belief an almost exclusively moralistic trait (269f.).

Jesus, who was probably not a Jew by blood (228ff.), is 'not the consummation of the Jewish religion but its negation' (246). In religion he puts all the emphasis on sensitivity, which had almost been buried away among the Jews (246). He has reservations about the Jewish law; in place of the hard-hearted God whom men have to fear like slaves, he puts the heavenly Father whom one can love whole-heartedly (149).

On the other hand Christ's teaching is unthinkable without the presupposition of Judaism. Not only does the Old Testament recognition of the weakness of mankind and the pitifulness of reason striving heavenwards form the background for the tragic greatness of the work of civilization carried out by the Greeks and Romans (48f.), but Israel (rather than Greece) was the place where the idea of human freedom also came into being. There, 'even in transgression, we find character and perseverance and faithfulness to one's own people' (102). Only against the background of the Jewish understanding of God could Jesus arrive at his view of the personal relationship of God to the individual (267). Christ is also governed by Jewish conceptions in his belief in divine omnipotence, his stress on the moral nature of man and the equality of all men before God. The change of will which he taught takes up the Semitic stress on the will: 'Christ becomes a Jew, and his appearance can only be understood if we have learned a critical understanding of these particular Jewish views which he found and made his own' (269f.).

On the one hand Christ cannot be understood apart from the basic doctrines of Judaism (271); on the other, he diverges from them totally (270).

The two main pillars in the development of Christianity (591ff.) were Jewish historical faith and Indo-European mythology (which in a distorted form, especially after the fourth century, led to a disfiguring of Christianity by dogmas, relics, monasticism and so on, whereas its authentic mythical nucleus is the religion of redemption which is essential to it, 620ff.). The Jewish contribution to Christian faith was significant and indispensable and consisted in that way of thinking in terms of the will which was characteristic of Judaism (630). However, the great figures of faith, particularly Paul, were far removed from the Jewish spirit in crucial questions. Paul, who was probably far from being a racially pure Jew (643), is a thoroughly ambivalent phenomenon. 'In his deepest, innermost being, in his view of the significance of *religion*, Paul is so un-Jewish that he even deserves to be called anti-Jewish' (647); his mysticism, his idea of redemption are completely Indo-European. However, it was Paul above all, especially in Romans, who outlined on the basis of the Old Testament and with the help of the anthropomorphic Jewish conception of God the scheme of a saving plan embracing ideas like the Fall and the birth of the second Adam understood as historical events; this contained the idea of a final judgment based on an arbitrary law and bound up with reward and punishment, in which the punishment can only be expiated by an appropriate sacrifice (649f.). There is an irresolvable contradiction between the two views of religion in Paul, and this necessarily leads to struggles (651). One can support only one of the two Pauls (653f.). The history of Christianity is not rooted in the figure of Jesus Christ but in 'the coupling of the Aryan spirit with the spirit of Judaism, and of both with the follies of a chaotic mass of peoples without a nation and without faith' (656). Therefore a new beginning is needed towards an authentic Aryan, German national religion.

An outright devaluation of Judaism is far from Chamberlain's mind, and here he differed from his subsequent admirers:'The Jews deserve to be recognized, for (in the extension of their influence in Europe) they have acted with complete assurance in accordance with the logic and truth of their nature' (354), which is conditioned by the distinctiveness of their race (378f.). In this respect, however, they represent an alien body in Europe; their growing influence creates the urgent problem of the Jewish question (353ff.).

Numerous other supporters of the nationalist movement and later of the German Christian movement which arose from it fought against the 'Jewish peril' and the Old Testament, identified with Judaism, on the basis of Chamberlain's ideas. There were also those who actually used the Old Testament as a weapon *against* Judaism, like the notorious T.Fritzsch, who not only claimed that the Jewish Yahweh was utterly different from the Christian God of love but also asserted that there was a contrast between Israelites and Jews which was conditioned by race (16ff.). Not only was Christ not a Jew (24), but the prophetic writings were also directed against the Jews (21). For Niedlich, too, who understood Aryan-Germanic and Semitic religion as opposites, Jesus, the representative of an inward, purely moral religion, the man in search of God, is the embodiment of Germanic faith; Jeremiah, Deutero-Isaiah and Job are outsiders of the same kind, though they did not exercise any decisive influence on the development of Semitic religion. For Dinter (22), Yahweh is the personification of evil; the Jews are not 'the elect people of God but the elect people of the devil' (25). By contrast Aryan primal religion is the highest stage of religion (20). The mania for everything Aryan occasionally led to absurd statements, like Wendrin's attempt to locate Paradise in the Swedish Tanum (Bohuslän). Age-old moral objections to the Old Testament dating from the Enlightenment again revived. Thus A. Rosenberg, chief ideologist of National Socialism, mocked the alleged heroism of the Jewish people (in a way that Chamberlain never did): 'The Jewish people begins with stories about cattle-rearing which lack any kind of heroism; the Bible itself associates their later exodus from Egypt with the tale of the jewellery stolen from the Egyptians; anything but a heroic attitude is displayed in the deceit and the sponging attitude of the peoples of the promised land' (*Der Mythos des 20. Jahrhunderts*, 152). Yahwistic belief combines materialism with the most 'wearisome philosophical superstition, for which the so-called Old Testament, the Talmud and Karl Marx provide equal insights' (142). In their countless pamphlets, the Ludendorffs, husband and wife, rejected Christianity root and branch along with the whole Bible as deception on the part of Judaism and priestly belief.

The striking two-volume work by the respected Assyriologist F.Delitzsch, *Die grosse Täuschung*, appeared relatively early. Its most important points of criticism are: 1. the unreliability of the historical books of the Old Testament as a historical source because of the way in which they have been worked over; 2. the moral inferiority of all the principal characters including the great prophets; 3. the erroneous belief that Jaho (*sic*) is to be identified with God when he is the god of a particular people and is at too low a moral level to be capable of being recognized as the supreme world God; 4. hence the crazy idea of a Jewish mission to the world; 5. unfulfilled prophecies which demonstrate the uselessness of prophecy; 6. lower religious and moral notions in the Psalter; 7. Jesus' hostility to Judaism. Although Delitzsch could rightly be accused of having said nothing new in making these points, his academic reputation (he was well known from the Babel-Bible dispute at the turn of the century) assured him an enormous hearing which became all the greater because his attack found a target in the credulousness about inspiration which was still widespread in the parishes, where people still had hardly any notion of the results of critical scholarship. For many people a whole world collapsed, and for others he provided the arguments they wanted for their long smouldering discontent over the Old Testament.

Now writers began to come forward to defend the Old Testament against Delitzsch's publications. However, the conservative position represented by E.König was not very convincing; whereas he found Delitzsch's pseudo-scientific arguments easy to cope with, his attempt to prove the historical reliability of the Pentateuchal sources and the other historical sources of the Old Testament (*Die grosse Täuschung*, 6ff.) or his defence of the religious contribution of the prophets (80ff.) were far from convincing. By contrast, E.Sellin, the renowned representative of the historical-critical movement, stressed against the doctrine of verbal inspiration that revelation was communicated historically (1921, 19). He repeated much that was already common knowledge about the legendary character of the Old Testament historical tradition, errors in prophecy, and the inferiority of ethics and belief in God in the Old Testament as compared with the New (10ff.); he then, however, pointed out that for all their achievements, Old Testament scholars had failed to ask about the divine revelation to be found in the Old Testament (17ff.). His definition of revelation is surprisingly modern: 'Revelation is the self-communication of the living God for the purpose of personal communion with him' (18). Otherwise, however, it is easy to see in the book the liberal exegete's view of the religious significance of the Old Testament: the prophets are the heart of the Old Testament or of the religions of the Old Testament; they, 'these unique men' (22), 'are unique in the whole of the history of the religion of the ancient East' (21) and grasp the nature of God in a completely new way: ' he requires of men only morality, only justice, only love' (ibid). The prophets are the 'great, classical figures of religion' (30); they belong not only to their people but to humanity. By contrast, with the 'fateful step' of the introduction of Deuteronomy, a beginning was made along the 'way to Judaism' (55); the post-exilic law represents popular religion which took the place of the religion of the spirit. With this view (taken over from Wellhausen) Sellin opposes all those who identify the Old Testament lock, stock and barrel with the law: 'The law is not at the beginning but at the end of the history of the Jewish religion' (90). The 'distinction between the popular religion which finally became the religion of the Judaic law and the prophetic, divine revelation' (72) makes it possible for Sellin, with Kähler, to recognize in the Bible, even in the Old Testament, the word of God which goes out directly to the individual (86). With Jesus' differentiated attitude to the Old Testament which is normative for Christians (63ff.), with Paul and the Apostles (70ff.), the Old Testament is not to be identified wrongly with the New (96f.); a distinction is to be made between the Israelite Jewish side and the aspect of religious progress in the Old Testament (83). The whole history of Israelite religion must be understood as the struggle 'of two factors, a higher and a lower; the transcendent spirit of God and the popular religion which has grown up naturally' (63).

Because of its dualism, the liberal position which emerges in Sellin's comments could not cope with the antisemitic attacks on the Old Testament which came to a head even before the National Socialist seizure of power; indeed it provided fuel for these flames. We can see that clearly from Sellin's own comments in 1932, which clearly reflect a situation which had intensified dramatically in the meantime. However, the nucleus of the argument lies even more decisively in the contrast between 'national cultic religion' and 'prophetic moral religion' (19ff.) as a 'double perspective' of Israelite religion (19). The national cult religion proved victorious in the Jewish community, but Jesus takes up prophetic religion (20; for the 'continuation of prophecy theory' of the literary-critical school see K.Koch, *Ratlos vor der Apokalyptik*, Gütersloh 1970, 35ff. = ET *The Rediscovery of Apocalyptic*, SBT II, London 1972, 36ff.). By referring to the part of the Old Testament which he counted as 'prophetic religion', Sellin thought that he could rescue this from antisemitic attacks; the 'marked Israelite and Jewish tone' in the Old Testament was abolished by the gospel (37). But when he draws the conclusion from the insight that all divine revelation is historically progressive that 'it had the levels and limitations of its time'(37), the insensitivity of the Enlightenment to history and its moral prejudices, which underlay all the attacks on the Old Testament, seem as clear as the idealistic emphases in the view that by reading or hearing the words of the Old Testament one can experience 'beyond the bounds of the millennia' how the living God stands before us, 'not Yahweh or the like' (38).

In Meinhold's work *Das Alte Testament und evangelisches Christentum*, the framework is already clear in the structure: 'Israel's delinquency' (41-58) and the (obsolete) 'world-view of Israel' (58-81) are made to contrast with the section 'What abides' (95-147), in which the Old Testament is discussed as a 'foundation document of the religion of revelation' and as the 'holy scripture of the Protestant Christian'.

One can trace a similar mode of argument in many works which seek to defend the Old Testament with subjective honesty, but in so doing make fatal concessions to the spirit of the time. This is the case e.g. with M.Kegel, who dissociates the Old Testament as an Israelite book (15) in which the trend towards truthfulness (17) and the heroic (21) is to be stressed from the 'distorted Judaism' (14) of the present time (similarly Hempel, *Fort mit dem Alten Testament?*, 19ff.: 'That early Israel... and Judaism are two historically different entities'); Hertzberg, who notes an intrinsic closeness between the 'German-Aryan church' and the world-affirming attitude of the Old Testament (24), to its God, for whom power is a characteristic, along with righteousness and goodness (28); and Begrich, who thinks 'that the Old Testament is at one with antisemitic polemic in what it rejects (examples of this are the prophetic accusations against 'Jewish' commercialism, corruption and so on, 15ff.) and far-reaching in what it regards as right and ideal' (examples are the Decalogue and so on, 17ff.). A few only had the strength and courage openly to attack the idolizing of the race (thus Herntrich, 1933; Vischer, *EvTh* 1934; cf. also Hempel, *Fort mit dem Alten Testament?*, 12: 'religion as a criticism of folk tradition').

A theological discussion was also carried on over the Old Testament at a higher level, the presuppositions of which, though, could not disguise their origin in the liberal theology of the turn of the century. Chief among those who rejected the Old Testament as a source of revelation but were willing to accord it a limited place in the church were A.von Harnack, E.Hirsch and R.Bultmann. Harnack (*Marcion. Das Evangelium vom fremden Gott*, Leipzig [2]1924) already believed that he was only drawing the consequences of his insight into the nature of the Christian concept of God (222; according to K.Holl, 'Urchristentum' [above 30], 10f., Jesus had introduced a completely new notion of God which was opposed to that of the Old Testament), when he said against the canonicity of the Old Testament: '...to reject the Old Testament in the second century was a mistake which the mainstream church rightly rejected; to retain it in the sixteenth century was a fate which the Reformation was still unable to avoid; but to retain it as a canonical document in Protestantism after the nineteenth century is the consequence of a crippling of religion and the church' (X, 217). He believed that he could maintain its high standing in the context of the history of religions ('the prophets', 223) precisely by refusing to maintain its canonical authority (he resolutely dissociated himself from Delitzsch, 212 n.1). That a similar position has not yet died out is shown by publications like H Crönert, 'Plädoyer für den Ketzer Markion', *DtPfrBl* 81, 1981, 562-4.

E.Hirsch, *Das Alte Testament und die Predigt des Evangeliums*, Tübingen 1936 (for a criticism cf. Strathmann, *ThBl* 1936 [above 22]; O. Procksch, 'Marcion redivivus', *AELKZ* 70, 1937, 218-26;

G. von Rad, 'Gesetz und Evangelium im Alten Testament', *ThBl* 16, 1937, 41-7; H.Seebass, *Biblische Hermeneutik* [above 19], 13-25) is a very different matter. He deliberately takes up Luther and chooses as the criterion for his judgment on the Old Testament the dialectic between law and gospel along with Kierkegaard's existential approach (cf. the Introduction, III). Here of course the Old Testament (or 'the religion of the Old Testament and Judaism') stands one-sidedly for the law ('that we have to regard the Old Testament *in its totality* as a document of a religion of the law which Christian faith has done away with', 26), and the New Testament (or 'the Christian religion') for the gospel (11,76). Further differences can be recognized from a 'preliminary meditation which is clearly focussed on the opposition between the two Testaments' (11, cf. 77f.), in which the *overall meaning* of the Old Testament is to be interpreted one-sidedly from the standpoint 'of the post-exilic Jewish national and religious community' (72): the Old Testament does not know the doctrine of the two kingdoms but only the earthly rule of God (13); the God of Abraham (in Gen.22) is other than the Father of Jesus Christ: he requires blind obedience even to nonsensical demands; his promise holds only for this life; he appears as the 'uncanny, demanding power to deal with whom shatters man' (25).

The Old Testament is therefore no longer the testimony to a binding revelation: 'Old Testament religion is to be classified as a special instance of non-Christian religion' (ibid.), it is 'a special case of non-Christian people's religion' (70, where he also dissociates himself from Luther's view. The background of the history-of-religions perspective to which Hirsch was introduced by his Old Testament teachers, above all Gunkel and Gressmann, is clear). To begin with, the difference between it and other pagan religions is only that it is the historical ground on which Christianity grew (27). However, Hirsch thinks that this does not finally do away with the Old Testament for Christians. Rather, he thinks that his book is an important contribution in its defence ('The reason for it is not the vigour of the attacks on the Old Testament but the quite inadequate way in which they are countered', 15). The Old Testament is continually relevant for Christians because in it the dark uncanny power, the *deus absconditus*, which is continually to be encountered as the mysterious background in all human religion, also presents itself to the Christian (so Luther) in the guise of sin, death and temptation (27-30). The God of the Old Testament has already been overcome through the God of love and truth, the Father of Jesus

Christ; however, he must always be stripped first, in faith, of his power over the individual (30f.).

This basic opposition between Old and New Testaments leads to a series of further differences: that the Old Testament is bound up with the temple and the cult (72f.), that it is related to a people (74), and unlike Christian faith does not know an eternal life (a similar list is still to be found in W. Bodenstein, 'Verheissung im Alten und Neuen Testament', *Zum Beispiel* 6, 1971, 90-7). One could probably find all these features in other non-Christian religions. Old Testament and Jewish religion has a special place for Hirsch, because although in other respects it was a typical religion of the law, it was the first to experience the conflict between the self-assertion of man in the service of the law and his encounter with the living God and therefore 'is the historical phenomenon in which the relationship of Christian faith to the religion of the law, i.e. to the true possibility of non-Christian religion, is made manifest more than anywhere else' (82). 'So precisely because the Old Testament is historically the most powerful counterpart to the New it fits so well as the first part of the Christian Bible' (83).

By way of criticism R. Abramowski already pointed out (*TR* 1937, 75) that Hirsch's basic mistake lay in his mechanical identification of the Old Testament with the law and the New Testament with the gospel. 'Law and gospel are no longer held together by the one revelation of God. They are no longer the twofold understanding of the one Word, but two different phases in the history of religion.' The primary concern is not the recognition of law and gospel but the devaluation of the Old Testament. W. Zimmerli later observed that Hirsch's position takes over the late-Jewish misunderstanding of the Old Testament. 'The reduction of the Word of the Old Testament to the concept of law is quite simply false exegesis and should not be taken over from the synagogue' ('Das Alte Testament in der Verkündigung der christlichen Kirche', in id., *Das Alte Testament als Anrede*, BEvTh 24, Munich 1956, [62-88] 80). In a different way from Vischer, but equally *a priori*, in Hirsch a dogmatic viewpoint has triumphed over exegesis.

Hirsch's existentialist interpretation recurs in a different way with R. Bultmann in his article 'The Significance of the Old Testament for the Christian Faith' (in id., *Glauben und Verstehen* I, Tübingen 71972, 313-36, ET in *The Old Testament and Christian Faith*, ed. B. W. Anderson, New York and London 1963, 8-35).

For criticism see also Marlé, R., 'Bultmann and the Old Testament', in T.E.O'Meara and D.M.Weiser (eds.), *Rudolf Bultmann in Catholic Thought*, New York, Evanston and London 1963, 49-63; Richardson, A., 'Is the Old Testament the Propaedeutic to Christian Faith?,' in B.W.Anderson (ed.), op.cit., 36-48; Geyer, H.G., 'Zur Frage nach der Notwendigkeit des Alten Testaments', *EvTh* 25, 1965, 207-37; Seebass, H., *Biblische Hermeneutik* [above 19], 55-73; Baker, D.L.,*Two Testaments* [above 1], 157-87; Müller, P.-G., 'Altes Testament, Israel und das Judentum in der Theologie Rudolf Bultmanns', in *Kontinuität und Einheit. Festschrift F.Mussner*, Freiburg, Basle and Vienna 1981, 439-72. In defence of Bultmann (though not successful in giving a basically revised picture of his position): Hübner, H., 'Rudolf Bultmann und das Alte Testament', *KuD* 30, 1984, 250-72.

For Bultmann, too, the pattern of law and gospel, with reference to Luther and Paul, provides the criterion (319 = ET 14) for a genuinely 'historical' investigation of the Old Testament, which can only interpret it 'in terms of the question what basic possibility it presents for an understanding of human existence' (318 = ET 13). Being under the law (as depicted by the Old Testament) is the presupposition for being under grace, and to this extent the Old Testament is the presupposition of the New; however, this is not so in terms of a historical view, 'but rather in the *material* sense that man must stand under the Old Testament if he wants to understand the New' (319 = ET 15; agreement with this 'preunderstanding' is also expressed by K.Michalson, 'Bultmann against Marcion', in B.W.Anderson (ed.), *Old Testament*, 49-63). Bultmann himself then answers the question whether it has to be the Old Testament itself which embodies 'standing under the law' in the negative: 'The pre-understanding of the Gospel which emerges under the Old Testament can emerge just as well within other historical embodiments of the divine Law' (17). In this connection it is not decisive *theologically* that Bultmann sees a *historical* development leading from the Old to the New Testament, approaching the question from a viewpoint restricted to the history of religion (cf. P.G.Müller, op.cit., 445ff.).

It is remarkable how with Hirsch and Bultmann an existentialist approach concerned with the direct relevance of the Old Testament for Christian faith, and a phenomenology of religions perspective as held by the liberal school, are in competition. The latter comes off best. This approach does not make it clear in what way the Old Testament is binding on Christian faith.

E. Würthwein criticized this very point, even before Hirsch's book appeared, in his article 'Vom Verstehen des Alten Testaments' (*Festschrift G. Beer*, Stuttgart 1935, 128-46 = id., *Wort und Existenz*, Göttingen 1970, 9-27). It is possible to treat the Old Testament in terms of the history of religion as a historical source document, but in that case the scholar remains a detached observer. 'I do not experience anything new in principle which makes a claim on me; I am dealing with the past, not the present' (131/12). 'I only understand a claim fully when I feel myself affected by it, when I know that it applies to me and that I am challenged by it' (136/17). The goal of Old Testament exegesis is defined (along with that of kerygmatic theology) as: 'working out the proclamation, the message of the Old Testament' (133/14). However, the content of this message is a particular form of existentialist theology. Penetrating to the inner concern of the text means penetrating 'to the form of existence which is expressed in it' (146/27). An anthropological approach resolves the difficulty that it is old Israel which is being addressed in the Old Testament: there are different types of people – 'they are all the same in one thing: in their position before God' (137/18). This position, which is described in exemplary fashion in the Old Testament as that of sinful man confronted with the demands of God, is used as the basis for the distinctive understanding of existence in the situation of the New Testament: 'The message of the gracious God can be heard in all its depth only where one is aware of the demands of God and the sin of man' (144/25).

The works of F. Baumgärtel (cf. e.g. Seebass, *Biblische Hermeneutik*, above 19, 26-42; Baker, *Two Testaments*, above 1, 191-201) are to be seen in a similar perspective though the tone in them is quite different: it is a warm revivalist piety, a serious concern for a truly 'evangelical' (a favourite word of the author's) understanding of the Old Testament in the service of proclamation. Alongside earlier occasional writings (above 13, 28) and contributions to the hermeneutical discussion after the Second World War (see below 41–3f.), emphasis should be laid on Baumgärtel's study of the history of piety (*Die Eigenart der alttestamentlichen Frömmigkeit*, Schwerin 1932) and his theological *magnum opus*, *Verheissung. Zur Frage des evangelischen Verständnisses des Alten Testaments*, Gütersloh 1952 (for criticism cf. G. von Rad, 'Verheissung', *EvTh*

13, 1953, 406-13). Here, too, we find the same subjectivism as in the existentialist interpretation of the Old Testament: the starting point in the person of the author, who expresses himself in a kind of experiential piety (in the tradition of Erlangen Lutheranism, cf. Baumgärtel's defence against this charge with reference to Hofmann, *Verheissung*, 70f.). The decisive factor in assessing the significance of the Old Testament is the degree to which the figures of the Old Testament are touched by the basic promise of the Old Testament – Baumgärtel understands the term salvation history in this subjectivist sense ('Das alttestamentliche Geschehen als "heilsgeschichtliches" Geschehen', *Geschichte und Altes Testament*, Alt Festschrift, Tübingen 1953, 13-28), as an 'inward event to be investigated in terms of the history of piety' (theses 4-13). The basic promise of the Old Testament, 'I am the Lord your God', 'affects our own existence before God to the degree that this encounter is also our own encounter... under the gospel' ('Das alttestamentliche Geschehen', 14): 'the history of Israel is our own history of salvation and disaster' (*Verheissung*, 58). Old Testament man experiences the basic promise at three points: 1. the experience of the revelation of God as a transcendent power; 2. the experience that this revelation of God is directed towards me, along with the experience that I try to avoid this unconditional truth; 3. the experience that here there is a judgment on my sin and that in this way I am in a hopeless position, along with the experience (which primarily culminates in an unsatisfied longing for salvation) that the way to a living communion with God is opened up to me as the only possibility of existence (*Verheissung*, 37f.). The Christian experiences the same thing in faith in Jesus Christ (cf. id., 'Das hermeneutische Problem des Alten Testaments', *TLZ* 79, 1954, 199-212 = *Probleme alttestamentlicher Hermeneutik*, ed. C.Westermann, TB 11, Munich 1960 [³1968], 114-39, 208/131). In all this we are 'companions of the men of the Old Covenant' (*Verheissung*, 55). However, in the light of the promise in Christ the basic promise becomes the gospel for us. For the burden of the old covenant is fulfilled in him (67). The specific realizations of the promise in the old covenant (in the physical existence of the people in Palestine and the historical course of its existence and in the life of the individual Israelite) are finished with as far as we are concerned (*Verheissung*, 49ff.) – here we find the reservations over, say, the 'this-worldliness' and the 'cultic and nationalistic conditioning' of Old Testament piety apply (cf. *Eigenart*, passim; 'Das alttestamentliche Geschehen', 21; and already *Die Bedeutung des Alten Testaments*, above 28, passim; *Die Nation vor Gott*, ed. W. Künneth and H.Schreiner, above 28, 103f.). Already in the Old Testament there are signs of a 'breakthrough towards something new'; this conditioning is transcended at the periphery (*Eigenart*, 94ff.). However, the main thing is that even in the tribulation and hopelessness within the Old Testament the promise 'I am the Lord your God' rings out (*Verheissung*, 67f.). The important thing is the experience, being encountered: that alone is salvation history which is experienced by us as 'the forgiveness of sins, being children of God, eternal life – justification', 'which is experienced by us as being directed towards us and forming the basis of our existence' (*Das alttestamentliche Geschehen*, 14f.).

For Baumgärtel, too, the real meaning of the Old Testament for Christian faith can only be grasped in a negative way: looking to the promise which is not fulfilled (*Verheissung*, 51ff.), the lostness of man before God's claim in judgment, in the law (ibid., 54ff.), the hopelessness, the failure (cf. also 'Das hermeneutische Problem', 208/131). Here Baumgärtel stresses 'that the Old Testament is primarily testimony to a "religion", that this religion is a non-Christian religion and that in its self-understanding it originally has *nothing to do* with the gospel' ('Der Dissensus im Verständnis des Alten Testaments', *EvTh* 14, 1954, [298-313] 312); 'It remains an alien word from an alien religion…'('Das hermeneutische Problem', 209/132). Only by means of existentialist understanding can it become a testimony which speaks to Christians. Baumgärtel too retains the dualism of the history-of-religions approach.

The disclosure of man's hopeless situation before God is also the nucleus of the Old Testament as a 'book of promise' for A.Jepsen ('Die Botschaft des Alten Testaments', in *Festschrift H.Schreiner*, Gütersloh 1953, 149-63). Man's need awakens the expectation of a final history which will bring redemption. The New Testament bears witness to this redemption. Cf. also the position of D.Barthelemy (*Dieu et son Image. Ébauche d'une Théologie biblique*, Paris 1964), who defines the Old Testament as 'la loi de mise à mort de l'homme ancien' (2) which shows us man characterized by original sin in his idolatry and his flight from God (21): 'Car l'Ancien Testament est avant tout le grand dépistage de l'idolatrie, le grand dépistage des contrefaçons du Dieu vivant.' However, it also portrays the action of God who as the hidden one persists in his plan of a perfect community which he realizes in the new covenant. For the position of F.Hesse, which is in many respects similar to his teacher Baumgärtel, cf. below 105f.

II

The Problem of a Systematic Account

Simultaneously with this controversy over the Christian use of the Old Testament (cf. also my *Problems of Biblical Theology*), the discussion was continuing in the sphere of the descriptive understanding of Old Testament theology over the form of presentation and the structure of such a systematic outline.

Eichrodt's article, 'Hat die alttestamentliche Theologie noch selbständige Bedeutung innerhalb der alttestamentlichen Wissenschaft?' (*ZAW* 47, 1929, 83-91, cf. also Bjørndalen, below 45, 23ff.) was a direct answer to the contribution by O.Eissfeldt (above 17f.). Eichrodt clearly recognized the demand that the selection of material for an Old Testament theology must correspond to the goal of revelation in Christ (he referred to the contemporary discussion among the secular historians E.Spranger, C.H.Becker and others of the principle that all historical research must be done from the perspective of particular principles of selection which derive from an evaluative basic attitude). He therefore argued that the nature of Old Testament religion can only be understood if one grasps its connection with the centre of revelation, because this is the only way of penetrating to the meaningfulness of Old Testament history. But that does not mean that such an understanding must consist purely of kerygmatic statements of faith. The Old Testament scholar is in no way forced to existential verdicts on all sides. 'He does make his statements on the presupposition of an existential judgment. In other respects, though, he is engaged in describing empirical facts and leaves it to the dogmatic theologian, as the representative of the normative discipline, to evaluate the connections which he demonstrates between God and man in the Old Testament in the system of Christian belief as normative knowledge' (90). This statement in some ways takes up Steuernagel's programme of 1925 (above 12); the methodological principle used is the distinction in principle between an objectifying ('empirical') description of history and a level of evaluation which has a limited influence merely as a principle of selection and arrangement for the material at a first level.

Dentan (*Preface*, above 1, 63) notes that the term 'Old Testament theology' is used in an ambiguous way because of the contrast between the systematic theological efforts described in I.2 and 3 and the investigations on a strictly historical basis. We shall go on, first, to consider this second area.

As we saw, the programme of providing a systematic framework for any detailed account of a 'theology of the Old Testament' was developed as a reaction to the increasing collapse of such outlines in the nineteenth and at the beginning of the twentieth century, with the result that they became mere 'histories of Israelite and Jewish religion'. However, detailed accounts in the new form only began to appear in 1933.

Summary literature:

Alonso Schöckel, L., 'Biblische Theologie des Alten Testaments', *StZ* 172, 1962-63, 34-51 = 'Tendencias actuales en la teologia biblica del Antiguo Testamento', *SelTeol* 3, 1964, 209-16; Baumgärtel, F., 'Erwägungen zur Darstellung der Theologie des AT', *TLZ* 76, 1951, 257-72; Bjørndalen, A.J., 'Det Gamle Testaments Teologi. Metodiske hovedproblemer', *TTK* 30, 1959, 22-38, 92-116; Boschi, B.G., 'Per una teologia dell'Antico Testamento', *SacDot* 21, 1976, 147-74; R.E.Clements, 'The Problem of Old Testament Theology', *LQHR* 6, 1965, 11-17; Festorazzi, F., 'Rassegna di Teologia biblica dell'Antico Testamento. Il problema metodologico (I)', *RivBib* 10, 1962, 297-316; Goldingay, *Approaches* (above 1), 24ff.; Gross, H., 'Was ist alttestamentliche Theologie?', *TTZ* 67, 1958, 355-63; Hamp, V., 'Neuere Theologien des Alten Testaments', *BZ* NF 2, 1958, 303-13; Hasel, G.F., 'Methodology as a Major Problem in the Current Crisis of Old Testament Theology', *BTB* 2, 1972, 177-98; Jepsen, A., 'Theologie des Alten Testaments. Wandlungen der Formen und Ziele', in *Bericht von der Theologie*, ed. G.Kulicke/ K.Matthiae/P.P.Sänger, Berlin 1971, 15-32 = id., *Der Herr ist Gott*, Berlin 1978, 142-54; Loretz, O., 'Israel und sein Gottesbund. Die Theologie des Alten Testaments auf neuen Wegen', *WuW* 15, 1960, 85-92; Nielsen, E., 'Det gamle Testamente', in B.Noack (ed.), *Teologien og dens fag*, Kopenhagen 1960, 13-42, esp. 38-42; Otto, E., 'Erwägungen zu den Prolegomena einer Theologie des Alten Testaments', *Kairos* 19, 1977, 53-72; Ramlot, R., 'Une décade de théologie biblique', *RThom* 64, 1964, 65-96; 65, 1965, 95-135; Rendtorff, R,.'Alttestamentliche Theologie und israelitisch-jüdische Religionsgeschichte', *Zwischenstation*, Festschrift E.Kupisch, Munich 1963, 208-22 = id., *Gesammelte Studien zum Alten Testament*, Munich 1975, 137-51; Würthwein, E., *TR* 1971, above 2; Zimmerli, W., 'Erwägungen zur Gestalt einer alttestamentlichen Theologie', *TLZ* 98, 1973, 81-98 = *Studien zur alttestamentlichen Theologie und Prophetie. Gesammelte Aufsätze* II, TB 51, Munich 1974, 27-54. Cf. also above 1f.

We already find the beginnings of a systematic form of presentation in the nineteenth century. Thus for example in the Old Testament Theology by E.Riehm (above 4) there is a historical division into the three periods of Mosaism, prophetism and Judaism, but within these main sections the sub-sections, chapters and paragraphs are arranged from the perspective of systematic theology. The material about 'Mosaism', for example, is arranged under the headings: "God and God's state' (86ff.), 'The people of Yahweh...'(100ff.), 'The religious communication between Israel and its God' (the sacrificial cult, 114ff.), 'The arrangements for preserving communication between Yahweh and his people' (sin and atonement, 124ff.). We find the same thing with Stade (above 5f.), who divides the history of Israelite religion into three periods: a pre-prophetic stage, the age of prophecy, and Judaism; here, at least for the first section, he provides a phenomenology of early Israelite religion arranged according to themes. With H.Schultz (above 6) we find for the first time a division which was to be followed by many successors: he begins in a First Part (81-278) with a historical account of 'the development of the religion of Israel to the time of Ezra', but then goes on to present in two further Parts a systematically arranged account of Israel's 'consciousness of salvation' (278-439) and 'religious world-view' (440-758) on the basis of what he assumes to be the stage of development 'at the end of the prophetic period'. In the Third Part he chooses a division which is clearly dependent on the classical dogmatic arrangement of *loci*: God and world (440-579), man and sin (579-664), the hope of Israel (664-758). The development towards Judaism is then presented in an appendix (758-831), clearly set apart. Similarly, in Dillmann (above 6) we find the division between a 'historical' (76-202) and a doctrinal part (202-544). H.Wheeler Robinson, *The Religious Ideas of the Old Testament*, New York/London 1931, [8]1949, has a division by 'ideas': Chapter II 'The Idea of Religion', Chapter III 'The Idea of God', Chapter IV 'The Idea of Man', Chapter V 'The Approach of God to Man', Chapter VI 'The Approach of Man to God' (here we meet the dogmatic scheme); then follow: 'The Problems of Sin and Suffering', 'The Hope of the Nation' and a concluding Chapter, 'The Permanent Value of the Old Testament'. E.König (above 11f.) begins in a first part with considerations of the 'special position, origin and main stages in the general life of the legitimate religion of Israel' (17-110); here Chapter III (84-110) contains a sketch of developments in the history of religion. The second main section, 'the history of the development of the individual factors of the true religion of Israel' (111-306) is then similarly divided into the following chapters: 'Theology in the stricter sense' (the doctrine of God), 'The relationship of the world and original man to God', 'Sin.,.', 'The ways of restoring lost humanity' (a summary chapter containing a great variety of themes like salvation history, cult and prophecy).

1933 saw the appearance of the first outlines in accordance with the new systematic programme. The first volume of W.Eichrodt's *Theology of the Old Testament* was published (see above); the two thin volumes of E.Sellin's *Alttestamentliche Theologie auf religionsgeschichtlicher Grundlage* (Leipzig 1933, [2]1936) appeared in the same year. Sellin deliberately chose to divide his work into a 'History of Israelite and Jewish Religion' (Vol.I) and an 'Old Testament Theology' proper (II); in his view the theology of the Old Testament was 'a discipline of Christian theology' and a 'historical' discipline, so that the two parts were organically connected. The 'history of Israelite and Jewish religion' has to depict the whole course of the history of Israelite religion. By contrast, the task of a 'theology of the Old Testament' in the strict sense is to give a systematic account of the faith and teaching in the Old Testament, 'but only in so far as it has recognized Jesus Christ and his apostles as the presupposition and basis of its gospel, as the revelation of the God proclaimed by them', 'the spiritual and religious world which the Old Testament has in common with the New Testament' (*Theologie* I; cf. *Religionsgeschichte*, 1f.). Alongside this we also find the various trends within Judaism which similarly – and rightly – refer to the Old Testament. However, the traditions continued by them in the Old Testament are not to be left out of account, as 'national cultic religion' and 'prophetic-moral-universalist-eschatological religion' fight together in a long historical process. However, it is very easy to stress the prophetic religion 'and present it in summary form from theological perspectives, since it is a unity, the religion which Jesus and his apostles also found in the Old Testament' (*Theologie*, 3).

The division of the material follows the traditional system of *loci*: Chapter I: The Doctrine of God; Chapter II: The Doctrine of Man; Chapter III: The Doctrine of Divine Judgment and Salvation (eschatology). It is the same, but on a smaller scale, in L.Köhler's *Theology of the Old Testament* (Tübingen 1936, [4]1966, = ET London and Philadelphia 1958, cf. Würthwein, *TR* 1971, above 2, 199-202): 'God', 'Man', 'Judgment and Salvation'. One can see more clearly in Köhler than in Sellin the difficulties which liberal Protestantism found with the Old Testament. Whereas Sellin coped with the problem very rigorously by dividing the whole of the material into two forms of religion and distributed it between volumes on the history of religion and theology, Köhler has one paragraph with the title 'Man's Expedient for his Own Redemption: The Cult' (section 52, 169-88 = ET 181-98), which he can only find a place for in the second part, 'Man'! (For the judgment on the cult which underlies this cf. also P.Volz, 'Die radikale Ablehnung der Kultreligion durch die alttestamentlichen Propheten', *ZST* 14, 1937, 63-85, and R.Hentschke, *Die Stellung der vorexilischen Propheten zum Kultus*, BZAW 75, Berlin 1956.)

In Köhler we also find the classic definition of a theology of the Old Testament understood as a systematic descriptive account: 'One may give a book the title Old Testament Theology if it manages to bring together and to relate those ideas, thoughts and concepts of the Old Testament which are or can be theologically significant, justified by their content and in their right context' (Foreword, V = ET 7; cf. also the definition in E.Jacob [below 53], 10 = ET 11. Dentan, *Preface* [above 1], 94, still defines Old Testament theology as 'that Christian theological discipline which treats of the religious ideas of the Old Testament systematically...' [cf.also 122]). On the basis of these presuppositions and in view of the general structure of such a work the real question can only be which principle of division is best suited to an appropriate arrangement of the material. Whereas Sellin and Köhler still drew on classical dogmatics for their division, O.Procksch was the first to devote more serious attention to the question of a division which would be more appropriate to the material in the Old Testament. His posthumously published *Theologie des Alten Testaments*, Gütersloh 1950 (which he in fact finished in 1942; he died in 1947) reflects the many tensions which previous developments had caused in the outward and inward form of the account. (For Procksch cf. especially C.A.Simpson, 'Professor Procksch's Theology of the Old Testament', *ATR* 34, 1952, 116-22; J.N.Schofield, 'Otto Procksch', in *Contemporary Old Testament Theologians*, ed. R.B.Laurin, Valley Forge 1970, 91-120; Würthwein, *TR* 1971, above 2, 202-5; and his own account in *Religionswissenschaft der Gegenwart*, ed. E.Stange (above 16), 161-94). Following the structure in Schultz and Sellin, but for other reasons (the history of religion is to be included in the theology of the Old Testament, because the history is the form in which the self-revelation of God is disclosed, 17), Procksch, too, prefaces his systematic account of the 'thought-world' of the Old Testament with a detailed historical outline of the 'historical world' (48-419). For his account of the 'thought-world' (420-712) Procksch is the first to use relational terms: 'God and the world', 'God and the people', 'God and man'; these were later taken over by Eichrodt (who owed them to the lectures of Procksch, his teacher, cf. *Theologie des Alten Testaments* I, Leipzig 1933, 6 n.1 = Stuttgart/Göttingen [5]1957 [[8]1968], 7 n. 19, not in the ET).

In Procksch's work one can note a hidden division between the descriptive method of his account and a theological concern which he formulates right at the beginning of his work (cf. already id., *NKZ* 1925, above 14): 'All theology is christology' (1); Christ is the centre point of the theology of history; the Old Testament has him as its goal; he can only be understood in his historicity in the light of the Old Testament (7ff.). The Old Testament is brought into an indissoluble connection with the New through the figure of Christ. Between the history of Israel and church history there is the double relationship of causality and analogy (11). However, as has been rightly observed (Dentan, *Preface*, above 1, 74) these principles are not implemented in his account.

The form of systematic presentation then reaches a climax (Hasel, *BTB* 1972, 187ff.; id., *Old Testament Theology*[2], 42ff., 'Cross-Section-Method') in Walther Eichrodt's three-volume work (which appeared as two volumes in later editions and in the ET: *Theologie des Alten Testaments* I-III, Leipzig 1933-1939 [I, cf. above; II[4]

1961, [7]1974] = ET *Theology of the Old Testament*, London and Philadelphia I, 1961 [[5]1978]; II, 1967 [[4]1982]).

For Eichrodt see especially F.Festorazzi, 'Rassegna di Teologia dell'Antico Testamento. Il problema methodologico (II). La Teologia dell'AT di W.Eichrodt e di G. von Rad', *RivBib* 12, 1964, 27-48; N.K.Gottwald, 'Recent Biblical Theologies. IX. Walther Eichrodt's *Theology of the Old Testament*', *ExpT* 74, 1963, 209-212; id., 'W.Eichrodt, *Theology of the Old Testament*', in *Contemporary Old Testament Theologians*, ed. Laurin, 25-62; W.G.Nesbit, *A Study of Methodologies in Contemporary Old Testament Biblical Theologies*, PhD Milwaukee 1968 (Ann Arbor microfilm), 11-173; E.Würthwein, *TR* 1971, above 2, 195-9; D.G.Spriggs, *Two Old Testament Theologies. A Comparative Evaluation of the Contributions of Eichrodt and von Rad to our Understanding of the Nature of Old Testament Theology*, SBT II 30, London 1974.

In the prefaces and in the introductory paragraphs, 'Old Testament Theology: The Problem and the Method' (I[5], 1-8 = ET I, 25-35) Eichrodt gives a clear account of his aims: on the presupposition that Old Testament theology is a historical and not a normative question (Preface to the Fifth Revised Edition, I[5], vi = ET I, 13), but in distinction to the earlier historical and genetic forms of account (I[5], 2ff. = ET I, 27ff.) he is concerned 'to present the religion of which the records are to be found in the Old Testament as '*A self-contained entity exhibiting, despite ever-changing historical conditions, constant basic tendency and character*' (from the Preface to the first edition, ET I, 17; the italics are Eichrodt's own, original ones). As Old Testament religion is on the one hand connected with the religions of the ancient Near East and on the other is not only historically but also in essence bound up with the living reality of the New Testament ('That which binds together indivisibly the two realms of the Old and New Testaments – different in externals though they may be – is the irruption of the Kingship of God into the world and its establishment here', I, 2 = ET 26); defined more closely, the problem is 'how to understand the realm of OT belief in its structural unity and how, by examining on the one hand its religious environment and on the other its essential coherence with the NT, to illuminate its profoundest meaning' (I, 6 = ET 31). Eichrodt thus aims at a systematic account. However, in his view this principle cannot be carried through in its purity: the element of the historical process of growth in Israelite religion has to be noted carefully (though it should not make us lapse into a purely historical and genetic account): 'the right way to make allowance for this is to have the historical principle operating side by side with the systematic in a complementary role' (I, 6 = ET 32). Moreover such lines of development have constantly to be discovered in the process of writing the Theology (though Eichrodt is well aware of the inconsistency with which he has been often charged, as the quotation shows).

In all this Eichrodt has a further central concern: 'One thing... must be guarded against and that is any arrangement of the whole body of material which derives not from the laws of its own nature but from some dogmatic scheme' (ibid.). Therefore all conceptuality deriving from Christian dogmatics is to be rejected (I, 6 = ET 33). The purpose must be 'to plot our course as best we can along the lines of the OT's own dialectic' (I,7 = ET 33). This leads to the whole account being presented in three main groups of themes (taken over from Procksch, see 49f.): 'God and the People', 'God and the World', 'God and Man'.

However, Eichrodt goes on to choose another principle, around which the whole theological content of the Old Testament is to be grouped: the idea of the covenant. After an introductory section 'The Covenant Relationship' (I, 9-32 = ET 36-69), the whole of the subject matter of the first half is in fact arranged under the heading of covenant, at least by title ('The Covenant Statutes', 'The Nature of the Covenant God', 'The Instruments of the Covenant', 'Covenant-Breaking and Judgment', 'Fulfilling the Covenant: [The Consummation of God's Dominion']). However, even at this point it is questionable whether Eichrodt has also retained a reference to the covenant concept right through the content of all the sections of the first part (he answers this criticism in the Preface to the Fifth Edition, I[5], VIf. = ET 13f., by saying that the decisive factor is not the occurrence of the word but the assurance of the fundamental free act of God in history as the foundation of faith which is expressed through the word covenant. However, the concept is itself vague and is used in different ways, cf. e.g. the criticism by Gottwald in Laurin, above 49). In Parts Two and Three the word is then completely abandoned in the headings, and the reference of the content to the basic principle also becomes increasingly loose.

Of course there is a problem here to which we must return later, cf. Chapter IV, 125ff.

Even after Eichrodt, the question of how to divide up a theology of the Old Testament constructed on systematic lines remained an unsolved problem. Further works appeared which, despite his call for a principle of division to match the material, were again more markedly arranged along dogmatic lines. Thus there was the (Roman Catholic) *Theologie des Alten Testaments* by P.Heinisch, Bonn 1940, divided into the sections: God, Creation (sub-divisions: spiritual beings, world, man), way of life (ethics, cult, sin and conversion), the beyond (death and resurrection) and redemption (judgment, expectation of the end, Messiah). O.J.Baab, *The Theology of the Old Testament*, New York 1949, was warmly welcomed as the first new Theology of the Old Testament since that of Davidson (1904) to be published in English in the Anglo-Saxon world; it is easy to see how the way in which the chapters are arranged (God, Man, Sin, Salvation, Kingdom of God, Death and the Afterlife, the Problem of Evil) is only a slight variation on the classical arrangement. The same thing happens over the division of the subject-matter in T.C.Vriezen (*Hoofdlijnen der Theologie van het Oude Testament*, Wageningen 1949 [³1960] = ET *An Outline of Old Testament Theology*, Oxford 1958, ²1970, translation of the third Dutch edition). A first part with Prolegomena (on the problem of 'History and the Word of God') is followed by 'God, Man, The Intercourse between God and Man, The Intercourse between Man and Man (ethics), God, Man and the World in the Present and the Future'. This is still the tripartite division into theology, anthropology and eschatology. However, Vriezen attempts to indicate the dialectical character of the biblical statements by using relational expressions and by prefacing the work with an account of its principles, to indicate 'The nature of the knowledge of God in the Old Testament as an intimate relationship between the Holy God and Man'. In content his work is close to that of Eichrodt, but he avoids stressing the term 'covenant'. The way in which H.Wheeler Robinson arranged his article on the subject in *Record and Revelation*, above 2 (God, Man, Sin and Grace, the Judgment of History), should also be mentioned.

In *The Religious Ideas of the Old Testament*, London and New York 1913 (⁹1952), Robinson had looked for four basic ideas in the Old Testament: the idea of God, the idea of man, the idea of suffering and the idea of the kingdom of God. For Robinson cf. also M.E.Polley, 'H.Wheeler Robinson and the Problem of Organizing an Old Testament Theology', in *The Use of the Old*

Testament in the New and Other Essays. Studies... W.F.Sti-nespring, Durham, NC 1972, 149-69.

If we look through the other general accounts which have appeared we find (with the exception of von Rad, see below) either the classical scheme or more or less independent attempts at a division taken from the Old Testament itself. The (Roman Catholic) account by P. van Imschoot, *Théologie de l'Ancien Testament* (two vols, Tournai 1954 = ET New York 1965) divides its material under the two main themes 'God' and 'Man', each of which occupies a separate volume, but this division seems very formal, especially when the individual chapters then present very different material; the titles also include terms of relationship ('God and the world', 'God and his people') which again serve as vehicles for the most varied themes. The arrangement is not at all convincing, especially as theological concepts alternate with themes relating to subject-matter (angels, demons, prophecy, etc.). The division in E.Jacob (*Théologie de l'Ancien Testament*, Neuchâtel [1955] ²1968 = ET London and New York 1958; cf. already id., *Les Thèmes essentiels d'une Théologie de l'Ancien Testament*, Neuchâtel 1955) is essentially stricter: he arranges the whole material under the main headings of the action of God in creation and history, but prefaces the relevant main section on 'The Action of God according to the Old Testament' (97-223 = ET 121-275) with a shorter one on the nature of God: 'Characteristic Aspects of the God of the Old Testament' (27-95 = ET 37-120). The fact that this is in turn followed by a conclusion, 'Opposition to and Final Triumph of God's Work' (225-75 = ET 281-342) once again shows the influence of the old scheme with its third theme, that of eschatology. Moreover, one might ask here whether the formal unity is not purchased by subordinating the material with excessive violence to a few themes, indeed to just one theme. Ultimately one could indeed say that God is the sole theme of the Old Testament (see ch.IV below), but is this recognition also appropriate to a thematic arrangement of the material?

In G.A.F.Knight, *A Christian Theology of the Old Testament*, London 1959, all the material is arranged under the heading of 'God'; although the intention is quite different (see below Ch.VI), the division of content is in fact similar to that in Jacob: Part I, 'God' (his revelation and his being, 17-104), is followed by 'God and Creation' (107-45), 'God and Israel' (149-93) and finally a section which collects up all the other themes like covenant, sacrifice, messianology and eschatology under a heading which is more like a slogan: 'The Zeal of the Lord' (197-348). The short outline by J.N.Schofield (*Introducing Old Testament Theology*, London 1964 [1966]), has headings which are used in strict parallel: 'The God Who Acts', 'The God Who Speaks', 'God's Kinship with Man', 'The Glory of God'. The division in I.P.Seierstad (*Gammeltestamentlig bibelteologie* I, Oslo 1957) should also be mentioned: 'The Old Testament testimony to God, the Old Testament testimony to humanity, the Old Testament testimony to the religious and ethical communion between God and man' (45). Even after the basic objections which von Rad made to a systematic arrangement of the materials for an Old Testament theology (see ch.III below), attempts at such a division were not abandoned. The authors of earlier accounts maintained their principles when new editions became due (thus Eichrodt, Preface to the Fifth Edition [I[5], I, VII = ET 13] when he still did not know von Rad's account in its extended form, and in his extended reaction to it in the German fourth edition of Volume II, Preface, esp. XIf. [not in the ET] and Jacob, Preface to the Second Edition, V-VII [not in the ET] – who did not think it convincing). However, the newer outlines, too, almost all follow systematic arrangements. Thus M.G.Cordero (*Teologia de la Biblia I. Antiguo Testamento*, Madrid 1970) adopts a system largely determined by dogmatics: I. The Content of Faith ('Las creencias'). A. God ('Dios', 33-372); B. The manifestations of God ('Las manifestaciones divinas', 373-429); C. Angels ('Los espiritus angélicos', 430-68); D.Anthropology (469-534). II. The Hopes ('Las esperanzas': messianic expectation, kingdom of God, eschatology, 535-82). III. The religious and moral obligations ('Las obligaciones religiosas y morales', 583-656). IV. Fall and rehabilitation of man ('Caida y rehabilitación del hombre', 657-730). After meticulous consideration (cf. 10f. = ET 13f., and id., 'Erwägungen [above 46]), W.Zimmerli (*Grundriss der alttestamentlichen Theologie*, Stuttgart 1972 [[2]1976] = ET *Old Testament Theology in Outline*, Atlanta, Ga and Edinburgh 1978) decides again to give his account a systematic structure, beginning from the revelation of the name of God (see below, Chapter IV: for the work cf. C.Westermann, 'Zu zwei Theologien des Alten Testaments [Zimmerli and G.Fohrer, *Grundstrukturen*]', *EvTh* 34, 1974, 96-112; E.Osswald, 'Theologie des Alten Testaments – eine bleibende Aufgabe', *TLZ* 99, 1974, [641-58] 647-9; E.Otto, *Kairos* 1977, above 46, 57ff.). However, this presupposition leads to an unexpressed division into two parts: 1. *Of God*: I. 'Fundamentals' (name and nature of Yahweh, 12-48 = ET 17-58), II. 'The Gifts Bestowed by Yahweh' (War, the land, the divine presence, charismata [offices], 49-93 = ET 59-108), III. 'Yahweh's Commandment' (94-122 = ET 109-140). 2. *Of man*: IV. 'Life before God' (obedience, righteousness, love; praise and cry for help, wisdom, 123-46 = ET 142-66); V. 'Crisis and Hope' (judgment and salvation, 147-207 = ET 167-240). The basic division – Part I, God; Part II, Man, has recently been suggested again by Boschi (above 45). It also appears in the TEF Study Guide by D.F.Hinson, *Old Testament Introduction 3: Theology of the Old Testament*, London 1976: 1. God; 2. Other spiritual beings; 3. Man; 4-7: Fall, redemption, new life, ultimate destiny; 8. The Old Testament in the New Testament. By contrast, A.Deissler, *Die Grundbotschaft des Alten Testaments. Ein theologischer Durchblick*, Freiburg/Basle/Vienna 1972, uses the message of the one God (cf. Deut.6.4) as a scarlet thread to be traced throughout the testimony of the Old Testament, including wisdom. However, this is a very brief account. J.L.McKenzie, *A Theology of the Old Testament*, London 1974, chooses the ways in which Israel encountered Yahweh as the principle for his thematic arrangement (cf. 32f.). This produces an unusual sequence of areas of subject-matter (though here, as a Roman Catholic, the author is clearly less constrained): I. Cult; II. Revelation (especially prophecy); III. History; IV. Nature; V. Wisdom (for the arrangement cf. 33f.). At the end there remain topics which cannot be subsumed under these headings: VI. Political and Social Institutions and VII. Eschatology (a last influence of the dogmatic arrangement which is otherwise abandoned).

We find a mixed division, but one which is essentially composed of the usual *topoi*, in R.E.Clements, *Old Testament Theology. A Fresh Approach*, London 1978 (cf. my review in *VT* 30, 1980, 369-73). The brief account of the content (chs.3-6) is framed here by detailed prolegomena to Old Testament theology (chs.1,2,7,8). The central part is divided on the one hand into the themes 'God' (Ch.3) and 'People' (ch.4), which relate to subject matter, and on the other into the dogmatic pattern of law (ch.5) and promise (ch.6). Clements asks how far the broken lines of the Old Testament can be connected with those of later ages (24), which leads him to fall back on this solution. This is an example of how it is possible to have a mixed form consisting of themes taken from the Old Testament itself and headings from dogmatics. At the same time, however, this situation shows the general uncertainty surrounding the whole discussion of the question of the structure of an Old Testament theology.

The most recent example is C.Westermann, *Theologie des Alten Testaments in Grundzügen*, ATD Ergänzungsheft 6, Göttingen 1978 (cf. also the account by W.Brueggemann, 'A Convergence in Recent Old Testament Theologies', *JSOT* 18, 1980, 2-18). As with other famous names in the field of Old Testament theology (above all von Rad and Zimmerli) the construction of this work, too, can only be understood against the background of a system developed in many preliminary studies on the Old Testament (for a discussion of its content cf. Chs. IV and V below). In accordance with a particular form of existential approach, the work is characterized by various overlapping polarities, e.g. by the opposition between God's action in saving and blessing (or in history and creation), Parts II (28-71) and III (72-101), between God's judgment and mercy (Part IV, 102-33: prophecy of judgment and salvation, and apocalyptic), and between the activity (and word) of God and the response of humanity (on two levels: within part I ['What does the Old Testament say about God?'] and again as an overall title to Part V, 134-91, sub-divided into three ['The response in discourse', 'The response in action', 'The response in thinking or reflection']. It should be noted that the concept of 'Israel's response' also plays a role in von Rad's theology [see 63f. below], though there it is a siding into which material [psalms and wisdom] that evades the author's historical approach can be shunted off. In Westermann the keyword has a much more major role and is one of the pillars of the dialectic which forms an overall foundation.) The hermeneutical considerations to follow later will have to illuminate the background to this. However, it is striking to what extent a glance at the arrangement of a work of Old Testament theology already makes the author's approach clear. But Westermann sees not only a dialectic but also a 'centre' (cf. Ch.IV below) in Old Testament theology: it is 'the oneness of God which makes the connection possible' (25-27); here he has the same reference to Deut.6.4 that we already found in Deissler (cf. on this Ch.IV below).

As an appendix to this survey I should note that here and there one still finds individual supporters of a historical and genetic presentation of the theology of the Old Testament. It is probably no coincidence that these are in part prompted by a fundamentalist approach. The tension between history and tradition (see Ch.III below) cannot appear if events and accounts of them coincide (because the authors are regarded as eye-witnesses). One example of this kind of presentation is C.K.Lehman, *Biblical Theology* I. *Old Testament*, Scottdale, Pa 1971. In this volume the division of the Massoretic canon itself (Pentateuch, Prophets, Writings) provides the division in the presentation, and the assumption of an unbroken and reliable historical tradition from Adam to the post-exilic period makes historical events and theological significance coincide. By contrast the equally fundamentalist book by J.B.Payne, *The Theology of the Older Testament*, Grand Rapids 1962, ³1971, has a dogmatic division: God, man, grace, commitment (penitence, faith, ethics and cult), reconciliation. This trend, which is still widespread above all in the USA (cf. recently J.Barr, *Fundamentalism*, London [1977], ²1981, with further literature; id., *Escaping from Fundamentalism*, London and Philadelphia 1984), is not to be regarded as a serious contribution to the discussion.

Cf. also E.J.Young, *The Study of Old Testament Theology Today*, London 1958; id., *An Introduction to the Old Testament*, Grand Rapids 1949 (²1953, reprinted 1965); id., 'What is Old Testament Biblical Theology?', *EvQ* 31, 1959, 136-42; H.Lindsell, *The Battle for the Bible*, Grand Rapids 1976.

The attempt by R.Rendtorff ('Alttestamentliche Theologie', above 46), to revive the demand for a historical presentation of the theology of the Old Testament as opposed to the systematic outlines, is to be taken more seriously; here he refers above all to J.Köberle.

The secondary quotations used by Rendtorff come from Köberle's work *Sünde und Gnade im religiösen Leben des Volkes Israel bis auf Christum*, Munich 1905. Köberle had already investigated the theological content of the Old Testament and Judaism in a historical account and declared 'that the reality of the divine revelation does not mean that the religion of this people did not follow a truly historical course; rather, the revelation shows itself precisely in this course. The divine revelation does not have its history alongside and outside the "profane" history of Israel but in it... The more fully we see the connections in the... history of Israel, the more completely will we also be able to recognize the reality of the divine influence in it...' (2).

To work out a 'theology of the Old Testament' and a 'history of Israel' which is at the same time an account of the history of the religion of Israel is basically the same enterprise (Rendtorff,

Gesammelte Studien, 150). This looks like a return to the position beyond which Eichrodt and others wanted to go with their systematic account; on the other hand, this move can only be understood in the context of the discussion over the question raised by von Rad of the significance of history for Old Testament theology (see ch.III below).

Finally, F.Baumgärtel's comments on the systematic presentation of an Old Testament theology should not be overlooked, even if he did not carry them out in a complete work. Baumgärtel, too, proposes (*TLZ*, 1951) a system related to content; it is to comprise three parts: I. As introduction, a history of Old Testament religion, conceived as an investigation of the history of piety; II. a systematic, scientific account which would be an investigation, in terms of the phenomenology of religion (following the pattern of those by R.Otto, F.Heiler and G. van der Leeuw), of Old Testament religion as a Semitic religion and a comparison between it and religion in general; III. the theological part proper, in which the Old Testament event is depicted in terms of 'salvation history' (see above 40f.) and to this extent is a present event in which God discloses himself in judgment and promise, and into which Christ is sent as the Word. If we leave aside the special character of Baumgärtel's theological position, this proposal would then combine a historical presentation with a specifically theological one. There is a similar dualism in E.Nielsen (*Det gamle Testamente*); he sees two equally important, but separate tasks of an Old Testament theology as being to provide a systematic account of the main theological notions of the Old Testament (with the Old Testament picture of God at the centre) and a christologically based discussion of its place in the church's proclamation of the church, starting from the way in which the Old Testament is understood in the New.

The contrast between the proposals by Rendtorff and Baumgärtel shows us that the problem of a systematic presentation of a theology of the Old Testament is not merely a question of form but deeply affects the question of content, namely what one understands by a 'Theology of the Old Testament'.

III

The Problem of History

1. The position of Gerhard von Rad

von Rad, G., *Das formgeschichtliche Problem des Hexateuch*, BWANT 4.F., 26, Stuttgart 1938 = id., *Gesammelte Studien zum Alten Testament*, Munich 1958, ⁴1971, 9-86 = ET 'The Problem of the Hexateuch', in *The Problem of the Hexateuch and Other Essays*, Edinburgh 1966, reissued London 1984, 1-78; id., 'Grundprobleme einer biblischen Theologie des Alten Testaments', *TLZ* 68, 1943, 225-34; id., 'Kritische Vorarbeiten zu einer Theologie des Alten Testaments', in *Theologie und Liturgie*, ed. L.Hennig, Kassel 1952, 11-34; id., *Theologie des Alten Testaments* I, *Die Theologie der geschichtlichen Überlieferungen Israels*, Munich 1957, ⁴1962 (⁶1969); II, *Die Theologie der prophetischen Überlieferungen Israels*, Munich 1960, ⁴1965 (⁷1980) = ET *Old Testament Theology*, I, *The Theology of Israel's Historical Traditions*, Edinburgh 1962, reissued London 1975 (⁴1982); II, *The Theology of Israel's Prophetic Traditions*, Edinburgh 1965, reissued London 1975 (⁴1982; for the various editions and translations see the bibliography by von Rabenau, K., *Probleme biblischer Theologie*, *Von Rad Festschrift*, Munich 1971 [665-81], no.13, 667f.); id., 'Offene Fragen im Umkreis einer Theologie des Alten Testaments', *TLZ* 88, 1963, 401-16 = *Gesammelte Studien zum Alten Testament II*, Munich 1973, 289-312 = ET 'Postscript' in *Old Testament Theology* II, 410-29.

Barr, J., 'Gerhard von Rad's *Theologie des Alten Testaments*', *ExpT* 73, 1961/2, 142-6; Baumgärtel, F., review, *TLZ* 86, 1961, 801-16, 895-908; Crenshaw, J., *Gerhard von Rad*, Waco, Texas 1979; Davies, G.H., 'Gerhard von Rad, Old Testament Theology', in *Contemporary Old Testament Theologians*, ed. Laurin, (above 49) 63-90: Festorazzi II, above 50; Fruchon, P.,

'Sur l'herméneutique de Gerhard von Rad', *RSPT* 55, 1971, 4-32; Greig, A.J., *Geschichte and Heilsgeschichte in Old Testament Interpretation with Particular Reference to the Work of G. von Rad*, typescript dissertation, Edinburgh 1974, 75-168; id., 'Some Formative Aspects in the Development of Gerhard von Rad's Idea of History', *AUSS* 16, 1978, 313-31; Groves, J.W., *Actualization and Interpretation in the Old Testament*, PhD Dissertation, Yale University 1979 (Ann Arbor microfilm), 8-71, cf. 118-95; Koch, K., 'Gerhard von Rad', in *Tendenzen der Theologie*, ed H.J.Schultz, above 7, 483-7; Martin-Achard, R., 'La théologie de l'Ancien Testament après les travaux de G. von Rad', *ETR* 47, 1972, 219-26; Nesbit, W.G.(above 50), 174-264; Ramlot, R., *RThom* 1965 (above 46f.); Rendtorff, R., 'Gerhard von Rads Beitrag zur alttestamentlichen Wissenschaft', *Gesammelte Studien* (above 46), 296-303 = ET 'Gerhard von Rad's Contribution to Biblical Studies', in *Proceedings of the Sixth World Congress of Jewish Studies, 13.-19.8.1973*, Jerusalem 1977, 351-6; Seebass, H., *Biblische Hermeneutik* (above 19), 43-54; Spriggs, D.G., (above 50); Wolff, H.W./Rendtorff, R./Pannenberg, W., *Gerhard von Rad. Seine Bedeutung für die Theologie. Drei Reden*, Munich 1973; Wolff, H.W., 'Gespräch mit Gerhard von Rad', *von Rad Festschrift*, 1971, 650-8; von Rad, G., 'Über Gerhard von Rad', in W.E.Böhm, *Forscher und Gelehrte*, Stuttgart 1966, 17f. = *von Rad Festschrift*, 1971, 659-61.

In 1938 von Rad produced his study 'The Form-critical Problem of the Hexateuch'. It was a first attempt at analysing from the perspectives of form criticism and tradition criticism the historical traditions of Israel as they are now to be found in the 'baroque' final form of the Hexateuch (this was von Rad's classification), with a view to discovering their origin, their earliest expressions, their cultic *Sitz im Leben* and the whole process of the tradition until they became the literary work of the Yahwist. According to von Rad, the 'short historical creed' in Deut 26.5b-9 is the earliest form of an Israelite confession of faith in which the most important stages of the salvation history are mentioned, from the stay in Egypt to the conquest. There are similar confessional summaries in Deut.6.20-25; Josh.24.2b-13 and other texts. Originally the Sinai tradition was quite separate from this salvation-historical tradition: it has its cultic *Sitz im Leben* in the Feast of Tabernacles which according to Josh.24

was celebrated in Shechem, whereas the historical creed belongs to the Feast of Weeks, which was located in Gilgal.

Subsequent exegetical discussion has questioned both the separation of the exodus/conquest tradition and the Sinai tradition and the age of the credal formulation in Deut. 26 (for the history of research cf. G.Wallis, 'Die geschichtliche Erfahrung und das Bekenntnis zu Jahwe im Alten Testament', *TLZ* 101, 1976, 801-10; cf. also N.Lohfink, 'Heilsgeschichte', in id., *Unsere grossen Wörter*, Freiburg im Breisgau/Basle/Vienna 1977, 76-91). For discussion in the English-speaking world cf. E.Nicholson, *Exodus and Sinai in History and Tradition*, Oxford 1973; G.W.Ramsey, *The Quest for the Historical Israel*, Atlanta, Ga 1981 and London 1982. This set of problems must be left on one side here.

The traditio-historical investigation of this material was continued by M.Noth; following von Rad (48f. = ET 46f.), his *Überlieferungsgeschichte des Pentateuch*, Stuttgart 1948 (^{3}1966) = ET *A History of Pentateuchal Traditions*, Englewood Cliffs, NJ 1972 reprinted Chico, Ca 1981, begins from the orientation of the Pentateuchal tradition on the whole of Israel (45-8 = ET 42-5) and attempts to understand the origin of the various groups of themes in the Pentateuch and the way in which they grew together to produce the final literary form of the Pentateuchal narrative as a whole (267-71 = ET 248-51; though he arrives at an almost completely negative conclusion about their historical reliability, cf. 276-9 = ET 256-9). A further sphere of Old Testament historical traditions, the so-called Deuteronomistic History, was opened up to traditio-historical investigation in M.Noth's *Überlieferungsgeschichtliche Studien*, Halle 1943, Stuttgart/Darmstadt ^{3}1967; ET of pp.1-110 = *The Deuteronomistic History*, Sheffield 1981.

Von Rad also developed his *Old Testament Theology* from this traditio-historical approach. As early as 1952 he argued that, in contrast to previous outlines, 'an Old Testament theology must have a historical and not a systematic basis' (*Theologie und Liturgie*, ed. L.Hennig, 31). However, he was moved by the scepticism, expressed especially by Noth, about the historical content of the historical traditions, particularly of the Pentateuch, to divide his work into two parts, following the lines of e.g. Sellin and Procksch. His only objection to this was that it was questionable 'whether an Old Testament theology should see its distinctive subject-matter as being that of describing a "thought-world", "views, notions and

concepts"' (id., 30). Rather, both parts are historical: the testimony
to belief in Yahweh expressed in the second part, too, does not
consist of static statements about God, the world, man and so on,
'but it goes by way of facts, and notes divine ordinances which are
manifested successively in history' (ibid., 31). 'An Old Testament
Theology must keep to what the testimonies of the books themselves
say about Yahweh, his Word and his actions' (ibid.,32). The
questions of religion or piety (ibid., 30), which have still to be
answered, are out of place: 'Elements of the history of piety have a
place in it only insofar as they are kerygmatically involved in these
statements.' Beyond question, in his theological thinking von Rad
was influenced by dialectical theology. That is clear in a programmatic statement like this: 'Thus if it sought to be more than a history
of religion or piety, it would have to begin from the word of Yahweh
which went out to Israel, and would have to define this phenomenon
theologically, in particular in accordance with its creative power'
(ibid., 31). However, this demand is later fulfilled only indirectly;
first under the pattern of 'promise and fulfilment' (cf. my *Problems
of Biblical Theology* II,4), and secondly by way of history and the
process which von Rad calls 'testimony', using a formula which
belongs to the same theological thought-world (ibid.). The traditio-
historical approach is decisive for the whole outline; this is what
gives it its epoch-making character and determines the questions
which von Rad leaves open for subsequent discussion.

In accordance with what he has indicated, von Rad prefaces the
first volume of his *Old Testament Theology* with a 'History of
Jahwism and of the Sacral Institutions in Israel in Outline' (I⁴, 17-
115 = ET 3-102). In the 'Methodological Presuppositions' which
follow (I⁴, 117ff. = ET 105ff.), he repeats some of the things he had
already said in 1952, but is more precise about the subject of a
theology of the Old Testament: this is not the spiritual and religious
world of Israel, nor even its world of faith, but 'it is simply Israel's
own explicit assertions about Jahweh. The theologian must above
all deal directly with the evidence, that is, with what Israel herself
testified concerning Jahweh, and there is no doubt that in many
cases he must go back to school again and learn to interrogate each
document, much more closely than has been done hitherto, as to its
specific kerygmatic intention.' Despite all their individual differences, these testimonies have one thing in common: they 'confine
themselves to representing Jahweh's relationship to Israel and the
world in one aspect only, namely as a continuing divine activity in

history... Israel's faith is grounded in a theology of history... It regards itself as based upon historical acts, and shaped and reshaped by factors in which it saw the hand of Jahweh at work' (I⁴, 118 = ET 106). 'The Old Testament is a history book', a statement which was made as early as 1952 (G. von Rad, 'Typologische Auslegung des Alten Testaments' [see below 75], *Gesammelte Studien* II, 278, cf. *Theology* II, 370 [⁴380] = ET 357 – id., 'Aspekte alttesta-mentlichen Weltverständnisses', *EvTh* 24, 1964, [57-73] 57 = *Gesammelte Studien* I, [311-331] 311 = ET 'Some Aspects of the Old Testament World-view', in *The Problem of the Hexateuch*, [144-65] 144, is differently expressed) governs the whole of von Rad's outline. Now as the Old Testament witness to its history is recorded in a manifold variety of sources and complexes of tradition, there is no appropriate systematic way of describing it. 'Thus re-telling remains the most legitimate form of theological discourse on the Old Testament... So a theology of the Old Testament will also have to practise this retelling...if it is appropriately to raise the content of the Old Testament' (I⁴, 134f. = ET 121f.). Accordingly the nucleus of Volume 1 is made up of the theology of the Hexateuch in the various periods of salvation history which it portrays (I⁴, 143-317 = ET 129-305). The main section which follows, 'Israel's Anointed' (I⁴, 318-65 = ET 306-54), is arranged in a mixture of a theological and a thematic treatment (unexpectedly the traditional theme of 'messianology' emerges here), along with an account of the connection between the sources; the discussion is mainly of the Deuteronomistic and Chronistic history works (but also of the royal psalms, 331-6 = ET 318-23). It is noteworthy that there is extensive material from the Old Testament which von Rad cannot sum up under the theme of 'historical traditions': the prayers and psalms, the sphere of law and above all of wisdom. He puts them under the heading 'Israel before Yahweh (Israel's Response)' without thinking the dialectic through to the end (I⁴, 366-473 = ET 355-459). (C. Barth, 'Die Antwort Israels', *Festschrift von Rad*, 1971, 44-56, now gives the term a much narrower meaning limited by form criticism.)

A further step which can be explained by the ongoing influence of earlier judgments is the 'definite break between the message of the prophets and the ideas held by earlier Jahwism' (II⁴, 13 = ET 3), which is expressed in the division of the material into two volumes, the second of which comprises the 'Theology of Israel's Prophetic Traditions'. However, von Rad rejects a 'classical' picture of prophecy modelled on Duhm and stresses that the prophets too were dependent on early traditions at the heart of their message (II[4], 14 = ET 4). Nevertheless, von Rad makes something completely new begin with the prophets as over against the earlier historical traditions: starting from the events in world history to which they were witnesses (the pattern of correspondence between the prophets and world history is in fact the 'key to understanding them correctly', II[4], 122 = ET 112f.) they see the emergence of a completely new historical action on the part of God which will do away with the old: the relating of eschatology to history (II[4], 121ff. = ET 112ff.) is the great new beginning in prophecy. We might again suppose that this assessment of the prophetic message as ' eschatological' would not withstand close exegetical examination – unless one wants to define all belief in Yahweh, and specifically that of the 'historical traditions', as eschatological (thus H.D.Preuss, *Jahweglaube und Zukunftser-wartung*, BWANT 87, Stuttgart 1968). In terms of the history of traditions there is a need for a critical investigation of the separation between the prophetic and the historical traditions (thus especially W.Zimmerli, review, *VT* 13, 1963, 100-11, esp. 107ff.). However, this point was not the centre of the discussion which followed von Rad.

Rather, von Rad himself had already shaped this discussion by the problems which he was the first to see in the centre of his account. As early as *Theologie und Liturgie* (ed. L.Hennig, above 59, 31), he had mentioned the division between the *de facto* history of Israel, the history of belief in Yahweh, its institutions, and so on, and the historical picture which Israel itself had drawn of Yahweh and his actions. In Volume 1 of the *Theology* he stresses this division even more strongly: the picture which historical criticism has gained of the history of the people of Israel is largely irreconcilable with the picture which Israel itself drew of its history with Yahweh. 'Critical historical scholarship regards it as impossible that the whole of Israel was present at Sinai, or that Israel crossed the Red Sea and achieved the Conquest *en bloc* – it holds the picture of Moses and his leadership drawn in the traditions of the Book of Exodus to be as unhistorical as the function which the Deuteronomistic book of Judges ascribes to the "judges"' (I[4], 119 = ET 106f.).

Just as the dilemma arose from the traditio-historical perspective (in both *Theologie und Liturgie*, 31, and in the *Theology* [I[4], 119 = ET 107], von Rad recalls Noth's results), von Rad also sees its solution in the sphere of the history of traditions. The picture which

Israel itself drew of its history also exists in history and as such is of theological significance: 'Historical investigation searches for a critically assured minimum – the kerygmatic picture tends towards a theological maximum' (I⁴, 120 = ET 108). It follows from this for the account itself that 'In the Old Testament it is thus this world made up of testimonies that is above all the subject of a theology of the Old Testament' (I⁴, 124 = ET 111).

A first criticism of von Rad was that his procedure of merely retelling the manifold historical testimonies of Israel put paid to the immediacy of faith at a stroke: 'Thus the result of von Rad's pre-understanding is that he does not, like Israel, retell the acts of God, but the stories which Israel retold' (C.A.Keller, review, *TZ* 14, 1958, [306-9] 308). The diastasis between descriptive account and confessional context is also preserved in von Rad, despite his theological commitment. 'Basically von Rad's book is not a theology but an introduction.' His approach avoids raising the question of truth, 'without – and this is the original, misleading thing - being theologically insignificant' (ibid., 308). This touches on a series of questions which need to be clarified further.

2. 'Actual' history or believed history?

First of all, however, we must pursue further the discussion around the question which von Rad put in the centre: on what view of history must the theology of the Old Testament be based?

Alonso Schökel, L., above 45; Amsler, S., 'Texte et événement', *Maqqél Shaqedh. Hommage à W.Vischer*, Montpellier 1960, 12-19; Barbour, R.S., 'The Bible – Word of God?', *Biblical Studies, Essays... W.Barclay*, ed. J.R.McKay/J.F.Miller, London 1976, 28-43; Barth, C., 'Grundprobleme einer Theologie des Alten Testaments', *EvTh* 23, 1963, 342-72; Baumgärtel, F., *TLZ* 1961, above 59; Conzelmann, H., 'Fragen an Gerhard von Rad', *EvTh* 24, 1964, 113-25; Festorazzi II (above 50); Franzmann, M.H., 'The Hermeneutical Dilemma: Dualism in the Interpretation of the Holy Scripture', *CTM* 36, 1965, 502-33 (review of K.Frör, *Biblische Hermeneutik*, Munich 1961 [new edition under the title *Wege zur Schriftauslegung*, Düsseldorf ³1967]); Greig, A.J., *Geschichte*, above 60, 261ff.; Gilkey, L., 'Cosmology, Ontology and the Travail of Biblical Language', *JR* 41, 1961, 194-205; Goldingay, J., ' "That You May Know that Yahweh is God": A

Study in the Relationship between Theology and Historical Truth in the Old Testament', *TynB* 23, 1972, 58-93; id., *Approaches*, 66ff.; Gross, H., *TTZ* 1958, above 45; Hamp, V., *BZ* 1958, above 45; id., 'Geschichtsschreibung im Alten Testament', in *Speculum Historiale. Festschrift J.Spörl*, Freiburg and Munich 1965, 134-42; Harvey, J., 'The New Diachronic Biblical Theology of the Old Testament (1960-1970)', *BTB* 1, 1971, 5-29 (short version: 'A Decade of Development in Biblical Theology', *ThD* 20, 1972, 137-40); Hasel, G.F., 'The Problem of History in Old Testament Theology', *AUSS* 8, 1970, 23-50; id., *Old Testament Theology* (above 1), 57-75; Hempel, J., *Altes Testament und Geschichte*, Gütersloh 1930; id., 'Alttestamentliche Theologie in protestant-ischer Sicht heute', *BiOr* 15, 1958, 206-14; id., Review, 'G.von Rad, *Theologie des Alten Testaments*. Bd.II', *BiOr* 19, 1962, 267-73; id., 'Faktum und Gesetz im alttestamentlichen Geschichts-denken', *TLZ* 85, 1960, 824-8; id., 'Die Faktizität der Geschichte im biblischen Denken', *Biblical Studies in Memory of H.C.Al-leman*, Locust Valley, NY 1960, 67-88; id., *Geschichte und Geschichten im Alten Testament bis zur persischen Zeit*, Gütersloh 1964; Hesse, F., 'Die Erforschung der Geschichte Israels als theologische Aufgabe', *KuD* 4, 1958, 1-20; id., 'Kerygma oder geschichtliche Wirklichkeit? Kritische Fragen', *ZTK* 57, 1960, 17-26; cf. also id., 'Zur Frage der Wertung und der Geltung alttestamentlicher Texte', *Festschrift F.Baumgärtel*, Erlangen 1959, 74-96 = ET 'The Evaluation and the Authority of OT Texts', in *Essays...*, ed. C. Westermann, below 75, 285-313; id., *Das Alte Testament als Buch der Kirche*, Gütersloh 1966, 115-34; id., 'Bewährt sich eine "Theologie der Heilstatsachen" am Alten Testament?', *ZAW* 81, 1969, 1-18; Honecker, M., 'Zum Verständnis der Geschichte in Gerhard von Rads Theologie des Alten Testaments', *EvTh* 23, 1963, 143-68; Jepsen, A., *Wissenschaft vom Alten Testament*, AVTRW 1, Berlin 1958 = *Der Herr ist Gott* (above 45), 13-38, abbreviated ET = 'The Scientific Study of the Old Testament', in *Problems*, ed. C.Wester-mann, 246-84; Koole, J.L., 'Het soortelijk gewicht van de histori-sche stoffen van het Oude Testament', *GTT* 65, 1965, 81-104; Lakatos, E., 'Por una Teologia basada en los hechos', *RevBib* 21, 1959, 83-6, 142-4, 197-200; 22, 1960, 140-5; Maag, V., 'Historische oder ausserhistorische Begründung alttestamentlicher Theo-logie?', *STU* 29, 1958, 6-18 (cf. also id., 'Das Gottesverständnis des Alten Testaments', *NedThT* 21, 1966/67, 161-207 = id.,

Kultur, Kulturkontakt und Religion, *Gesammelte Studien*, ed. H.H.Schmid/O.H.Steck, Göttingen 1980, 256-99); Murray, J., 'Systematic Theology', *WTJ* 25, 1963, 133-42; North, C.R., *The Old Testament Interpretation of History*, London 1946; Osswald, E., 'Geschehene und geglaubte Geschichte in der alttestamentlichen Theologie', *WZ (J).GS* 14, 1965, 705-15; Pfeiffer, R.H., 'Facts and Faith in Biblical History', *JBL* 70, 1951, 1-14; Porteous, N.W., 'Magnalia Dei', in *Festschrift von Rad*, 1971, above 60, 417-27; id., 'Old Testament and History', *ASTI* 8, 1970/1, 21-77; von Rad, G., 'Antwort auf Conzelmanns Fragen', *EvTh* 24, 1964, 388-94; id., 'Offene Fragen' (above 59); Soggin, J.A., 'Alttestamentliche Glaubenszeugnisse und geschichtliche Wirklichkeit', *TZ* 17, 1961, 385-98; id., 'Geschichte, Historie und Heilsgeschichte im Alten Testament', *TLZ* 89, 1964, cols.721-36; de Vaux, R., 'Peut-on écrire une "Théologie de l'Ancien Testament"?', *Mélanges M.Chenu*, Paris 1967, 439-49 = *Bible et Orient*, Paris 1967, 59-71 (= ET 'Is it Possible to Write a "Theology of the Old Testament"?', in *The Bible and the Ancient Near East*, London 1972, 49-62. Cf. also P.Mamie, 'Peut-on écrire une "Théologie de l'Ancien Testament"?', *NV* 42, 1967, 298-303); Vawter, B., 'History and Kerygma in the Old Testament', in *A Light unto my Path. Studies... J.M.Myers*, Philadelphia 1974, 475-91; Vischer, W., 'Das Alte Testament und die Geschichte', *ZZ* 10, 1932, 22-42; Vriezen, T.C., 'Geloof, openbaring en geschiedenis in de nieuwste Oud-Testamentische Theologie', *KeTh* 16, 1965, 97-113, 210-18; Zimmerli, W., 'Die historisch-kritische Bibelwissenschaft und die Verkündigungsaufgabe der Kirche', *EvTh* 23, 1963, 17-31. For the background to the discussion, Wolf, E., 'Leoni 1963', *EvTh* 24, 1964, 165-9; Sauter, G., 'Josefstal 1964', *EvTh* 25, 1965, 273-8.

Hardly had the first volume of von Rad's *Theology* been published than massive criticism of his concept of history erupted (survey of the debate e.g. in E.Osswald, *WZ (J).GS* 1965). One of the most resolute critics was F.Hesse, who in a number of articles put forward the view that what is significant for theology is the real history of Israel, i.e. its actual course (*ZTK* 1960, 24; *KuD* 1958, 12f.) as discovered by historical-critical research, and not the view which Israel itself had of the course of its history, for if Yahweh has in fact acted in history, then only the facts can be of interest to us. Therefore research into the history of Israel is a theological task (hence the title of the article in *KuD* 1958), 'for the salvation history which culminates in Jesus Christ as its telos happens in, with and under the history of Israel' (*KuD* 1958, 19). Insofar as the Old Testament describes events which did not really take place like that in reality, these accounts have significance for us in that they reflect particular notions and conceptions which Israel had of its history and a particular understanding of God; however this is no longer testimony to a history (*ZTK* 1960, 25). V.Maag put his criticism of von Rad even more strongly: anyone who wants, say, to claim that the Deuteronomistic account of history in the book of Judges is theologically binding, although the course of history was quite different, 'plants fictions of God's action instead of an adequate conception. He plants... a pious lie and presents it as the word of God' (*STU* 1958, 13). 'It would be better for us to have no theology at all rather than a theology which teaches falsely about the action of God in history by attributing to God rules according to which he never acted in historical reality and never thinks of acting'(14). Hempel thinks that it is the 'tragedy' of von Rad's theology that 'his ultimate intention comes to nothing', because: 1. we have no knowledge of historical events, above all in the early period, apart from the traditions of the Old Testament itself; 2. the traditio-historical view of this period modelled on Noth has left behind a 'vacuum' which could hardly serve as an adequate basis for presenting the action of God in history as the foundation of Yahwistic belief and; 3. this raises the question of the truth of revelation and thus of God himself (*BiOr* 1957, 213; cf. *BiOr* 1962, 271f.). Eichrodt (*Theologie* I[4], VIIIf. [not in the ET]), similarly sees in von Rad's 'methodological presuppositions' the gulf between the two pictures of history 'opened up with such violence that it seems no longer possible to make an intrinsic connection between them'. This raises the question 'whether a testimony of faith which has no certain connection with historical reality can be valid as a testimony to historical revelation'. The same view has been expressed more recently by G.Kaufman ('What Shall We Do with the Bible?', *Int* 25, 1971, 95-112). For him, too, the Bible is to be seen as a historical source to be examined critically, from which we must discover 'what actually happened'(105), for as one who acts in history God can be known only through his actions (103), which are reported in the Bible. We need not believe what is reported, but must investigate the reports with all the historical-critical means at our disposal.

Von Rad responded to these charges not only by observing that it is by no means so easy to detach fact from interpretation (I³, 473), but in the second volume of his *Theology* (Preface, 1960, esp.8ff. = ET viff.), above all with a reference to the quite different philosophical presuppositions of modern historians. On their premises they are not in a position to say anything about God, so their picture of the course of the history of Israel has no theological relevance when, say, it is a matter of interpreting the events of 587 as an act of God. Of course there is also much to be learned from modern historical study. 'But there is no substitute for Israel's own word about what has happened to it at the hands of God; nor is there anything to authenticate it' (10). The important thing, therefore, is to take seriously the picture which Israel constructed of its history as an object of science and analysis. And one can see that von Rad feels himself under attack : 'As opposed to all this cavilling and meddling I begin from the assumption that it could be promising to let the Old Testament speak for itself and plead its cause more than has happened hitherto, instead of constantly interrupting it' (11).

Underlying this position is an additional problem which F.Baumgärtel, of all the critics, has detected most acutely; quite apart from the fact that it often does not correspond with real historical events, the picture which Israelite faith made of history is itself a piece of history and as such the subject of historical research. 'When von Rad investigates the "theological" discourse of the Old Testament and the Old Testament picture of history produced by Old Testament faith, he is investigating historical matters, and rightly does that with the means of contemporary historical criticism, in this case with the help of introductory disciplines' (*TLZ* 1961, 804). Baumgärtel also severely criticizes von Rad's programme of 'retelling'; he argues that it is a direct translation into proclamation, which avoids the work of theological thinking (903f.). Whether this charge is justified is doubtful, but beyond question von Rad himself has provoked it by inadequate reflection on the relationship between a historical view of history and its kergymatic dimension.

C. Barth attempts to mediate between the two opposed positions by stressing that the 'course of history worked out as being *probable* by a *truly* historical-critical discipline' is 'an indispensable means for understanding and handing on the biblical testimonies of faith' (*EvTh* 1963, 363). Here we have signs of a matter-of-factness which could not hope for much response in view of the scepticism over the history of traditions evoked by Noth; however, it does deserve further thought in the context of basic hermeneutical considerations.

Remarkably, W.Vischer had already written about the problem in 1932 (in any case it is a very old one, cf. Hesse, *KuD* 1958, 2ff.): for him the gulf between the account and the factuality of what is reported is a proof of the human character of scripture: no history can be written without selection and evaluation, so the historical testimony of the Old Testament must above all be heard as a whole (*ZZ* 1932, 25ff.; cf the similar conclusion in Osswald, *WZ (J). GS* 1965, 711). C.R.North expresses himself in much the same way: 'What concerns us... is not the literal accuracy of this or that happening, but whether the interpretation as a whole is valid for the events in their broad totality' (XIII). Jepsen, similarly, thinks that it is enough if the general view in the Old Testament that God is the Lord and Director of specific history is correct; it is not important that all the details should have been presented correctly (*Der Herr*, 26). At all events, the history writers of the Old Testament sought to report what had really happened. (Cf. Hempel, *Geschichten und Geschichte*, 12ff. Vawter, 483ff., does not think that any of the facts discovered by historical research refute the Old Testament interpretation of any of the central events of salvation history, and de Vaux, 'Peut-on écrire...?', takes the same view.) Koole's position is also similar: he regards the factuality of the event as an indispensable element of its relevance to the historical kerygma, but at the same time wants to take account of the character of the genre of popular narrative. Barbour (31ff.) even goes so far as to assert that an event could be reported quite unreliably and yet be interpreted theologically in a way that was vital for the relationship between God and people. Even then, such an event is a proper ingredient of salvation history.

I should just mention in passing that there is also a fundamentalist criticism of von Rad which claims that everything in the Old Testament happened exactly as it is reported (e.g. Murray). The conviction, along the same lines, that the believer is enabled to transcend the 'dualism' as the Word of God discloses to him the objective reality of history (Franzmann, *CTM*, 1965, 522; Goldingay, *TynB* 1972, esp.92f.; id., *Approaches*, 72ff.), also cuts the Gordian knot before reflecting adequately on the hermeneutical problem. Finally, we should remember the comments by L.Gilkey, though they do not arise directly from the discussion of von Rad's work, but from the similar positions of Wright and Anderson: in view of the modern picture of the world, which differs from that of the Bible, he asks that there should be new reflection on the meaning of analogous language about the 'activity' or 'action' of God in our experience of reality. The whole debate indicates the frequent lack of clarity in discussions of the problem of epistemology, particularly in biblical theology.

3. History and revelation

Davidson, R., 'Faith and History in the Old Testament', *ExpT* 77, 1965/6, 100-4; Eichrodt, W., 'Offenbarung und Geschichte im Alten Testament', *TZ* 4, 1948, 321-31; Ferré, N.F., 'Living Light and Dedicated Decision: Comments on the Relation between Biblical and Systematic Theology', *Int* 6, 1952, 1-16; Fohrer, G., 'Tradition und Interpretation im Alten Testament', *ZAW* 73, 1961, 1-30 = id., *Studien zur alttestamentlichen Theologie und Geschichte*, BZAW 115, Berlin 1969, 54-83; id., 'Prophetie und Geschichte', *TLZ* 89, 1964, 481-500 = id., *Studien zur alttestamentlichen Prophetie (1949-1965)*, BZAW 99, Berlin 1967, 265-93; Gese, H., 'Erwägungen zur Einheit der biblischen Theologie', *ZTK* 67, 1970, 417-36 = id., *Vom Sinai zum Zion. Alttestamentliche Beiträge zur biblischen Theologie*, BEvTh 64, Munich 1974, 11-30; Galling, K., 'Biblische Sinndeutung der Geschichte', *EvTh* 8, 1948/9, 307-19; Goldingay, J., *TynB* 1972, above 65f.; Greig, A.J., *Geschichte*, above 60, 297ff.; Groves, above 60; Guthrie, H.H., Jr, *God and History in the Old Testament*, London 1961; Hasel, G.F., above 1; Harvey, J., above 66; Hesse, F., 'Zur Frage der Wertung und Geltung', above 66; Honecker, M., above 66; Kaufman, G., *Int*. 1971, above 68; Keller, C.A., 'L' Ancien Testament et la théologie de l'histoire', *RTP* 13, 1963, 124-37; Knierim, R., 'Offenbarung im Alten Testament', *Festschrift von Rad*, 1971, above 59, 206-35; Knight, D.A., 'Revelation through Tradition and Theology in the Old Testament', in *Tradition and Theology in the Old Testament*, ed. D.A.Knight, Philadelphia 1977, 143-80; Kraus, H.J., 'Zur Geschichte des Überlieferungsbegriffs in der alttestamentlichen Wissenschaft', *EvTh* 16, 1956, 371-87; Lemke, W.E., 'Revelation through History in Recent Biblical Theology', *Int*. 36, 1982, 34-46; Loretz, O., *Die Wahrheit der Bibel*, Freiburg im Breisgau 1964; McKane, W., 'Tradition as a Theological Concept', in *God, Secularization and History. Essays... R.Gregor Smith*, ed. E.T.Long, Columbia, SC 1974, 44-59; Mildenberger, F., *Gottes Tat im Wort*, Gütersloh 1964; Murphy, R.E., 'Eschatology and the Old Testament', *Cont* 7, 1969/70, 583-93; North, C.R., *Old Testament Interpretation*, above 67; Östborn, G., *Yahwe's Words and Deeds: A Preliminary Study into the Old Testament Presentation of History*, UUÅ 1951, 7, Uppsala/Wiesbaden 1951; Otto, E., *Kairos* 1977, above 46; Porteous, N.W., *ASTI* 1970/1, above 67; Preuss, H.D., *Das Alte Testament* (above 2), 98ff.; von Rad, G., 'Offene Fragen/Postscript', above 59; Rendtorff, R., 'Hermeneutik des Alten Testaments als Frage nach der Geschichte', *ZTK* 57, 1960, 27-40 = id., *Gesammelte Studien*, above 46, 11-24; id., ' "Offenbarung" im Alten Testament', *TLZ* 85, 1960, 833-8; id., 'Geschichte und Überlieferung', in *Studien zur Theologie der alttestamentlichen Überlieferungen*, ed. K.Koch and R.Rendtorff (*Festschrift von Rad*), Neukirchen 1961, 81-94 = *Gesammelte Studien*, 25-38; id., 'Geschichte und Wort im Alten Testament', *EvTh* 22, 1963, 621-49 = *Gesammelte Studien*, 60-88; id. 'Die Offenbarungsvorstellungen im Alten Testament', in *Offenbarung als Geschichte*, ed. W.Pannenberg, Göttingen (1961) [2]1963 ([4]1970), 21-41 = *Gesammelte Studien*, 39-59 = ET 'The Concept of Revelation in Ancient Israel', in *Revelation as History*, New York 1968 and London 1969, 23-53; Richardson, A., *Christian Apologetics*, London 1947 [[8]1970], 89ff., 133ff.; Robinson, James M., 'Revelation as Word and as History', in *New Frontiers in Theology* III, *Theology as History*, New York, Evanston and London 1967, 1-100; Robinson, H.W., *Inspiration and Revelation in the Old Testament*, Oxford 1946, [5]1960, reprinted 1979, cf. also the review by N.W.Porteous, *JTS* 48, 1947, 75-8; also M.E.Polley, above 52; Roscam Abbing, P.J., *Inleiding in de bijbelse theologie*, Amsterdam 1983, 102ff.; Saebø, M., 'Offenbarung in der Geschichte und als Geschichte', *StTh* 35, 1981, 55-71; Seeligmann, I.L., 'Erkenntnis Gottes und historisches Bewusstsein im alten Israel', *Beiträge zur alttestamentlichen Theologie. Festschrift W.Zimmerli*, Göttingen 1977, 414-45; Smend, R., 'Überlieferung und Geschichte. Aspekte ihres Verhältnisses', in *Zu Tradition und Theologie im Alten Testament*, ed. O.H.Steck, BThSt 2, Neukirchen 1978, 9-26 = ET 'Tradition and History: A Complex Relation', in *Tradition and Theology*, ed. D.A.Knight, 49-68; Soggin, J.A., 'God and History in Biblical Thought', in *Old Testament and Oriental Studies*, BibOr 29, Rome 1975, 59-66; Stoebe, H.J., 'Das Verhältnis von Offenbarung und religiöser Aussage im Alten Testament', *Acta Tropica* 21, 1964, 400-14; id., 'Überlegungen zur Theologie des Alten Testaments', *Festschrift H.W.Hertzberg*, Göttingen 1965, 200-20; de Vaux, R., 'Presence and Absence in History: the Old Testament View', *Conc* 5, 1969, 5-12; Vriezen, T.C., *KeTh*, 1965, above 67; Weiser, A., *Glaube und Geschichte im Alten Testament*, BWANT 55, Stuttgart 1931 = id., *Glaube und Geschichte im Alten Testament und andere ausgewählte Schriften*, Göttingen 1961, 99-181; cf. also id., 'Das theologische Gesamtverständnis des Alten Testaments', *DT* 10, 1943, 50-70 = *Glaube und Geschichte*, 257-79; Wright, G.E., *The Old Testament against its Environment*, SBT 2, London 1950; id., *God who Acts. Biblical Theology as Recital*, SBT 8, London 1952. [8]1966 (cf. also id., 'The Old Testament. A Bulwark of the Church against Paganism', *IRM* 40, 1951, 265-76; Wright, G.E. and Fuller, R.H., *The Book of the Acts of God*, Garden City, NY 1957; id., 'Reflections concerning Old Testament Theology', *Studia Biblica et Semitica T.C. Vriezen Dedicata*, Wageningen 1966, 376-88; id., *The Old Testament and Theology*, New York and London 1969; Zimmerli, W., 'Das Alte Testament in der Verkündigung der christlichen Kirche' (above 38); id., 'Einzelerzählungen und Gesamtgeschichte im Alten Testament, ibid., 9-36; id., 'Das Wort des göttlichen Selbsterweises (Erweiswort)', in *Mélanges rédigés en l'honneur de André Robert*, Paris 1957, 154-64 = *Studien* (above 46), 120-32 = ET 'The Word of Divine Self-manifestation (Proof-saying): A Prophetic Genre', in *I am Yahweh*, ed. W.Brueggemann, Atlanta, Ga 1982, 99-110; id., ' "Offenbarung" im Alten Testament', *EvTh* 22, 1962, 15-31; id., 'Alttestamentliche Traditionsgeschichte und Theologie', *Festschrift von Rad*, 1971 (above 60), 632-47 = *Studien*, 9-26; id., *TLZ* 1973 (above 46); id. 'Die kritische Infragestellung der Tradition durch die Prophetie', in *Zu Tradition und Theologie*, ed. O.H.Steck, op.cit., 57-86 = ET 'Prophetic Proclamation and Reinterpretation', *Tradition and Theology*, ed. D.A.Knight, 69-100.

Von Rad's work again brought the theme of 'history' as a medium of revelation fully into the perspective of Old Testament theology. However, the question was not completely new; it had been thematized e.g. by Weiser under the old rubrics of 'experience' and 'ideology of faith'. At about the same time as von Rad's preliminary considerations on his theology, G.E.Wright's provocative work *God who Acts* appeared. Its sub-title, 'Biblical Theology as Recital', indicated its central thesis: history is the real place of God's revelation (cf. already *The Old Testament against its Environment*, 20ff.); the objectivity of the external acts is decisive (and their inner effects on human consciousness are only secondary). These he performs by means of the election of Israel (the covenant ceremony on Sinai was the place of their confirmation and Christ is their goal), and the primary significance of theology is the confessional recitation of the acts of God in history.

(Cf. esp. 50ff. To begin with, this 'recital theology' found a number of followers, cf. e.g. C.Stuhlmueller, 'The Influence of Oral Tradition upon Exegesis and the Senses of Scripture', *CBQ* 20, 1958, [299-326] 301, 311 n.46. For criticism cf. e.g. F.B.Dilley, 'Does the "God Who Acts" really Act?', *ATR* 47, 1965, 66-80; D.H.Kelsey, *The Uses of Scripture in Recent Theology*, Philadelphia and London 1975, 33-8.)

In von Rad, too, the historical event itself, the 'facts', a term which he often uses, has absolute priority for Israel (cf.I⁴, 121 = ET 116), though this becomes significant in the form of tradition, i.e. as the message of the event (thus e.g. I⁴, 125, not in the ET): the subject of a Theology of the Old Testament is, 'the living word of Yahweh as it came down to Israel in the message of his mighty acts from time to time'. Later (II¹, 371 = ET 358), von Rad differentiates between words and acts of God and distinguishes between the revelation by Word (from the oracle given in the cult to the word of God addressed to the prophets) and the 'knowledge of God in the facts'; in the case of the latter he persists in the view: 'Here – of course always only at particular times – an event became addressed to Israel quite directly so that in it she could recognize God's historical will.' However, history and word are related to each other, for the way in which these historical actions are open to constantly new interpretations by later generations 'in a direct ratio to their understanding of their own position in the light of their fathers' history with God' (II, 375 = ET 361) provides an ongoing context of interpretation: 'History becomes word and word becomes history' (II, 371 = ET 358). Here the future, too, is always interpreted in the light of experiences of the past. In view of the connections which follow from this in the sequence of events as seen by Israel, retelling is the most legitimate form of theological discourse in the Old Testament (I⁴, 126 = ET 121 [cf. above 62ff.]).

Von Rad recognizes another important interpretative element

which characterizes the Israelite understanding of history for him: thought in the tension between 'promise' and 'fulfilment'. In contrast to the traditional use of this framework for an exclusive under-standing of the relationship between the Testaments (cf. my *Problems of Biblical Theology*, ch.II), for von Rad the relationship of fulfilment to promise expresses a 'periodizing of history' (I[4], 147-9, 182-6, 317 = ET 133-5, 168-75, 304) which can be seen even in the theology of the Hexateuch itself. The gradual progression in that theology from a promise to its fulfilment and from there to the next promise introduces an inner movement into history which keeps it open for the future.

Cf. already 'Typologische Auslegung des Alten Testaments', *EvTh* 12, 1952/53, 17-33 = 'Typological Interpretation of the Old Testament', *Int* 15, 1961, 174-92, 1952 original reprinted in *Gesammelte Studien* II (above 59), 272-88; there is an abbreviated version in *Essays on Old Testament Interpretation*, London 1963 = *Essays on Old Testament Hermeneutics*, Richmond, Va 1963, 17-39; also 'Offene Fragen/Postscript' [above 59] 415/309 = ET 414; for more details see Rendtorff (below 80ff.); C.Westermann, 'The Way of Promise through the Old Testament', in *Old Testament*, ed. B.W.Anderson (above 38), 200-24 = 'Der Weg der Verheissung durch das Alte Testament', in id., *Forschung am Alten Testament*, GS II, TB 55, Munich 1974, 230-49; W.Zimmerli, 'Verheissung und Erfüllung', *EvTh* 12, 1952/53, 34-59 = 'Promise and Fulfillment', in *Essays*, ed. Westermann, 69-101 = 'The Interpretation of the Old Testament III. Promise and Fulfilment', *Int* 15, 1961, 310-38. Cf. further the continuation of the notion by W.Pannenberg and R.Rendtorff (below 77f.). Jürgen Moltmann, *Theologie der Hoffnung*, BEvTh 38, Munich 1964, [10]1977 = ET *Theology of Hope*, London and New York 1967, has made the notion of the future in history, which in his view derives from Jewish-Christian messianism, into the basic principle of an overall theological approach (cf. also Porteous, *ASTI* 1970/1 [above 67], 66ff.).

Von Rad's ideas about the Hebrew concept of time (on this see especially Nesbit [above 50], 235ff.; Groves, *Actualization* [above 60], 147ff.) and the process of the cultic actualization of the central events of salvation history have a role here (II[1], 112ff., II[4], 108ff. = ET II, 99ff.). Whereas in this actualization (on it cf. also M.Noth, 'Die Vergegenwärtigung des Alten Testaments in der Verkündigung', *EvTh* 12, 1952/53, 6-17 = *Gesammelte Studien zum AT* II, TB 39, Munich 1969, 86-98, = ET 'The "Re-Presentation" of the Old Testament in Proclamation', *Essays on Old Testament Interpretation/Hermeneutics*, 76-88 – a detailed criticism in Groves, *Actualization* [above 60], 118-95) a first stage is already seen of the reshaping of natural and sacral cultic traditions by 'historicization' (cf. Weiser, 117ff., *Theology* II, 117ff. = ET 104ff.), the arrangement of saving facts of this kind in a historical sequence indicates an arrival at the conception of a linear course of history (a linear chronological view of history) which von Rad sees as 'one of this people's greatest achievements' (II, 121 = ET 107) since this linear understanding is radically opposed to the cyclical conception of time among the peoples of the ancient Near East.

The question of the Hebrew concept of time is a separate theme which can be mentioned here only in passing. However, it should be noted that both the view that Hebrew thought has its own concept of time (that of 'filled' time: time is not something given *a priori*, but time and event are directly related in the sense of the *kairos*) and the question whether Israelite historical thought is linear or cyclical, are much disputed. Literature: Barr, J., *Biblical Words for Time*, SBT 33, London 1962; Cullmann, O., *Christus und die Zeit*, Zollikon-Zurich 1946, ³1962 = ET *Christ and Time*, London and Philadelphia 1951; Eichrodt, W., 'Heilserfahrung und Zeitverständnis im Alten Testament', *TZ* 12, 1956, 103-25; Herrmann, S., *Zeit und Geschichte*, Stuttgart 1977, 85-110; Marsh, J., *The Fulness of Time*, London 1952; Momigliano, A., 'Time in Ancient Historiography', in *History and Concept of Time*, HTh Suppl 6, 1966, 1-23; Muilenburg, J., 'The Biblical View of Time', *HTR* 54, 1961, 225-52; Pannikar, R., 'Le Temps circulaire: temporisation et temporalité', in Castelli, E., et al., *Temporalità e Alienazione* (AF), Padua 1975, 207-46 = 'Die zirkuläre Zeit: Temporisierung und Zeitlichkeit', in E. Castelli et al., *Zeitlichkeit und Entfremdung in Hermeneutik und Theologie*, KuM 6,8, 1976, 32-58; Petitjean, A., 'Les conceptions vétérotestamentaires du temps', *RHPR* 56, 1976, 383-400; Pidoux, G., 'À propos de la notion biblique du temps', *RTP* III/2, 1952, 120-5; Ratschow, K.H., 'Anmerkungen zur theologischen Auffassung des Zeitproblems', *ZTK* 51, 1954, 360-87; Schmitt, R., *Abschied von der Heilsgeschichte?*, EHS.T 195, Frankfurt am Main and Berne 1982, 101ff.; Sekine, M., 'Erwägungen zur hebräischen Zeitauffassung', *SVT* 9, 1963, 66-82; Snaith, N.H., 'Time in the Old Testament', *Promise and Fulfilment*, ed. F.F.Bruce, Edinburgh 1963, 175-86; Vollborn, W., 'Studien zum Zeitverständnis im Alten Testament', Göttingen 1951; Wilch, J.R., *Time and Event*, Leiden 1969.

Von Rad's pupils developed his understanding of history in two particular directions. One line leads from the pronounced stress on 'facts' in von Rad to an anti-kerygmatic theology oriented on historical facts. Here at first sight there seems to be a close connection with the apparently opposite position held earlier by F.Hesse, although he very rapidly dissociated himself from it. This trend, associated above all with the name of W.Pannenberg and the slogan 'revelation as history', must be discussed next. The other, which to begin with is difficult to separate from the first, develops von Rad's ideas on the history of tradition and seeks to give tradition history itself theological relevance. Here the works of R.Rendtorff are of particular significance.

Pannenberg, W., 'Heilsgeschehen und Geschichte', *KuD* 5, 1959, 259-88 = id., *Grundfragen systematischer Theologie*, Göttingen 1967, 22-78 = ET 'Redemptive Event and History', in *Basic Questions in Theology* I, London and Philadelphia 1970, 15-80; id., 'Kerygma und Geschichte', *Festschrift von Rad*, 1961, above 72, 129-40 = *Grundfragen*, 79-90, = ET 'Kerygma and History', *Basic Questions* I, 81-95; id., 'Was ist eine dogmatische Aussage?', *KuD* 8, 1962, 81-99 = *Grundfragen*, 159-80 = ET 'What is a Dogmatic Statement?', *Basic Questions* I, 182-211; id., 'Hermeneutik und Universalgeschichte', *ZTK* 60, 1963, 90-112 = *Grundfragen*, 91-122, = ET 'Hermeneutic and Universal History', *Basic Questions* I, 96-136; id., 'Dogmatische Thesen zur Lehre von der Offenbarung', *Offenbarung als Geschichte* (above 72), 91-114 = ET 'Dogmatic Theses on the Concept of Revelation', ibid., 123-58; id., 'Einführung', ibid., 7-20 = ET 1-23; id., 'Nachwort zur zweiten Auflage', ibid., 132-48 = ET 'Postscript', 183-206; id., 'Einsicht und Glaube. Antwort an Paul Althaus', *TLZ* 88, 1963, 81-92, = ET 'Insight and Faith', *Basic Questions in Theology* II, London and Philadelphia 1971, 28-45; id., 'Die Krise des Schriftprinzips', *Grundfragen*, 11-21 = ET 'The Crisis of the Scripture Principle', *Basic Questions* I, 1-14; there is a longer version: 'Die Grundlagenkrise der evangelischen Theologie', *Radius* 4, 1962, 7-14 = 'Die Fragwürdigkeit der klassischen

Universalwissenschaften (Evangelische Theologie)', in *Die Krise des Zeitalters der Wissenschaften*, Frankfurt 1963, 173-88; id., 'Vorwort', *Grundfragen*, 5-9, = ET ' Preface', *Basic Questions* I, xv-xviii; id., 'Stellungnahme zur Diskussion', *Neuland in der Theologie* III, Zürich 1967, 285-351 = ET *New Frontiers in Theology* III (above 72), 221-76; id., *Wissenschaftstheorie und Theologie*, Frankfurt am Main 1973 (1977) = ET *Theology and the Philosophy of Science*, Philadelphia and London 1976; id., 'Der Gott der Geschichte. Der trinitarische Gott und die Wahrheit der Geschichte', *KuD* 23, 1977, 76-92; id., *Die Bestimmung des Menschen. Menschsein, Erwählung und Geschichte*, Göttingen 1978.

Althaus, P., 'Offenbarung als Geschichte und Glaube. Bemerkungen zu Wolfhart Pannenbergs Begriff der Offenbarung', *TLZ* 87, 1962, 321-30; Braaten, C.E., 'The Current Controversy on Revelation: Pannenberg and his Critics', *JR* 45, 1965, 225-37; Dufort, J.-M., 'Wolfhart Pannenberg et la théologie de l'espérance', *ScEs* 22, 1970, 361-77; Fuchs, E., 'Theologie oder Ideologie', *TLZ* 88, 1963, 257-60; Galloway, A.D., *Wolfhart Pannenberg*, Contemporary Religious Thinkers, London 1973; Geyer, H.G., 'Geschichte als theologisches Problem', *EvTh* 22, 1962, 92-104; Hamilton, W., 'The Character of Pannenberg's Theology', in *New Frontiers* III (above 72), 176-96; Henke, P., *Gewissheit vor dem Nichts. Eine Antithese zu den theologischen Entwürfen Wolfhart Pannenbergs und Jürgen Moltmanns*, TBT 34, Berlin 1978, 95-129; Hesse, F., 'Wolfhart Pannenberg und das Alte Testament', *NZST* 7, 1965, 174-99; Klein, G., 'Offenbarung als Geschichte', *MPT* 51, 1962, 65-88; id., *Theologie des Wortes Gottes und die Hypothese der Universalgeschichte*, BEvTh 37, Munich 1964; Kolden, M., *Pannenberg's Attempt to Base Theology on History*, Univ.Chicago Diss 1976; Mühlenberg, E., 'Gott in der Geschichte. Erwägungen zur Geschichtstheologie von W.Pannenberg', *KuD* 24, 1978, 244-61; Muschalek, G./ Gamper, A., 'Offenbarung in Geschichte', *ZKT* 86, 1964, 180-96; Obayashi, H., 'Pannenberg and Troeltsch: History and Religion', *AARG* 38, 1970, 401-19; Steiger, L., 'Offenbarungsgeschichte und theologische Vernunft', *ZTK* 59, 1962, 88-113.

The systematic theologian of the 'Revelation as history' movement is W. Pannenberg. He expresses his view of the relationship between the two most evocatively in the 'Dogmatic Theses on the Doctrine of Revelation', included in the book *Revelation as History*, which served as the programme for his group. According to Pannenberg, God's self-revelation (cf. Introduction, 7ff. = ET 9ff.) did not take place directly, as by a theophany, but indirectly, through God's acts in history. It is visible to all and has a universal character. As such, however, it is only manifest at the end of all history (here Pannenberg refers to the apocalyptic understanding of history – similarly also in the Preface to *Grundfragen/Basic Questions*, 5ff. = ET I, xvf. – cf. also R.Rendtorff, *TLZ* 1960 [above 72f.], esp. 836f.). Pannenberg copes with the difficulty that in the Christian view the fullness of revelation has already taken place in Jesus Christ by understanding the Christ event 'proleptically': the fate of Jesus Christ is 'the anticipation of the end, and thus the revelation of God' (*Offenbarung als Geschichte* [above 72], 106 = ET 143); 'with the resurrection of Jesus, the end of history has already occurred' (ibid., 104f./142). Now that means that 'God [is] finally and fully revealed in the fate of Jesus'. Here is a counter-blow to kerygmatic theology (cf. also id., 'Redemptive Event and History'). It is also important that the Christ event is completely taken up into the context of the history of God with Israel: 'The Christ event does not reveal the deity of the God of Israel as an isolated event, but rather insofar as it is a part of the history of God with Israel' (Thesis 5, 107/145).

Pannenberg's critics (for a survey of the debate cf. Braaten; in Robinson, 88ff.) have accused him above all of rationalism (Althaus, 327f.; Klein, *MPT* 1962, 66f.); of adopting an idealistic conception of universal history (cf. 'Introduction', 18ff. = ET 16ff., and Pannenberg's frequent references to Hegel); of levelling out the specific history of salvation to this (Klein, *Theologie*); and of excluding the character of revelation as Word (Steiger, 108f.). In this context I cannot go into the question how far these charges are justified; but in connection with the first accusation we should at least note Pannenberg's answer to Althaus, in which he refers to the psychological need for faith in arriving at this knowledge (*TLZ* 1963, 84f.) and to the sheltering power of faith as an act which follows what is first merely theoretical knowledge ('Nachwort', 145 = ET 197). Nor does Pannenberg exclude the Word from the realization of the history of revelation; he explicitly asserts: 'History is not composed of... so-called brute facts' (*Offenbarung*, 112 = ET 152). It retains its function as promise, instruction and (in the New Testament) kerygma. Moreover he has explicitly rejected the accusation that he uses an untheological concept of history which is not constituted by the action of God (cf. *New Frontiers* III, 250f. – in fact according to *KuD* 1977, 78f., the action of God is constitutive of history; cf. already *von Rad Festschrift*, 1971 [above 59]). As to the incorporation of the resurrection of Jesus into history, Klein's criticism is that in this conception the Easter event loses its eschatological character and is corrupted into a world phenomenon of the past (*MPT* 1962, 78). Here we have a sign of Bultmann's distinction between history and eschatology (cf. R.Bultmann, *The Presence of Eternity. History and Eschatology*, 1957 [the 1955 Gifford lectures]) which often makes conversation between Old and New Testament scholars difficult.

It must also be noted that the discussion has meanwhile moved forward. Pannenberg's own position in it has remained consistent, as we can see from his remarks in e.g. *Theology and the Philosophy of Science*. If here for a historical exegesis of scripture the 'framework of a *theologically* oriented history of religions, that is, a theology of religions', is commended as a basis for work, the underlying view is that 'the phenomena of the history of the Judaeo-Christian religion themselves require them to be interpreted as the self-manifestation of the divine power over everything' (381f. = ET 379). Their preservation down to the present is then looked for in a second act. Here the contribution of the group to Old Testament theology is particularly interesting. Its main representative in this sphere is R.Rendtorff. His most important concern is to go beyond the contrast suggested by von Rad between two forms of history, the history of facts which can be demonstrated by historical criticism and the history attested by the faith of Israel. He does this by arguing that history and tradition coincide, are one and the same. 'When we speak of God's action in history, that cannot mean that he acted only in particular facts of history and that these facts are now constantly interpreted afresh. Rather the tradition of the acts of God in history is itself history. It includes the facts, but it cannot be detached from them ...'(*Gesammelte Studien* [above 46], 23). Thus for example the traditions which the tribes brought with them are much more significant for the early history of Israel than the outward facts, which are largely unknown (28ff.). The *historical efficacy* of an event often consists in the experiences which those involved gained from it and the way in which they interpreted these experiences for their historical existence (33). But the consequence of that is also not only that the account of Israel's history is a testimony to God's action but that this history as a whole embraces God's action with Israel (35). For, 'The history of Israel takes place in the outward events which are traditionally the subject-matter of historical research, *and* in the manifold and many-layered inner events which we sum up in the concept of tradition' (37). (These ideas had already been anticipated by D.Lerch, 'Zur Frage nach dem Verstehen der Schrift', *ZTK* 49, 1952, [350-67] 358.)

Rendtorff elaborated on these comments by observations which, following the lines of the programme of *Revelation as History*, define the event itself as an event of revelation and exclude the (prophetic) word as an independent source of revelation. 'The knowledge (of Yahweh) is not achieved by the Word in isolation but first through the event announced in the Word in its context in the history of the tradition' (58). This corresponds to the 'unity of event and word (or significance)' in the event of tradition as stressed by Pannenberg (emphasizing his agreement with Rendtorff, *Offenbarung als Geschichte* 137 = ET 189f.). As Rendtorff here had referred e.g. to the formula *'ani yhwh* which W.Zimmerli had made the focal point of his theological approach to the Old Testament (in 'Ich bin Jahwe', *Alt Festschrift* [above 41], 179-209 = id., *Gottes Offenbarung*, TB 19, Munich 1963 = ET 'I am Yahweh', in *I am Yahweh* [above 73], 1-28 and further articles; cf. his *Outline* [above 54]), this led to a discussion with Zimmerli. In an article ' "Offenbarung" im Alten Testament', (*EvTh* 1962 [above 73]), the latter discussed Rendtorff's contribution in *Revelation as History*. After discussing the 'self-introductory formula' itself (which is not a predicate but a statement of self-disclosure; not a summary of Yahweh's claim to power but an introductory formula), Zimmerli goes on to discuss the relationship betwen history and the word as the bearer of revelation. According to Zimmerli, to suppose that history itself could be the revelation of God goes against the Old Testament understanding of history. Rather, history is 'always understood here as the creaturely instrument which is freely manipulated by God' (28). By contrast the proclamation of the word and the prophetic proclamation of the name of Yahweh play a central role: 'It is an impossible undertaking... for the Old Testament to isolate history from the word of proclamation and to give the word only an incidental and subsidiary role' (25). History 'has no hidden meaning within it which man could approach with his power of interpretation'. Rather, it is the prophets who announce God's action and call out the name of Yahweh over the event; it is they who bring about the knowledge of God and faith (28f.). (B.Albrektson, *History and the Gods* [below

113f.], 118ff., stresses the significance of the revelation in the divine word as an annoucement of the divine action without which the divine acts in history are incomprehensible; cf already Richardson, 139ff. [on the role of prophecy] and recently Greig, *Geschichte* [above 60], 297ff.; Goldingay, *TynB* 1972 [above 65f.], 62f., id., *Approaches*, 74ff.)

Thus Zimmerli counters the position of 'history as revelation' with the opposite position of the theology of the word which he had already put forward in 1956 in *Das Alte Testament als Anrede*. There he had already been concerned to stress the Old Testament as 'a book whose word is meant to be proclaimed' (76); the Pentateuchal narrative as 'the rendering of that basic history of Israel meant to be retold in proclamation' (69) and the prophetic proclamation of the imminent historical event as an expression of the divine claim on his people Israel (70ff.) are the two pillars which support the 'bow of tension' (75) in the Old Testament. Rendtorff (*History and Word*) then in turn replied to Zimmerli, separating various stages and areas (view of history and prophecy) with different roles for the word. For historiography (e.g. the succession narrative, 633f./72ff.) he maintains his view that an understanding of history emerges there which 'recognizes the action of Yahweh in the context of the event itself' (649/88).

Zimmerli's position has developed above all from his preliminary work on his Ezekiel commentary (BK XIII, 1955-69, ²1979 = ET Hermeneia, Philadelphia, I, 1979; II, 1983); according to the preface to his collection of articles, *Gottes Offenbarung* (8), these studies 'ask how in the testimony of the Old Testament God emerges from his mystery and how human knowledge can encounter this appearance'. In particular, the article 'The Word of Divine Self-manifestation (Proof-Sayings): A Prophetic Genre' combines the making known of Yahweh's name as the 'centre of the event of revelation' (160/127) with his demonstration of the truth in the historical event itself. So this demonstration of truth can only come about if it is confirmed by a prior prophetic announcement of the event. 'Yahweh's history with Israel is the place where the truth of his revelatory word becomes recognizable in its unfolding' (*I am Yahweh* [above 73], 190/22 = ET 11). The position of the 'Revelation *as* History' group dissolves this tension.

I.L.Seeligmann's contribution to the Zimmerli Festschrift offers a variant on this view; he distinguishes each specific generation of eye-witnesses (as indicated by the use of the term *yr'*) as those who have seen God's glory directly in his historical acts, from the later generations to whom this knowledge is granted only by oral tradition, through hearing. However, this leaves undiscussed the question whether the events already brought their interpretations with them or whether they do not themselves presuppose a 'tradition'. (For the problem cf. also J.H.Robinson, 'The Historicality of Biblical Language', in B.W.Anderson (ed.), *Old Testament* [above 38], 124-58, who refers to the *berakoth* and *hodayoth* formulae as bearers of the tradition of the direct experience of the salvation-historical event.)

Zimmerli's view that the interpretative and proclamatory Word of God must be added to historical events as a means of revelation is shared by a large number of other exegetes, e.g. Richardson; Eichrodt (*TZ* 1948); Östborn; Preuss (*MPT* 1961); Davidson; Fohrer, *Tradition*; id., *Prophetie*, 487/273; Mildenberger, 1964; E.Jacob, 'Possibilités et limites d'une théologie biblique', *RHPR* 46, 1966, (116-30) 123.

F.Mildenberger attempts to characterize this double-sidedness of 'act' and 'word' in history with a term taken over from H.Diem, (*Dogmatik*, Tübingen 1955, 102ff. = ET Edinburgh 1959, 116ff.; id., *Der irdische Jesus und der Christus des Glaubens*, SGV 215, Tübingen 1957, 8ff.): 'proclamation history' (82, 107ff.). 'In the proclamation of the divine history the God who acts in it makes himself present to each particular present, or better, draws this particular present into the time of his history'(113). For the discussion with Mildenberger cf. also K.Schwarzwäller, 'Das Alte Testament in Christus', *TS(B)* 84, Zurich 1966, 10ff. The recent proposal by T.Veijola, 'Finns det en gammaltestamentlig teologi?', *SEÅ* 48, 1983, 10-30, that the decisive element in the Old Testament should be seen as the divine challenge and human response (which can therefore be interpreted theologically) could be said to belong in the same group.

Cf. also G.E.Wright's own correction to his earlier position in *God who Acts*: 'The event-centered mode of God's revelation cannot be systematized, for it includes both the confessional recital of God's activity and the inferences and deductions which a worshipping community draws from it in the variety of historical situations in which it finds itself' (*Vriezen Festschrift*, 383). For the combination of 'act/deed' and 'word', cf. ibid., 382 n.1. *The*

Old Testament and Theology, 44: 'The historical happening and its interpretation, the deed and the word of God as its commentary, these constitute the Biblical event.'

R.Knierim has again investigated the relationship between revelation in act and revelation in word, taking up the discussion between Rendtorff and Zimmerli, and arrives at the conclusion, 'that in the revelation of Yahweh as Yahweh, two different processes of revelation coincide' (223), namely revelation through historical actions (which belief in Yahweh has in common with the Near Eastern religions) and the specific revelation of the name of Yahweh, through which the identity of the God who acts here first becomes known. So the distinction is also that between Yahweh and Elohim (221) or between the 'general history of religion and the specific history of Yahweh' (223). At the same time this leads to doubts about the thesis of 'revelation as history', cf. below.

The question is whether it is not wrong to see 'revelation as history' and 'history and revelation' as alternatives. As early as 1947 A.Richardson pointed out that the distinction between objective historical event and later subjective interpretation is a simplification. We know of history only through the written report which in turn is interpreted. So revelation, too, cannot be divided into history and interpretation. For C.H.Dodd, *History and the Gospel*, London 1964, 19ff., history means two things: 1. a sequence of events; 2. an interpretation of this sequence of events. Since then the hermeneutics of history has made considerable progress which confirms the traditio-historical view. Reference should be made in particular here to H.G.Gadamer's concept of 'effective-history' (cf. *Wahrheit und Methode*, Tübingen 1960 = ET *Truth and Method*, London and New York 1975, ²1979), which since then has become very influential.

H.Wheeler Robinson was doubtless ahead of his time in developing in his (posthumous) work, *Inspiration*, above 00f. (which was envisaged as a prolegomena volume to an Old Testament theology), the main thesis that the form of revelation in Israel's faith was determined by two factors: the means by which God acts and the interpretative response of those who received the revelation: 'The divine revelation in Nature, Man and History is through acts, which need to be interpreted through human agency to make them *words* in our ordinary sense' (159). This also provides a bridge to the parts of the Old Testament which do not fit into von Rad's scheme. It is also worth noting the model of 'dynamic transcendence' developed by P.D.Hanson (*Dynamic Transcendence. The Correlation of Confessional Heritage and Contemporary Experience in a Biblical Model of Divine Activity*, Philadelphia 1978). Using the exodus event (28ff.) and the interpretation of Cyrus' victorious progress by Deutero-Isaiah (38ff.) as examples, he demonstrates that a happening representing a broad nexus of social, political and historical events on the synchronous level can be understood as divine action only through the visionary perspective which the living belief of a community develops as it takes up its confessional heritage. Thus the exodus event could not be understood without the patriarchal traditions; nor would the victorious progress of Cyrus have become transparent for faith in its significance for the future of the Jewish community without the exodus traditions. N.W.Porteous, *Living the Mystery* [2 above], Introduction, 2 (cf. also id., 'The Old Testament and Some Theological Thought-Forms', *SJT* 7, 1954, 153-69 = *Living the Mystery* [31-46] 42) has a similar view. However, it would go beyond the limits of this account to develop this theme.

De Vaux's view (*Conc* 1969, above 73) should also be mentioned as an interpretation of the problem of history which does more justice to the totality of the Old Testament than the one-sided position of Pannenberg. De Vaux points out that the Old Testament is as often aware of the hiddenness of God in history as it is aware of his manifestation. At times he even seems to withdraw completely from history. The suppliants in the psalms and the prophets seek to come to terms in different ways with this difficult problem (for example by explaining that it is a temporary absence as a punishment). Cf. also 4 below.

Since then the traditio-historical perspective has largely become established as an important way of solving the problems of Old Testament theology (cf. Zimmerli, *Alttestamentliche Traditionsgeschichte*, and D.A.Knight, *Rediscovering the Traditions of Israel*, SBLDS 9, Missoula ²1975). There is evidence of this in the newest contributions to Old Testament theology which choose the very theme of 'tradition' as a framework. They are contained in the volume *Tradition and Theology*, ed. D.A.Knight (above 71). The contribution on the theme of 'Tradition and History' by R.Smend (49-68) is really no more than a confirmation of the validity of the traditio-historical perspective for the exegesis and thus also for the theology of the Old Testament. The theological relevance of the tradition (as a place of revelation) is more directly visible in the contribution by D.A.Knight to the same volume. It is important because it shows most clearly the effect of traditio-historical scholarship on the understanding of the reciprocal relationship between tradition and revelation within the Old Testament. Knight points to the place of revelation in tradition as a living movement carried on by successive generations, which produces both pre-understanding and the occasion for the origin and interpretation of revelation, and in so doing stresses the active role of the human side in the process of revelation (168). Without wanting to infringe the sovereignty of God in his revelation (ibid.) and the ultimate mystery which lies in this (149, 180, where he makes the important comment: 'For this reason also theology must not be equated with the history of tradition... tradition can constitute only one, albeit a very important contribution to our understanding of theology'), he stresses the special significance of tradition for the development of revelation. There is no process of revelation at a particular point in an isolated sense (152f.); at least it is extremely difficult to make one out (161f.), and one cannot even speak of a deposit of revelation (164). As a consequence there is a traditum (179) which has the character of testimony to the original revelation but which immediately issues in the process of tradition, and indeed has its place of origin in it (173). One important comment by Knight coming from the more recent insights of textual exegesis relates to the 'democratization' of 'inspiration': in the prophetic books, it is no longer exclusively the 'authentic' words of the great individual prophet which are thought to be theologically significant; the later stages of the growth of the text are just as important (177).

W.McKane, op.cit., would similarly argue for a theological evaluation of tradition as the bearer of the tradition of faith which evokes in us the response of faith; here he dissociates himself from the spiritualizing of the history-of-religions school and also from the restriction of the kerygma to 'acts of God' in history (cf. further T.M.Raitt, 'Horizontal Revelation', *RelLife* 47, 1978, 423-9). One attempt, to be seen against the background of Catholic hermeneutics, is C.Stuhlmueller's contribution (above 74), which would allow the character of inspired word of God not only to the material coming from the earliest biblical writers but also to the redactional additions which arise from the actualizations at particular times, since the Bible reflects the whole process of the transmission of old traditions of salvation history actualized at particular times.

J.Scharbert ('Probleme der biblischen Hermeneutik', in J.B.Lotz, *Neue Erkenntnisprobleme in Philosophie und Theologie*, Freiburg im Breisgau 1968, [180-211] 195ff.) takes a similar view, at the same time criticizing earlier Catholic doctrinal statements on the question of scriptural inspiration (cf. my *Problems of Biblical Theology* Ch. II, 3).

It should be noted that Knight in no way identifies tradition with revelation (see above) and even mentions the possibility that tradition can be an obstacle to revelation, especially when it results in a fossilization of earlier revelation (174f.) or raises false hopes (the false prophets, 176).

Nor have the reservations about attaching too great importance to tradition for Old Testament theology been removed. W.Zimmerli has again recently emerged as the spokesman here (in his contribution to the same collection; cf. also P.R.Ackroyd, 'Continuity and Discontinuity' , ibid., 215-34). In some respects with a similar arrangement to that given by von Rad to the 'prophetic traditions of Israel' in the second volume of his *Theology*, Zimmerli puts more stress on the prophetic 'no' to the fossilized tradition of the people, the collapse in their function of making present salvation in judgment and the antitypical move beyond judgment to a new action of Yahweh which in language and content takes up the old traditions.

One might ask whether dialectic should not be introduced even more markedly into the process of tradition and whether the supposed antithetical structure between the 'historical' and the 'prophetic' sphere is not the survival of the old personalistic understanding of the prophets. This must be regarded as outdated both in terms of the exegesis of the prophetic books themselves, which prove to be the result of a long-drawn-out process of tradition, and the 'extra-prophetic' traditions which are taken up in them. – For Gese's position see my *Problems of Biblical Theology*, III.

4. The problem of salvation history

Baumgärtel, F.,'Das alttestamentliche Geschehen als "heilsgeschichtliches" Geschehen' (above 41); Blank, J., 'Geschichte und Heilsgeschichte', *WuW* 23, 1968, 116-27; Bultmann, R., 'Heilsgeschichte und Geschichte. Zu Oscar Cullmann, *Christus und die Zeit*', *TLZ* 73, 1948, 659-66 = id., *Exegetica*, Tübingen 1967, 356-68 = *Das Problem der Theologie des Neuen Testaments*, ed. G.Strecker (above 3), 294-308; id., 'Weissagung und Erfüllung' *StTh* 2, 1949, 21-44 = *ZTK* 47, 1950, 360-83 = *Glauben und Verstehen* II, Tübingen 1952, 162-86 = ET 'Prophecy and Fulfilment', *Essays. Philosophical and Theological*, London 1955, 182-208 = *Essays in Old Testament Hermeneutics/Interpretation* (above 75), 50-75; id., 'Geschichte und Eschatologie im Neuen Testament (History and Eschatology in the New Testament)', *NTS* 1, 1954, 5-16 = id., *Glauben und Verstehen* III, Tübingen 1960, 91-106; id., ' "The Bible Today" und die Eschatologie', *The Background of the New Testament. Festschrift C.H.Dodd*, Cambridge 1956, 402-8 (cf. Ott, H., *Geschichte und Heilsgeschichte in der Theologie Rudolf Bultmanns*, BHT 19, Tübingen 1955, and the retort by Biehl, P., 'Welchen Sinn hat es, von einer "theologischen Ontologie" zu reden?', *ZTK* 53, 1956, 349-72); id., *History and Eschatology* (above 80); Burrows, M., 'Ancient Israel', in R.C.Dentan (ed.), *The Idea of History in the Ancient Near East*, New Haven and London (1955) [3]1966, 99-131; Conzelmann, H., *EvTh* 1964 (above 65); Cullmann, O., *Christ and Time*, above 76; id., *Heil als Geschichte: Heilsgeschichtliche Existenz im Neuen Testament*, Tübingen (1965), [2]1967 = ET *Salvation in History*, London and New York 1967 (see Braun, D., 'Heil als Geschichte. Zu Oscar Cullmanns neuem Buch', *EvTh* 27, 1967, 57-76); id., 'Gottes Heilsplan in der Weltgeschichte', *EK* 7, 1974, 730-3; Darlap, A., 'Fundamentale Theologie der Heilsgeschichte', *MySal* I, 3-156; Dodd, C.H., *The Authority of the Bible*, London (1928) [2]1960, reprinted 1978, 227ff.; id., *The Bible Today*, Cambridge 1946/New York 1947; Ehlen, J.A., 'Old Testament Theology as Heilsgeschichte', *CTM* 35, 1964, 517-44; Fangmeier, J., 'Heilsgeschichte?', in J.Fangmeier and M.Geiger, *Geschichte und Zukunft*, TS 87, Zurich 1967, 5-27; Flückinger, F., 'Heilsgeschichte und Weltgeschichte', *EvTh* 18, 1958, 37-47; Fritsch, C.T., 'Biblical Typology II: The Bible as Redemptive History', *BS* 103, 1946, 418-30; Fuchs, E., 'Christus das Ende der Geschichte', in *Vorträge der Ev.Studentengemeinde Marburg*, H.2, Giessen 1946 = *EvTh* 8, 1948/49, 447-61 = id., *Zur Frage nach dem historischen Jesus*, Gesammelte Aufsätze II, Tübingen 1960, 79-99; Gélin, A., *Les idées maîtresses de l'Ancien Testament*, Paris 1948 = ET *The Key Concepts of the Old Testament*, New York 1955; Gloege, G., 'Der Heilsplan Gottes als geschichtliches Problem', *ELKZ* 2, 1948, 115-18 = id., *Heilsgeschehen und Welt*, Theologische Traktate I, Göttingen 1965, 11-26; id., 'Vom Sinn der Weltgeschichte', *LM* 2, 1963, 112-22 = *Heilsgeschehen*, 27-

52; Goldingay, J., *Approaches* (above 1), 66ff.; Gunneweg,
A.H.J., 'Über die Prädikabilität alttestamentlicher Texte', *ZTK*
65, 1968, 389-413; id., *Vom Verstehen des Alten Testaments. Eine
Hermeneutik*, ATD Erg.R.5, Göttingen 1977, 164-75 = ET
Understanding the Old Testament, OTL, London and Philadelphia
1978, 196-208; Hasel, G.F., *Old Testament Theology* (above 1);
Heller, J., 'Die Etappen der alttestamentlichen Heilsgeschichte',
in *Oikonomia. Festschrift O.Cullmann*, Hamburg-Bergstedt
1967, 3-10; Herberg, W., 'Biblical Faith as "Heilsgeschichte"',
Christian Scholar 39, 1956, 25-31 = *Faith enacted as History*,
Philadelphia 1976, 32-42; Hesse, F. 'Zur Frage der Wertung'
(above 66); id., *Das Alte Testament als Buch der Kirche* (above
66), 141-50; id., *Abschied von der Heilsgeschichte*, TS 108, Zürich
1971; id., 'Zur Profanität der Geschichte Israels', *ZTK* 71, 1974,
262-90; Jacob, E., *Grundfragen alttestamentlicher Theologie*,
Stuttgart 1970, 32-40; Käsemann, E., 'Rechtfertigung und
Heilsgeschichte im Römerbrief', in *Paulinische Perspektiven*,
Göttingen 1969, 108-39 = ET 'Justification and Salvation History
in the Epistle to the Romans', *Pauline Perspectives*, London and
Philadelphia 1969, 60-78; Klein, G., 'Römer 4 und die Idee der
Heilsgeschichte', *EvTh* 23, 1963, 424-47 = id., *Rekonstruktion
und Interpretation*, BEvTh 50, Munich 1969, 145-69 (shorter
version 'Heil und Geschichte nach Römer IV', *NTS* 13, 1966/7,
43-7); id., 'Individualgeschichte und Weltgeschichte bei Paulus.
Eine Interpretation ihres Verhältnisses im Galaterbrief', *EvTh*
24, 1964, 126-65 = *Rekonstruktion*, 180-224; id., 'Bibel und
Heilsgeschichte. Die Fragwürdigkeit einer Idee', *ZNW* 62, 1971,
1-47; id., 'Die Fragwürdigkeit der Idee der Heilsgeschichte', in
Spricht Gott in der Geschichte?, ed. F.T.Tenbruck et al., Freiburg
im Breisgau 1972, 95-153 (cf. also id., 'Präliminarien zum Thema
"Paulus und die Juden"', in *Rechtfertigung. Festschrift E. Käse-
mann*, Tübingen and Göttingen 1976, 229-43); Kraus, H.J.,
Biblische Theologie (above 1), 185-8, 240-53; id., 'Das Problem
der Heilsgeschichte in der *Kirchlichen Dogmatik*', in *Antwort.
K.Barth zum 70. Geburtstag*, Zürich 1956, 69-83; Kümmel, W.G.,
'Heilsgeschichte im Neuen Testament?', in *Neues Testament und
Kirche. Festschrift R.Schnackenburg*, Freiburg im Breisgau 1974,
434-57 = id., *Heilsgeschehen und Geschichte* 2, Marburg 1978,
157-76; Ladd, G.E, 'The Search for Perspectives', *Int.* 25, 1971,
41-62; Löwith, K., *Meaning in History*, Chicago 1949, esp. 182-
90; Lohff, W., 'Heil, Heilsgeschichte, Heilstatsache', *HWP* 3,

1031-3; Lohfink, N., *Freiheit und Wiederholung. Zum Geschichts-*
verständnis des Alten Testaments? Die religiöse und theologische
Bedeutung des Alten Testaments, Würzburg 1964, 79-103;
Malevez, L., 'Les dimensions de l'histoire du salut', *NRT* 86,
1964, 561-78 (on Cullmann and Bultmann); id., *Histoire du salut*
et philosophie: Barth, Bultmann, Cullmann, Paris 1971; Maly,
E.H., 'The Nature of Biblical History', *BiTod* 1, 1962, 278-85;
Muñoz Iglesias, S., 'Old Testament Values superseded by the
New', *Conc* 3.10, 1967, 50-5; Noth, M., 'Vergegenwärtigung',
above 75f.; Pannenberg, W., 'Redemptive Event' (above 77); id.,
'Preface', *Basic Questions* I (above 78); id., 'Weltgeschichte und
Heilsgeschichte', *Festschrift von Rad*, 1971 (above 60), 349-
66 = *Geschichte – Ereignis und Erzählung*, ed. R.Koselleck/
W.D.Stempel, Munich 1973, 307-23; Phythian-Adams, W.J., *The*
Fulness of Israel. A Study of the Meaning of Sacred History,
London, New York and Toronto 1938; cf. the other works by this
author mentioned in my *Problems of Biblical Theology*, ch.I;
Piper, O., *God in History*, New York 1939; Procksch, O., *NKZ*
1925 (above 14); von Rad, G., 'Offene Fragen/Postscript', (above
59); id., 'Antwort auf Conzelmanns Fragen', *EvTh* 1964 (above
67); Rahner, K., 'Old Testament Theology', *SM* 4, 1969, 186-90;
id., 'Weltgeschichte und Heilsgeschichte', *Schriften zur Theologie*
V, Einsiedeln ²1964, 115-35 = ET 'History of the World and
Salvation-History', *Theological Investigations* 5, London and New
York 1966, 97-114; id., 'Altes Testament (als heilsgeschichtliche
Periode)', *HTTL* 1, 1972, 79-84; Reventlow, H.Graf, *Rechtferti-*
gung im Horizont des Alten Testaments, BEvTh 58, Munich 1971,
41-66; Richardson, A., *The Bible in the Age of Science*, London
1961, ³1968; Robinson, J.M., 'Heilsgeschichte und Lichtungsge-
schichte', *EvTh* 22, 1962, 113-41; Roscam Abbing, *Inleiding*
(above 72), 107ff.; Ruppert, L., 'Gottes befreiendes Handeln in
der Geschichtstheologie des Alten Testaments', *SPK* 28, 1977,
67-81; id., 'Jahwe, Israels Gott, als Gott der Geschichte', in *Die*
Botschaft von Gott. Orientierungen für die Praxis, ed. K.Hem-
merle, Freiburg, Basle and Vienna 1974, 94-111; Scharbert, J.,
'Heilsgeschichte und Heilsordnung des Alten Testaments', *MySal*
2, 1076-144; id., *Was ist Heilsgeschichte?*, SBEsp 26, Madrid
1970, 21-34; Schmitt, R., *Abschied* (above 76); Schütz, F.,
'Anmerkungen zu einer Theologie der Heilsgeschichte', *NZST*
12, 1970, 103-13; Seeligmann, I.L., 'Menschliches Heldentum
und göttliche Hilfe. Die doppelte Kausalität im alttestamentlichen

Geschichtsdenken', *TZ* 19, 1963, 385-411; Sekine, M., 'Vom Verstehen der Heilsgeschichte', *ZAW* 75, 1963, 145-54; Soggin, J.A., *TLZ* 1964 (above 67); Steck, K.G., *Die Idee der Heilsgeschichte*, TS 56, Zürich 1959; De Vaux, R., *Conc* 1969 (above 73); Vielhauer, P., 'Paulus und das Alte Testament', in *Studien zur Geschichte und Theologie der Reformation*, Festschrift E.Bizer, Neukirchen-Vluyn 1969, 33-62 = id., *Oikodome. Aufsätze zum Neuen Testament* 2, ed. G.Klein, TB 65, Munich 1979, 196-228; Weth, G., *Die Heilsgeschichte*, FGLP IV,2, Munich 1931; Wolff, H.W., 'Heilsgeschichte und Weltgeschichte im Alten Testament', *EvErz* 14, 1962, 129-36 = *Wegweisung*, Munich 1965, 78-94.

The theme of 'salvation history' was introduced into modern study of the Bible in the nineteenth century above all by the so-called Erlangen school (also in the sphere of Swabian pietism by J.T.Beck: earlier origins refer to Reformed federal theology and the group of Swabian pietists around J.A.Bengel. – For the prehistory see esp. Weth and the survey in Ehlen). Its most important representative is J.C.K. (von) Hofmann.

For Hofmann see G.Flechsenhaar, *Das Geschichtsproblem in der Theologie Johannes Hofmanns*, Diss. Theol. Giessen 1935; M.Schellbach, *Theologie und Philosophie bei v.Hofmann*, BFCT 38,2, Gütersloh 1935; E.W.Wendebourg, *Die heilsgeschichtliche Theologie J.C.K. von Hofmanns kritisch untersucht als Beitrag zur Klärung des Problems der 'Heilsgeschichte'*, Diss. theol. Göttingen 1953, typescript; partial reprint, 'Die heilsgeschichtliche Theologie J.C.K.von Hofmanns in ihrem Verhältnis zur romantischen Weltanschauung', *ZTK* 52, 1955, 64-104; E.Hübner, *Schrift und Theologie*, FGLP 10 R.VIII, Munich 1956; Steck, *Idee*, 19-30; Kraus, *Biblische Theologie* (above 1), 247-53; for an evaluation from a confessional and conservative perspective see also C.Preus, 'The Contemporary Relevance of von Hofmann's Hermeneutical Principles', *Int* 4, 1950, 311-21.

Hofmann already developed in his various writings the most important features of the concept of salvation history which were to play a role in the later discussion of this theme (bibliography in P.Wapler, *Johannes von Hofmann*, Leipzig 1914), above all in his early work: *Weissagung und Erfüllung im alten und im neuen Testamente* (I and II, Nördlingen 1841/4 – cf. also his interesting review of himself in *Mecklenburgisches Kirchenblatt* 1, 1844, 54-82 =

Grundlinien der Theologie J.C.K. von Hofmanns, ed. J. Haussleiter, Leipzig 1910, 1-29). In the latter he talks about the twofold motive which led him to his conception of salvation history: 'I see only two ways which are worthy of an independent discipline. The first and nearest goes from the most general experience of salvation to personal experience... and leads from the directly certain fact which forms its content to the presuppositions of this fact, which therefore must also be facts...; thus the theologian finds comprised in the fact of rebirth the whole sacred history in accordance with its most important events. The other way is the historical one; here one brings together the whole of sacred history as this has been transmitted in scripture, in the sense of scripture, i.e. in the light of what scripture declares to be the centre of this history' (in Haussleiter, 2f.). Hofmann takes the second way in his work: 'Jesus is the end but also the middle of history; his appearance in the flesh is the beginning of the end' (*Weissagung und Erfüllung*, I, 58). The history which precedes the Christ event takes on the character of prophecy as such by its very goal: 'Thus we have in the self-portrayal of Christ in the world both history and prophecy: history, namely the constantly progressing formation of the finite form of the communion of God and man; prophecy, the ever more definite indication of the final form of the communion of God and man' (ibid., 40). Hofmann decisively rejects the secular notion of development in its usual form; but it cannot be denied that he immediately takes it over again: 'Thus all the progress of the history of this people is explained (with the coming of Jesus) to be progress in the history of salvation, for its result was a condition of the birth of Jesus' (ibid., 36; for the problem of Hofmann's relationship to historicism, particularly that of Ranke, cf. Wendebourg, *ZTK* 1955, 66f., 77f.). On the other hand he has no objection to the assumption that the events of salvation history had a supernatural character: 'The reality of what is a matter of faith cannot be proved by means which are taken from outside the sphere of faith' (*Theologische Ethik*, Nördlingen 1878, 13). So it is true of the Old Testament event that the aim of giving a description of Christ in advance at the same time provides the criterion for the facticity of the event which is above historical criticism: 'When God walks in the Garden of Eden, when Moses divides the waters of the sea, when Balaam predicts the downfall of Assyria, it is vain to declare all this as impossible as soon as it can be shown that it had to happen' (*Weissagung und Erfüllung* I, 55). For this assurance Hofmann simply refers to the testimony of the

Holy Spirit which guarantees scripture for the community; a scientific proof is subsequent confirmation of this certainty, but as such it always remains fragmentary (ibid. 50). The theologian, too, 'does not bring the academic systematic knowledge of salvation which he possesses to scripture, because first he wants to test it by scripture... but he brings his state as a Christian, by virtue of which he is certain that he possesses his salvation, namely the forgiveness of his sins and the capacity to love God, in Jesus Christ. Precisely through this he knows Israel's calling to be the people of salvation history and recognizes in scripture a testimony to the same salvation that he has in Christ' ('Die Aufgabe der biblischen Hermeneutik', *ZPK* NF 45, 1863 = *Vermischte Aufsätze*, ed. H.Schmid, Erlangen 1878, [114-22] 115). This *testimonium spiritus sancti internum* holds together the two ways of individual subjectivity and objective history mentioned above (for the underlying 'naive' Hegelianism here cf. Wendebourg, *ZTK* 1955, 75f.). For the former, Hofmann refers to the experience given to the individual Christian. (Cf. Steck, *Idee*, 19ff., and e.g. *Theologische Ethik*, 13: 'But the reponse to the question "what kind of an object of knowledge Christianity is" is the expression of a fact of experience, and it is impossible to go beyond this fact of experience as it is found in nature', or *Der Schriftbeweis*, I, Nördlingen 1852, 9: 'The knowledge and expression of Christianity must therefore be above all the Christian's self-knowledge and self-expression.')

It is also important for the salvation-historical understanding of the Old Testament that Hofmann revives typology as a perspective: the orthodox pattern of 'prophecy' and 'fulfilment' introduced in the title of his work is reinterpreted. Instead of referring, as it once did, to the prophetic proclamation understood as a prediction of Christ, it refers to a general relationship between salvation history and salvation itself understood in universal terms; here attention is focussed not so much on the words as on the events: 'Anyone who recognizes the gradual character of the divine revelation, the progress in the achievement of salvation, cannot think it strange to find the whole sacred history... depicted as prophecy or as a reference to the final, eternally abiding relationship between God and man. And again, he will call each stage of the realization of this relationship a fulfilment of the prophecy that has gone before. Only thus, in its extension over the whole of sacred history, is typology, which has been so despised, true... ('Selbstanzeige', in Haussleiter, 4). Prophecy does not cease with Old Testament history (that would be the well-known 'caricature' of typology, ibid.), but continues to the end of history: 'the self-portrayal of Christ in the world' (it happens in the life of his community) is 'at the same time history and prophecy: history, namely the ever-progressing formation of the communion of God and man; prophecy, namely the ever more definite reference to the final form of the communion between God and man' (*Weissagung und Erfüllung* I, 40).

The salvation-historical school merely played the role of an outsider in the theological scholarship of its time. Historicism introduced questions with which it clearly could not cope, so it soon seemed old-fashioned and out of date. However, the revival of theological awareness in exegesis after the First World War made the theme of salvation history topical again (after it had first been decried by dialectical theology, cf. K.Barth, *Romans*[2] [above 14f.] 16 = ET 57; G.Weth [above 91] 11 and passim). (At the end of his criticism of the 'salvation history school', Weth declares, 'We must reconstruct a theology of salvation history', 230). The positions over it taken up in more recent debate can hardly be understood without Hofmann as a model (though people tended to dissociate themselves firmly from him); in a way which might almost be called dialectical he combined perspectives which in later times were often understood as alternatives: the concern for the experience of faith on the part of the individual Christian, corresponding to a tradition of Lutheran and pietistic devotion, and an overall view of salvation history as an organic unity, the two connected through the 'centre' formed by the Christ event which represents both the ground of faith for the individual piety of the Christian who encounters scripture and the goal of the salvation history which comes down from the Old Testament and goes on to the end of all history. Strikingly enough we can find Hofmann's twofold understanding of salvation history in Barth's *Church Dogmatics* (here we must remember that the two passages in which the theme is discussed in more detail, II/1, 569ff. = ET 506ff. and IV/4, 27ff. = ET 24ff., were composed with an interval of almost thirty years between them, though their dialectical unity is unmistakable). In II/1, 'salvation history' is the special relationship that God, who is first Lord of the whole creation, has established as direct communication and partnership by *choosing* particular people. This communication is first of all with the patriarchs, beginning in Gen.3: 'We can see this from Abel through Noah to Abraham, Isaac and Jacob. We can see a continual selection and separation in Israel. We can see the same thing in the calling and gathering of the Church and even within the Church itself' (II/1,

571 = ET 508). This, then, is a line which goes through world history and as such is always special. Now 'the meaning and mystery' of this salvation history which runs its course through the life of Israel and the church is Jesus Christ: because 'the history of salvation is first and last, at its centre and in its origin, the history of Jesus Christ' (II/1, 577 = ET 513). As Kraus, too, has shown (*Festschrift K. Barth* 1956), to understand these statements one has to begin from the role of christology in Barth's dogmatic system and also from the specific understanding of particular concepts like 'origin' (for the use of the term in 'early' Barth cf. W.Härle, *Die Theologie des 'frühen' Karl Barth in ihrem Verhältnis zu der Theologie Martin Luthers*, Diss.theol. Bochum 1969, 6f., esp. n.35; 98f.) and 'centre', in which the idea of transcendence, the famous 'vertical' in the 'vertical from above', is expressed in Barth. In this understanding 'salvation history' is a special history determined only by God's act of revelation and without analogy to ordinary history; the term 'covenant history' can also be used to denote its particular place. This beginning in the theology of revelation then leads to the statement that salvation history is the centre of all history (hidden, but still normative): 'The history of salvation is *the* history, the true history which encloses all other history... Salvation history is *the* history (III/1, 64 = ET 60). From that there then follows the other way of using the word 'salvation history', for the event of Christ 'which took place once in time [and] becomes in the life of a man, again once in time, the event of his renewing'. According to Barth that happens 'in its power to proclaim itself in all times and places and to all men as the salvation history accomplished for all, in its power as salvation history'. As such, it is promise and assurance to everyone whom it reaches (IV/4, 27f. = ET 25f.); it becomes 'his own salvation history' (IV/4, 30 = ET 27).

Seen from a distance in time, we have to recognize the weakness of Barth's position; just as he introduces an absolute concept of revelation, so he also introduces an absolute concept of (salvation) history and does not attempt any discussion with the general hermeneutics of history. This leads to an obscurity in the understanding of history which was not overcome in the Barth school either.

Mention should be made of the outline by G.Gloege, *Vom Sinn der Weltgeschichte*, which represents an independent systematic solution. Developing Löwith's views critically, from a New Testament eschatological perspective, he understands the whole of world history as (hidden) salvation history on the way to its final consummation.

In Catholic dogmatics the theme of 'salvation history' is usually taken up without being seen as problematical (for the literature cf. J.Scharbert, SBEsp 26 [above 90], 23 n.5). For K.Rahner, first of all history as a whole has an underlying sense of salvation history, for 'the same man who in his whole and entire being is faced with the decision regarding salvation in his historical existence has ultimately only one history, in the sense that there are no isolated sectors of his existence which are in no way co-determined by the history of grace and faith' (*Schriften zur Theologie/ Theological Investigations* 5, 118/100). 'Salvation and damnation are events of profane history, for wherever men achieve themselves in freedom, they stand before God and decide their salvation' (ibid., 119 = ET 100). However, secular history as such is still ambivalent: 'The content and reality proper to salvation history do indeed lie hidden in profane history, since immediately tangible historical events and realities do not of themselves give us any clear clue, as they themselves can be of a saving or a damning nature' (ibid., 117 = ET 99). Within the secular history in which it is hidden in this way, salvation history first becomes transparent through prophetic interpretation and above all through the Christ event (ibid., 118 = ET 100).Salvation history interpreted in this way is 'materially coextensive' with secular world history. 'It is part of the Catholic statement of Faith that the supernatural saving purpose of God extends to men of all ages and places in history' (ibid., 121 = ET 103). Now alongside this 'general revelation- and salvation-history' (ibid., 123, ET 105) there is also the 'real, special official history of salvation'(ibid., 125 = ET 107, cf.127 = ET 109). It is constituted by God through his 'word, which is an inner constitutive element of God's saving activity considered as an event of human history as such. Hence, wherever profane history is clearly interpreted by the word of God in history as to its saving or damning character... there is found the special, official history of salvation and revelation, immediately differentiated and standing out in relief from profane history' (ibid., 125 = ET 107). The history of Israel is special salvation history in such a sense; it remains the privilege of Israel 'that its tangible and to some extent distinct salvation-history was the immediate historical prelude to the Incarnation of the divine

Word, and that this history of Israel alone was interpreted authoritatively by the word of God in scripture in such a way that it was thereby distinguished from any other profane history..., and that only thus it became the official and special salvation-history in distinction to profane history (ibid., 128f. = ET 109f.). (A similar view is also taken by E.Schillebeeckx, *Revelation and Theology*, London and New York 1967, 11ff.). However, 'in the Old Testament, too, the dividing line between saving and profane history is still very fluid: it was only with difficulty that men in Old Testament times could distinguish between authentic and false prophets...The Old Covenant, taken as a whole, could have fallen away from its mission, and... become an empty sign, an illegitimate usurpation of the sign of God's grace to the world' (128 = ET 108f.).

Nevertheless, for Catholic dogmatics salvation history is an area so free from doubt that the encyclopaedic *Mysterium Salutis* can provide an all-embracing 'Outline of the dogmatics of salvation history'. In the Introduction the editors write: 'There can no longer be any question that it is justifiable to give a Catholic dogmatics the form of a salvation history' (*MySal* I, XXIII). Here they can refer to the Vatican II Constitution on Divine Revelation IV, 14 (cf. Abbott, *Documents of Vatican II*, London and New York 1975, [5]1980, 759, and E.Stakemeier, *Die Konzilskonstitution über die göttliche Offenbarung. Werden, Inhalt und theologische Bedeutung*, KKTS XVIII, Paderborn 1966, 165); there we are told tersely: *Oeconomia autem salutis ab auctoribus sacris praenuntiata, enarrata atque explicata, ut verum Dei verbum in libris Veteris Testamenti exstat* ('Now the economy of salvation, foretold, recounted and explained by the sacred authors, appears as the true Word of God in the books of the Old Testament'); for the role of the theme of 'salvation history' in Vatican II cf. also G.Müller-Fahrenholz, *Heilsgeschichte zwischen Ideologie und Prophetie*, ÖF.S IV, Freiburg 1974, 169ff.). It emerges from Stakemeier's commentary (166) that the focal point of this definition is to be found in the saving plan of God ('economy of salvation', cf. Vatican II and Muñoz Iglesias, *Conc* 1967, above 90), promised, realized and developed (this tripartite division is meant to indicate the three parts of the Old Testament canon: the prophetic books, the historical books and the wisdom books) in salvation history (for other hermeneutical problems in this section cf. my *Problems of Biblical Theology*, II, 3). Darlap (*MySal* I, 3) also points out that 'a widespread interest in salvation history can be discovered in more recent Catholic theology'. He even distinguishes (11-13) six different possible ways of understanding salvation history, the first (salvation history as the history of religion, 'i.e. as the history of all human experiences of salvation') and the fourth (salvation history 'understood more narrowly as biblical theology of the Old and New Testament') would correspond to Rahner's twofold division. (Darlap even sees the 'authorized prophetic interpretation' as being the only special feature of the salvation history of the Old Testament over against the general history of religion, ibid., 49). It is precisely the first version which seems initially to be a specifically Catholic possibility. However, it is taken up by W.Pannenberg, who sees world history as a whole as the field of divine action for human salvation ('the whole of humanity') and thus would see salvation history issuing in the history of religion (*von Rad Festschrift* 1971, esp. 362ff.; cf. also above 78ff.). Rahner's and Darlap's view (cf. Müller-Fahrenholz, *Heilsgeschichte*, 193ff.) is, however, in no way that of all Catholic theologians. J.Scharbert, SBEsp 26 (above 90) stresses: 'Salvation history in the biblical sense is not simply to be identified with human history' (25), and limits this to those facts 'in which the biblical tradents represent God's saving action and the human reactions to it' (26), and thus to 'biblical history' in the narrower sense, though he allows the church a part in it through its witness. Blank expressly dissociates himself from Darlap and argues that his conception of salvation history is 'basically nothing more than a "natural theology" supplemented by a few modern perspectives'(118). For him 'salvation history' is 'first and foremost the historical connection of the revelation of God in *Israel and in Jesus Christ* attested in the scripture of Old and New Testaments' (119).

In addition to the Catholic outlines of a theology of history cf. the surveys by R.Aubert, 'Discussions récentes autour de la Théologie de l'Histoire', *CMech* 18, 1948, 129-49; L.Malevez, 'La vision chrétienne de l'Histoire II. Dans la théologie catholique', *NRT* 71, 1949, 244-64; id., 'Deux théologies catholiques de l'histoire', *BPTF* 10, 1949, 225-41; J.David, 'Theologie der irdischen Wirklichkeiten', in J.Feiner, J.Trütsch and F.Böckle (eds.), *Fragen der Theologie heute*, Einsiedeln 1957, ³1960, 560-7 (bibliography); G.Thils, 'La théologie de l'Histoire. Note bibliographique', *ETL* 26, 1950, 87-95. In the Catholic theology of history there is also the contrast between a theology of history with a more eschatological orientation and a theology of history with a more incarnational orientation, cf. W.Kasper, 'Grundlinien einer Theologie der Geschichte', *TQS* 144, 1964, (129-69) = id., *Glaube und Geschichte*, Mainz 1970, [67-100] = id., *Glaube im Wandel der Geschichte*, Mainz 1973, [63-102] 129/67/63.

The problem of 'salvation history' is above all a hermeneutical question, in which perspectives from a systematic point of view play a decisive role. Discussion of it is carried on not only by systematic theologians but also above all by New Testament scholars, whereas the participation of Old Testament scholars is quantitatively smaller. The Old Testament scholars are often positive towards the concept as such, whereas the criticism, above all in the wake of R.Bultmann, comes most strongly from the New Testament side.

F.Baumgärtel is relatively close to Hofmann's individualist perspective in his understanding of 'salvation history' in the Old Testament: according to him, 'salvation history', understood in the light of the central Christ event, is an 'inner event which comes about in and with the outward event from God to Israel' (*Alt Festschrift* [above 41], 13); it is a matter of 'the people of the Old Testament being affected by the event from God, the attestation of the Old Testament experience of judgment and grace in and through the Old Testament event', which 'affects our own existence before God,... the fact that (along with Israel) we are addressed under the gospel' (ibid., 14). The Christian therefore has a dialectical relationship with the Old Testament salvation history: the Old Testament understanding of the history of the people of Israel, which sees this as a history of salvation and disaster in the light of its earthly conception of the promise which is bound up with the people, is irrelevant to the Christian. Nevertheless, the Old Testament testimonies affect us as our own history of salvation and disaster; we stand with Israel in the darkness of incurring guilt, and with Israel receive the promise which is fulfilled and made a certainty in Christ Jesus that 'I am the Lord your God' (cf. *Verheissung* [above 40f.], 54ff.). So in Baumgärtel we find a very arbitrary way of existentializing the conception of 'salvation history' which makes the aspect of its historical context as such fade well into the background.

More common is the understanding of 'salvation history' as a historical connection of outward events (which can even be divided into periods, Heller); they begin in the history of Israel as reflected in the Old Testament and move towards the Christ event, which is their conclusion and climax. For example C.H.Dodd outlines such a conception: for him the history of Israelite religion, despite many divergences along the way, is a development of revelation from lower religious forms to higher, which reaches its climax in the Christianity of the New Testament. For W.J.Phythian-Adams (*Fulness* [above 90]), salvation history is the history of Israel beginning with Abraham which extends to Jesus Christ and is continued in the history of the church (5); its eschatological goal is the accomplishment of humanity in reconciliation (8). The idea of reconciliation is the scarlet thread which runs through salvation history (cf. also id., *The Way of At-One-Ment. Studies in Biblical Theology*, London 1944 [cf. my *Problems of Biblical Theology*, ch.I]). Similarly, for Löwith, too, salvation history is a particular history, leading up to Christ, within the general history of the world. According to Blank, for whom salvation history is exclusively 'the history of Israel, Jesus and the early church' (119, cf.121), this is connected with the whole of history by its representative character, in that 'at the same time, in its concrete historicity it stands for the salvation of the whole'(120).

Scharbert (SBEsp 26 [above 90], 23f.) gives a closer definition. Salvation history is not history of salvation, for 'salvation' is a state of perfection which is to be hoped for only at the end of history; it is a history of the expectation of salvation, the longing for eschatological blessings, towards which God is leading humanity through history. However, this is an isolated view. In von Rad's work the term 'salvation history' plays a significant role as a summary of the acts of Yahweh in history as Israel presented them in its confessional summaries (cf. e.g. 'The Problem of the Hexateuch', [above 59], 3/12= ET 4, and passim, *Theology* II, Index s.v. 'history: saving history, ideas about saving history'). In the 'Retrospect and Prospect' of the fourth German edition of Vol.II (not in the ET), von Rad sums up the impulses which were provided by the form-critical method (even after the rejection of the developmental pattern of the history-of-religions school in the revival of Old Testament theology after the First World War) towards the discovery of larger summary accounts of historical connections through the great narrative works of the Old Testament. 'The Pentateuchal sources or the Deuteronomistic History are not limited to describing individual historical encounters with Yahweh... Here, rather, we have accounts of historical periods of considerable length, which were significant to their authors only because these periods of history were utterly under the disposition and rule of Yahweh in such a way that it would be possible to point to a logic of divine rule... From that point on I began to talk of "salvation history", of Yahweh's "rule in salvation history"'(*Theologie* II⁴, 441).

Of course in making these comments von Rad sees himself only at the beginning in terms of method. In addition to the problem of the two different pictures of history, that of modern historical criticism and that held by Israel, which we have already discussed (above 65ff.), the difficulties are caused above all by the juxtaposition of the various views of salvation history in the different sources of the Old Testament and the fact that 'the reinterpretation of an older text by a later is often a violent one' ('Offene Fragen' [above 59], 404/292f. = ET 413), e.g. the different traditions of the election and the 'continual actualization of the data of the saving history' (ibid., 405/293 = ET 414) which can be noted right through the Old Testament. Here von Rad also stresses the 'constant breaks in tradition, the new beginnings, which can be found in this process' (cf. *EvTh* 1964 [above 67], 390). This difficulty produces problems above all for the unity of the canon (see below). Within the salvation history von Rad masters this by assuming in his approach above all a progressive relationship of promise and fulfilment already within the framework of the Old Testament development (see above 74f.)

Von Rad stresses the distance between this new way of talking about 'salvation history' and the old 'salvation history school' of the eighteenth and nineteenth centuries (*Theologie* II⁴,441). The new approach seems to him to grow directly out of the text by the application of the form-critical (traditio-critical) method. However, the kerygmatic concern which calls forth the use of this particular term is also unmistakable.

That is even more markedly true for the New Testament scholar O.Cullmann (for his work cf. also Müller-Fahrenholz, *Heilsgeschichte* [above 97], 137ff.), whose two books *Christ and Time* and its sequel *Salvation in History* represent the clearest overall view of a system of salvation history. Cullmann's approach in *Christ and Time* is characterized by its starting point in a linear view of the biblical history of revelation, in contrast to what he assumes to be the cyclical view of Hellenism (31ff., 43ff. = ET ²1962, 37ff., 51ff., see also above 76). The Christ event represents the mid-point within the linear salvation history formed by the selection of *Kairoi* (33f. = ET 39ff.); the past and future of salvation history are related to it (93ff., 107ff. = ET 131ff., 139ff.). Here the concept of *salvation* history is clearly not decisive for Cullmann; he is principally concerned with the 'divine sequence of events' (or God's plan, cf. 'God's saving plan'. For criticism of this thought pattern, however, see Gloege, *Der Heilsplan Gottes*). 'Because of sin and judgment it can also be a history of disaster' (*Salvation in History*, 3 = ET 21 [and *EK* 1974, 732] but cf. 39 = ET 57f.). As Cullmann stresses in his later book, even the term 'salvation *history*' is only an expedient since (as he also stresses in the revision of his approach in *Christ and Time*, against Steck), 'salvation history' in the sense he intends is not an unbroken causal chain of demonstrable historical facts; but salvation-historical faith is 'faith in a connection revealed only by God, resting upon a completely uncalculable selection of individual events' (*Salvation as History* 37 = ET 55, cf. EK 1974, 732). So the term 'history' has to be put within quotation marks, although on the other hand there is also an analogy between history and salvation history (*Salvation in History*, 59 = ET 91). As we can see, the problems of the diastasis between 'actual' and 'kerygmatic' history (above 65-71) which emerge with von Rad also play a part with Cullmann (Bultmann's early criticism, *Exegetica*, 356ff., also focusses above all on this problem).

Vigorous criticism of the concept of 'salvation history' was made not only by some systematic theologians but above all by Bultmann and the Bultmann school (in the wider sense; Bultmann's influence goes far beyond the circle of his closest pupils). It was directed not least against Cullmann's position, since he was the first theologian after the Second World War to revive a developed system of salvation history. One can read the essence of Bultmann's objections to the recognition of 'salvation history' in his comments on *The Bible Today* in the Dodd Festschrift: for Bultmann, thinking in terms of salvation history is theologically illegitimate, 'since this latter approach understands history in terms of an idea which is immanent in the historical event, whereas theological understanding sees it... in the light of the end of history as given in the Christ event...'(ibid., 402, similarly also Fuchs, 'Christus das Ende', who reinterprets Rom.10.4 accordingly). In the New Testament understanding the church is certainly the goal of salvation history, but as 'an eschatological entity in the radical sense that it is not a worldly phenomenon and that those who belong to it no longer belong to the world but have been desecularized. For with Christ the history of the world has reached its end' (ibid., 404, cf. also *GuV* III, 102). '...as the body of Christ the church has no history, but is an eschatological phenomenon' (ibid., 408). So it is the contrast between history and eschatology (this is also the title of the 1955 Gifford lectures, above 80) which governs Bultmann in his rejection of the concept; for Jesus and the New Testament the (apocalyptic) eschatological message is the distinguishing feature (cf. *History and Eschatology*, 31ff.). Underlying this is the well-known contrast, typical of Bultmann, between history (which can be objectified and is at men's disposal), and 'historicity' (in the now of decision, which is not at men's disposal). Hence his question to Dodd: 'Must not a theological understanding of history begin from the understanding of historicity (as the essence of human being) and not from the understanding of history as the context of a past event?' (*Dodd Festschrift*, above 88, 407).

Historicity does not dissolve history but limits it to individual history; cf. *History and Eschatology*, 43: 'historicity of man, the true historical life of the human being, the history which every one experiences for himself and by which he gains his real essence'; ibid., 155: *'the meaning of history lies always in the present... do not look around yourself into universal history, you must look into your own personal history. Always in your present lies the meaning in history...'*

This presupposition also determines the understanding of the Old Testament: 'Now I will not deny that in the proclamation of the church the Old Testament, too, can be the word of God; however this is only in such a way that a word of the Old Testament can become a word which addresses us *sub specie Christi*, not in such a way that we can detect that the word of God came about in the history of Israel itself' (ibid.). Even in respect of passages like Acts 7.2-53 or Heb.11 Bultmann rejects the view that 'the early Christian community understood itself as a real phenomenon of history, or that the relation to the Israelite people was understood as real historical continuity. The continuity is not a continuity growing out of history but is one created by God... Now for the first time the divine counsel which was hitherto concealed is unveiled. It does not consist in the divine guidance of Israel's history... The content of the divine counsel is the eschatological events which have begun to happen with the incarnation of Christ...' (*History and Eschatology*, 35f.) For Bultmann, Paul's understanding of history in particular has an apocalyptic stamp, modified by his anthropology: so the whole of the past is not specifically the history of Israel but the history of humanity, and as such is essentially determined by sin, and therefore – like the law – the presupposition of grace which is ended by its coming (*History and Eschatology*, 40f.). The contrast between the event of faith (to be interpreted existentially) and salvation as a present reality disclosed only to faith on the one hand and past history (to be ascertained by historical scholarship) on the other is the heart of G.Klein's criticism of 'salvation history' (following Bultmann: e.g. *ZNW* 1971, 1f.: 'since salvation as a reality disclosed only to faith is not capable of verification historically, i.e. by means of a method which does not make faith a condition of its possibility, no possible *history* of salvation can be verified in this way, too'). Akin to this is Steck's objection that history is always past and therefore 'above all a cemetery and field of the dead' (op.cit., 53; the characterization of history by Löwith, *Meaning in History* 193, cf. 197, as 'a realm of sin and death' whose end has dawned in Christ, is similar). Alongside this central thought the contrast between actual and believed history which also emerges with Klein (see above – here he actually quotes Hesse in particular, *ZNW* 1971, 9ff.; *Spricht Gott in der Geschichte?*, ed. F.T.Tenbruck [above 89] 99f., etc.) is less important. For his existential understanding of faith detached from history Klein appeals above all to Paul (there is detailed criticism of Klein above all in Kümmel, *Schnackenburg Festschrift*), to a Pauline message understood as a contrast to the Old Testament understanding of salvation. The figure of Abraham according to Rom.4 becomes the example of a belief which is not understood in terms of salvation history but brings liberation from history: 'There is a continuity between Abraham as a historical figure and present-day faith, but it is not the product of a historical development and is in no way capable of demonstration by historical research. Rather, this continuity *arises* first of all where one believes like Abraham' (*Rekonstruktion*, 157; cf. *NTS* 1966/67, 44f.). Klein makes the same point in connection with the removal of the difference between Jew and Gentile, according to Gal.2.15f., in the event of justification with its christological foundation, which virtually breaks through the limits of a specific salvation history within secular history – 'the history *sui generis* which emerged within the delimitation *proves* equally to be an element in sinful secular history, which first acquires that character now as a consequence' (*Rekonstruktion*, 180ff., quotation 194). For H.Haag (*TQS* 1980, above 22), too, the event in the New Testament is 'not at all the organic aim and end of the Old Testament developmental history, but something new like a leap'.

P. Vielhauer's argument is on similar lines; e.g he stresses in connection with II Cor.3.7-18: 'Paul's comments are *not* oriented on a theology of history *but* on a soteriology; they do *not* seek to characterize the history of Israel from Moses to Christ from the perspective of salvation history, as a history of disaster... *but* make the present *either-or* unavoidable with the antithesis of old covenant/new covenant' (above 91, 48/212). Exegetically Paul's soteriological intention-for-decision is excellently observed and convincingly expounded. Nevertheless the basic criticism remains, whether on ideological grounds Vielhauer does not make the history of salvation and soteriology alternatives in a way which is profoundly un-Pauline, because the Jew Paul, like the Old Testament prophets, understands the *kairos* against the background of the constantly valid faithfulness of the God of Israel to his original institutions of salvation down to the present 'last of all' (cf. also below 107–9).

What is for the moment F. Hesse's final contribution to the problem of salvation history follows the same pattern as Klein's, as he indicates already in the title of his significant pamphlet *Abschied von der Heilsgeschichte*, cf. also *ZTK* 1974. For criticism, cf. above all R. Schmitt, *Abschied* (above 76). Where his argument is leading is eminently clear from the metaphor of 'astigmatism' which appears at the end (66); the saving event, in reality only a point, namely the event of Christ crucified, is seen by the theology of salvation history as a line, as a 'sequence of successive saving acts', together forming a salvation history which also includes the events of the Old Testament. However, the salvation associated with Christ, which represents forgiveness of sins for the godless, cannot be derived from elsewhere and is unforeseeable; it is not contained anywhere in history, does not fit into its continuity, and is not prepared by it. 'The resurrection of Jesus from the dead cannot be verified as a fact within history' (62); the saving significance of the cross can only be grasped through proclamation and its acceptance in faith (62f.). It follows from this that no extraordinary action of God breaking through causal connections can be seen in the history of Israel. 'That is why the history of Israel is not different in quality from the history of any other people' (59, cf. also *ZTK* 1974, 289, which also quotes with approval Bultmann's theory of contradiction between 'the idea of the people of God [and] ... an empirical national community' ['Prophecy and Fulfilment', *GuV* II, 183 = ET *Old Testament*

Interpretation/Hermeneutics, 73). This final conclusion is supported by a series of subsidiary arguments: e.g. the comment that the history of Israel is not a history of salvation but a history of disaster and that even Israel could only have seen it in this way (25ff.); the New Testament,too, is unaware of a continuum of salvation history leading up to the Christ event (31ff.); not even the position once put forward by Hesse (*Das Alte Testament als Buch der Kirche*, above 66, 141ff.) that salvation history did not run its course in the actual history of Israel or in the history in which Israel believed but 'in, with and under' the history experienced by Israel. Hesse now thinks that this solution, too, no longer works, since one cannot make it clear to anyone, not even the believer (41f.)

Hesse's most recent view represents the final point in one of the two lines which begin from Hofmann: he takes over from his teacher Baumgärtel the concept and content of 'promise' (*Das Alte Testament...*, 67ff.; *Abschied*, 43ff.), i.e. an idea which is appropriate to the individual experience of faith. The relationship of faith to the community is almost eliminated (as with Hirsch) and the other-worldliness of Christian salvation is stressed. So salvation cannot be realized in a soteriological sense in the context of the community of a people, which is what Israel was: 'According to the Old Testament, salvation for a a people is completely and utterly political salvation' (*Abschied*, 11), 'something explicitly material' (12). Over against this, Hesse makes the New Testament concept of *soteria* the only normative one: it has a purely future orientation, consists in the forgiveness of sins and the justification of the godless, 'and accordingly relates only to man's relationship with God and not to conditions in this world' (15).

It is striking how the lines from an internalized Lutheranism, the understanding of faith in existentialist terms as in the Bultmann school, and an isolated theology of the Word come together here. For what Hesse continues to affirm is that God is at work in the continuum of history with which the Old Testament deals; however, this happens exclusively through his word, and 'such a word of God comes about independently of any historical continuum'(54).

A.H.J.Gunneweg (*Understanding*, cf. already *ZTK* 1968) criticizes the concept of salvation history with similar arguments. The *saving event*, which is to be distinguished from *salvation history* (169 = ET 202) is not a continuous *process* but unconnected individual episodes (between which connections are drawn only at a later stage, as with the themes in the Pentateuch). There can be no question of a development, a process of salvation culminating in a goal. The argument in terms of the *kairos* as a moment of salvation (in the New Testament), standing outside the historical continuum and with an eschatological content, emerges again with Gunneweg (165 = ET 197). His position is more cautious and considered than those of Klein and Hesse, but it follows the general line of the Bultmann school. Common to Bultmann, Klein and Hesse is the fact that they appeal especially to Paul over the gap between the events of the Old Testament and the events of the New (cf. Hesse, *Abschied*, 32f., with references to Klein). Here I can only indicate that Pauline exegesis has recently begun to move slowly but surely away from this one-sided interpretation. E.Käsemann gave a first warning against it in 1969 ('Justification and Salvation History'). He called the debate over whether Paul had any view of salvation history 'a specimen of the entanglement of all exegesis in systematic prejudices'(116 = ET 65). 'Theology cannot begin and end with the individual, where world mission appears as the Christian task pure and simple...' (116f. = ET 65). 'It cannot be seriously disputed that salvation history forms the horizon of Pauline theology' (118 = ET 66). However, one may detect a profound paradox in the reality of salvation history. On the one hand there is a continuity in space and time, starting from the promise over Israel as a historical entity, from creation, the election of Israel and the Christ event to the parousia. On the other hand, history is not a continuum of salvation but a battlefield (Augustine), in that there salvation is hidden in disaster, and faith, sorely tried, lives in the shadow of the cross. Seen from close to, salvation history is a history of catastrophes. 'The man who places himself in its ranks does so hoping against hope, believing that God is constantly calling into being the things that are not, that he raises the dead, lifts up the fallen, forgives sinners and makes the ungodly the instruments of his grace' (124 = ET 69f.).

These basic considerations (which also include the view that Paul's doctrine of justification was polemic against Judaism, even if it does not just hold a subsidiary place in Pauline theology, but is central [125 = ET 70], as it is an interpretation of christology [130 = ET 72], and the fact that it is never oriented on the individual but has cosmic horizons [132 = ET 74]) must be qualified by more thorough exegesis of the letters of Paul.

Käsemann has recently commented that 'Paul's doctrine of

salvation history is a variation on his doctrine of the justification of the ungodly' (*An die Römer*, HNT 8a, Tübingen 1973, ³1974, 254 = ET *Commentary on Romans*, Grand Rapids and London 1980, ²1982, 266). The term 'salvation history' can only be used appropriately in theology when one is aware of the dialectic which prevails in the history of Israel. It is inappropriate to understand it in terms of an unbroken, continuous realization of salvation which took place in the life of the old people of God. To this degree, criticism of certain ways of using the term is justified (for criticism cf. also Conzelmann, *EvTh* 1964, above 65, 119f.; Westermann, *Theologie*, above 62, 10). The clear theological judgment of the Old Testament evidence itself (cf. Reventlow, *Rechtfertigung*) is that the history of Israel became what it represents in historical reality through the actions of the people, namely a single chain of disasters and catastrophes with very few bright moments. It can be called salvation history only if it is considered in the light of the action of God: in the light of his ever-new saving ordinances, through the disaster which is the consequence of human conduct, and of his faithfulness in keeping his promises and maintaining the election once expressed in them (cf. Blank, 123: 'Salvation history has its fundamental, theological basis, which supports and brings about salvation history as continuity, in that factor which the Bible calls the "faithfulness of God", *'emet Yahweh'*). This introduces a dialectic into the event which includes an aspect oriented on the future. Cullmann (*Salvation in History* [above 88], 147ff. = ET 166ff.) regards ' the salvation-historical tension between "already" and "not yet" as the key to the understanding of New Testament salvation history'. This brings him very close to von Rad, who understands the Old Testament salvation history as a 'ceaseless movement towards a [final] fulfilment' (*Theology* II⁴, 397 = ET 373), though he also puts great stress on the 'discontinuity between the revelations which it was Israel's lot to experience' (II⁴, 385 = ET 362). This last aspect in particular should be noted more strongly in talking of 'salvation history', since the concept of the continuum as a quality immanent in history (like the concept of history itself) is alien to the Old Testament (so too H.Seebass, 'Zur Ermöglichung biblischer Theologie', *EvTh* 37, 1977, [591-600] 591 n.5). Compared with the linear approach in Cullmann's *Christ and Time*, the account of salvation history in *Salvation in History* is more like a wave (cf. Braun [above 88, 62). However, the dialectic of a history of salvation *and* disaster is not expressed clearly enough in von Rad and Cullmann (but cf. Blank, 124). For Christian faith the future aspect connects the Old Testament salvation history with the Christ event, as forming its goal (cf. P.Pokorný, 'Probleme biblischer Theologie', *TLZ* 106, 1981, [1-8] 4: the context of the two Testaments is not an already given historical continuity. However, in the light of its experience of faith in Jesus Christ, 'the church has accepted the event attested in the Old Testament as its past and chosen the Old Testament tradition for its own..'); here the promise of God is finally fulfilled *sub contrario* (we need not discuss here the question of 'futurist eschatology' in the New Testament itself – for Cullmann the Christ event in this sense remains the 'mid-point of time').

Steck's description of history as a 'cemetery and field of the dead' (above 104) recalls one last aspect which makes it so difficult for thought shaped by a historical consciousness to gain access to the perspective of salvation history. For Israel, history had never been past in this sense. M.Noth has made this clear in his article 'Die Vergegenwärtigung des Alten Testaments in der Verkündigung' (above 75f.) by means of the cultic re-presentation of the events of salvation history, above all the exodus, at the three great pilgrimage festivals of Israel. The cultic presence of the past is also familiar to the Christian church; however, it needs also to be realized in thought and to be exploited for biblical and theological work on the testimony of the two Testaments to history. N.Lohfink, 'Freiheit', draws attention to the same perspective: there are two conceptions of history, one static and one dynamic. Neither of them is primitive. The static understanding of history, characterized by the repetition of the event, belongs in the cult; precisely in Israel there is this incorporation of history into the cult. Alongside this there is also the eschatologizing of history, which in Lohfink's view is the contribution of the great prophets. Despite the reservations one might have about this second notion, the first remains important. F.Schütz (*NZST* 1970) also refers back to the Old Testament understanding of history (against Cullmann's talk of a faith 'in' salvation history oriented on the past, cf. above 102) and from this perspective interprets Luke's outline of the 'middle of time': 'salvation history' always means certainty for belief in the present on the basis of historical experience, the certainty of the *presence* of the *person* of the *Christus praesens* and not faith in past events as an objective factor. In this sense, for the Old Testament, too, the nearness of God experienced in past salvation history is a reality in the present.

5. Is the Old Testament a history book?

Barr, J., 'The Problem of Old Testament Theology and the History of Religion', *CJT* 3, 1957, 141-9; id., *ExpT* 1961/2 (above 59); id., 'Revelation through History in the Old Testament and in Modern Theology', *Int* 17, 1963, 193-205 = *PSB* 56, 1963, 4-14 = M.E.Marty and D.G.Peerman (eds.), *New Theology* 1, New York 1964, 60-74; id., *Old and New in Interpretation*, London 1966 (cf. also the critical review by G.E.Wright, *Int*. 22, 1968, 83-9); id., 'Trends and Prospects in Biblical Theology', *JTS* 25, 1974, 265-82; *New Directions in Faith and Order, Bristol 1967. Reports-Minutes-Documents*, Geneva 1968, esp.9ff; Curtis, J.B., 'A Suggested Interpretation of the Biblical Philosophy of History', *HUCA* 34, 1963, 115-23; Halperin, J., 'Les dimensions juives de l'histoire', *RTP* 98, 1965, 222-40; Knierim, R., 'Offenbarung im Alten Testament', *von Rad Festschrift*, 1971 (above 60), 206-35; von Rad, G., 'Glaube und Welterkenntnis im Alten Israel', *Ruperto-Carola* (Heidelberg) 13 (vol.30), 1961, 84-90 = id., *Gesammelte Studien* II (above 59), 255-66; id., 'Aspects' (above 63); Rendtorff, R., *Festschrift W.Zimmerli* (above 72); id., 'Weisheit und Geschichte im Alten Testament', *EK* 9, 1976, 216-18; Schmid, H.H., 'Das alttestamentliche Verständnis von Geschichte in seinem Verhältnis zum gemeinorientalischen Denken', *WuD* 13, 1975, 9-21; Smend, R., *Elemente alttestamentlichen Geschichtsdenkens*, TS 95, Zurich 1968; id., *Tradition and History* (above 72); Westermann, C., 'Das Verhältnis des Jahweglaubens zu den ausserisraelitischen Religionen', *Forschung am Alten Testament*, TB 24, Munich 1964, 189-218; id., *Theologie* (above 56).

G. Ebeling once remarked that 'For modern man everything, the whole of reality, turns to history' ('Die Welt als Geschichte', in *Mensch und Kosmos*, Zurich/Stuttgart 1960, [103-14] 103 = id., *Wort und Glaube* (above 3), (381-92) 381, = ET 'The World as History' [1960], in *Word and Faith*, above 3, [363-73] 363) and spoke of the awareness of doom that lurks in it. However, the usual view that history is the centre of Israel's faith continued to hold unbroken sway e.g. at the 1967 Faith and Order Conference in

Bristol. Von Rad himself later became sceptical about his former remark that 'the Old Testament is a history book' (see above 63, cf. also R.Mack, 'Basic Aspects of Revelation in the Old Testament', *GBT* 4, 8, 1975, 13-23, and most recently H.-J.Zobel, 'Altes Testament – Literatursammlung und Heilige Schrift', *TLZ* 105, 1980, [81-92] 83-5): 'If I am right, we are nowadays in serious danger of looking at the theological problems of the Old Testament far too one- sidedly in terms of the theology of history' ('Aspects', [above 63], 57/311 = ET 144).

Massive expression has been given to this scepticism above all by J.Barr. After the reservations already expressed in his review of von Rad's work (cf. *ExpT* 1961/2, above 59, 145: 'It may be one of the effects of this book in the end that, by doing the very utmost to make Heilsgeschichte control everything, it may only prove the impossibility of letting Heilsgeschichte control anything') he developed his hesitations further in *Int* 1963 and listed the areas in which the theme of 'revelation in history' did not apply to the Old Testament: above all in the sphere of wisdom; in cases of direct communication from God, e.g. to Moses; and in divine action outside the sphere of history (e.g.Noah and the flood). It could even be objected that the concept of 'history' is not biblical, and is as artificial as the distinction between *Geschichte* and *Historie*, between salvation history and world history. Still, he would not want to give up the term 'salvation history'; there is a salvation history and it is the central theme of the Bible. However, alongside it there are also other axes, like the direct communication between God and man, in which the understanding of prophecy is particularly difficult (ibid., 206 n.6; here theology remained liberal in method). In his 1966 book *Old and New*, Barr has developed these comments in more detail (in particular prefacing them with a chapter on the many-layered character of the Old Testament tradition: Ch.I, 15ff., cf. esp. Ch.III, 65ff.); here he adds the sphere of creation (74ff., arguing against von Rad's position on this, see below 138–41). He again stresses verbal communication as being central to the event of revelation; here it is not a matter of subsequent interpretation of historical acts of God but of communications independent of the event or preceding it (77ff.). A further important comment is that the conception of a continuity running right through history is inappropriate to the Old Testament narratives: 'The texts do not build up a continuity in the form of a series of acts done by God; rather, these acts fall into a sequence with divine words and with human acts and human words'(77). The closeness of these narratives to what we would call history varies; the flood narrative is completely unhistorical, the story of David is almost historical in our sense. However, insofar as they provide dates, and so on, and refer to a chronological sequence, both the individual narratives and the larger narratives within which they are set are included in the framework of a 'history'.

In his return to the theme in *JTS* 1974, Barr can note that a series of scholars have taken up his view (he mentions Westermann, Smend and Fohrer, 268). For example, Smend 1968 stresses: 'History is not *the* thought-form of Old Testament faith but one among several; alongside it we find cult, law and wisdom.' However, he adds: 'It is and remains beyond dispute that history already occupies a predominant place among the thought-forms of the Old Testament simply because there is so much of it' (*Elemente*, 4). Similarly, R.Knierim, (*Festschrift von Rad*, 1971 [above 60], 228ff.) has attacked the one-sided stress on history as the only category in which reality is experienced in the Old Testament and referred to the realm of 'nature' as 'one of the most important modes by which Yahweh is manifested' (229). Zimmerli also stresses that in the sphere of its historical experiences Israel had a particularly impressive encounter with its God (*Erwägungen* [above 46], 86f./34f.). Further reflection has since fully confirmed this line (Smend repeats his remarks in a very similar form in 1978 (*Zu Tradition*, ed.Steck [above 72], 9f.= *Tradition*, ed. Knight [above 72], 49-51). H.H.Schmid (*WuD* 1975) asserts that in an earlier period Yahweh was understood, almost like the gods of neighbouring peoples, above all as creator of the world and thus as Lord over nature and history (cf. also below 179ff.), and that only the specific historical experiences of the latter period of the monarchy and above all of the process of coping theologically with the exile made history one of the basic elements of Israelite religion.

Von Rad's historically oriented unitary view of the theological structure of the Old Testament has thus become a pluriformity of spheres of life; even von Rad himself already recognized the plurality of evidence, but by forcing through his orientation on the focal point of history he exaggerated them out of all proportion and at the same time levelled them out.

This one-sided orientation was connected with a particular form of ideology which Barr similarly criticized at a very early stage. This ideology consisted in the view, once widespread and still alive even today, that the Old Testament differs from all surrounding ancient Near Eastern religions and cultures and even from the Greek view of history by virtue of its own understanding of history.

Albrektson, B., 'Främreorientaliska och gammaltestamentliga föreställingar om uppenbarelse i historien. Några preliminäre synpunkter', *TAik* 71, 1966, 13-34; id., *History and the Gods. An Essay on the Idea of Historical Events as Divine Manifestations in the Ancient Near East and in Israel*, CB.OT 1, Lund 1967 (cf. the reviews by Bleeker, C.J., *BiOr* 26, 1969, 228f.; Lambert, W.G., *Or* NS 39, 1970, 170-7); Cancik, H., *Mythische und historische Wahrheit. Interpretationen zu Texten der hethitischen, biblischen und griechischen Historiographie*, SBS 48, Stuttgart 1970; id., *Grundzüge der hethitischen und alttestamentlichen Geschichtsschreibung*, Wiesbaden 1976; Gese, H., 'Geschichtliches Denken im alten Orient und im Alten Testament', *ZTK* 55, 1958, 127-45 = id., *Vom Sinai zum Zion* (above 71), 81-98; Goossens, G., 'La philosophie de l'histoire dans l'Ancien Orient', *SacPag* 1, 1959, 242-52; Hanson, P., 'Jewish Apocalyptic against its Near Eastern Environment', *RB* 78, 1971, 31-58; Hempel, J., 'Altes Testament und Religionsgeschichte', *TLZ* 81, 1956, 259-80 (cf. also id., 'Biblische Theologie und biblische Religionsgeschichte I. AT', *RGG*[3], I, 1256-9); Koch, K., 'Der Tod des Religionsstifters', *KuD* 8, 1962, 100-23 (cf. Baumgärtel, F., 'Der Tod des Religionsstifters', *KuD* 9, 1963, 223-33; id., 'Das Offenbarungszeugnis des Alten Testaments', *ZTK* 64, 1967, 393-422; Rendtorff, R.,'Mose als Religionsstifter?', in id., *Gesammelte Studien* [above 46] 152-71); Krecher, J. and Müller, H.P., 'Vergangenheitsinteresse in Mesopotamien und Israel', *Saec* 26, 1975, 13-44; Lambert, W.G., 'Destiny and Divine Intervention in Babylon and Israel', *OS* 17, 1972, 65-72; Lindblom, J., *Den gammaltestamentliga religionens egenart*, Lund 1935; id., 'Zur Frage der Eigenart der alttestamentlichen Religion', *Werden und Wesen des Alten Testaments*, BZAW 66, Berlin 1936, 128-37; Noordzky, A., *Das Rätsel des Alten Testaments*, Brunswick 1928; Noth, M., 'Von der Knechtsgestalt des Alten Testaments', *EvTh* 6, 1946/47, 302-10 = id., *Gesammelte Studien* II (above 75f.), 62-70; id., *Geschichte Israels*, Göttingen [2]1954, 11 = ET *History of Israel*, London [2]1960, 2; Reventlow, H.Graf, 'Die Eigenart des Jahweglaubens als geschichtliches und theologisches Problem', *KuD* 20, 1974, 199-217; Ridderbos, N.H., 'Het Oude Testament en de geschiedenis', *GTT* 57, 1957, 112-20; Roberts, J.J.M., 'Divine Freedom and Cultic Manipulation in Israel and Mesopotamia', in *Unity and Diversity*, ed. H.Goedicke and J.J.M. Roberts, Baltimore and London 1975, 181-7; id., 'Myth versus History: Relaying the Comparative Foundations', *CBQ* 38, 1976, 1-13; Saggs, H.W.F., *The Encounter with the Divine in Mesopotamia and Israel*, London 1978; Sellin, E., *Die alttestamentliche Religion im Rahmen der anderen altorientalischen*, Leipzig 1908; Van Seters, J., *In Search of History. Historiography in the Ancient World and the Origins of Biblical History*, New Haven and London 1983; Smith, M., 'The Common Theology of the Ancient Near East', *JBL* 71, 1952, 135-47; id., 'The Present State of Old Testament Studies', *JBL* 88, 1969, 19-35; Speiser, E.A., 'The Biblical Idea of History in its Common Near Eastern Setting', *IEJ* 7, 1957, 201-16; Stolz, F., 'Monotheismus in Israel', in O. Keel (ed.), *Monotheismus im Alten Israel und seiner Umwelt*, BiBe 14, Fribourg 1980, 143-84; Westermann, C., 'Sinn und Grenze religionsgeschichtlicher Parallelen', *TLZ* 90, 1965, 489-96 = id., *Forschung am Alten Testament* II (above 75), 84-95; Wright, G.E., 'How did Early Israel differ from her Neighbours?', *BA* 6, 1943, 1-10, 13-20; id., *The Old Testament against its Environment* (above 73). Cf. also the composite volume: Dentan, R.C. (ed.), *The Idea of History in the Ancient Near East* (above 88, which includes Burrows, M., 'Ancient Israel' [above 88]).

The books by E.Sellin and A.Noordzky are examples of this view from an earlier period, but it also occurs unexpectedly in a historian like M.Noth, as an erratic 'theological block'. While in his article 'Von der Knechtsgestalt des Alten Testaments', Noth stresses the far-reaching dependence of the content of the Old Testament on the ancient Near Eastern cultures of its environment, and the way in which its history (of which he had expert knowledge) is woven into that of the ancient Near East, he then continues: 'the Old Testament as a whole still remained an alien body in the world of the ancient Near East which we now know so well, albeit a stranger wearing the garb of the environment and the time' (305/66f.). This, he argued, was evident from the three themes of the 'law' which is unique in the ancient Near East in that it is not associated with a state order but with the covenant relationship (cf. Noth, *Die Gesetze im Pentateuch*, SKG.G 17, H.2, Halle 1940 = *Gesammelte Studien zum Alten Testament*, TB 6, Munich 1957, 9-141 = ET *The Laws in the Pentateuch and Other Studies*, Edinburgh 1966 reissued London 1984, 1-107) but in content is an indissoluble mixture, first, of 'natural' law, ancient Near Eastern law and specifically Old Testament covenant law; then, of history ('Old Testament historiography is again something unique within the world of the ancient Near East',305/66f.; the 'cyclical thought of the ancient Near East' knows only constant repetition, and not an understanding of history directed towards a goal, the perspective which, through Augustine, became normative for the West); and thirdly, the prophets ('the prophets have no equal in the world of the ancient Near East or elsewhere in human history', 307/67f.). But in the Old Testament, history, too, is written on the presuppositions of the time, just as prophecy is also to be seen as conditioned by time and history. While in *The History of Israel* Noth begins with this presupposition, he then allows his remarks to build up to a climax, in a lyrical rhapsody, with the special character of Israel: ' "Israel" still appears a stranger in the world of its own time, a stranger wearing the garments and behaving in the manner of its age, yet separate from the world it lived in... so that at the very centre of the history of "Israel" we encounter phenomena for which there is no parallel at all elsewhere...' There is no doubt that the old idealistic view of the religion of Israel as 'the climax of the history of religion' influences this view, as we can also see from Kittel and Sellin (1921, above 10f., and 30-5).

Agreement is also expressed by H.W.Wolff, 'The Hermeneutics of the Old Testament', *Int.* 15, 1961, (439-72) 445 n.19 = *Essays/Problems*, ed. Westermann, above 75, (160-99) 167 n.19; similarly also H.Wildberger, 'Auf dem Wege zu einer biblischen Theologie', *EvTh* 19, 1959, (70-90) 77, who describes the Old Testament as an 'erratic block' and [like Noth] as a 'stranger', which its special character connects only with the New Testament.

In *Old and New* (above 110), J.Barr similarly attacks this view of the Israelite view of history as something unique. Here he can refer back to similar comments by H.Gese, who had put the beginnings of historical thought as early as Mesopotamia and among the Hittites; he argued that these beginnings had then been continued by Israel in the light of its special relationship with God and the theological view of history which had been conditioned by that. From these and other observations Barr concludes that 'it does not seem to me possible or wise to make a complete separation

between Hebrew historiography and that of the ancient Near East'
(71). Here, too, a difference in degree between Hebrew and ancient
Near Eastern thought is possible, but it is not to be exploited
theologically.

Since Barr's incidental remarks from that time, the evidence
against the assumption that only Israel knew serious historiography,
and that the ancient Near East and even Greece had only a cyclical
understanding of time, has grown much stronger. Here the book by
B.Albrektson, *History and the Gods*, led the way. The sub-title
gives the main focus: Albrektson demonstrates that in the ancient
Near East, too, history was seen as a divine sphere of activity (Barr
had already drawn attention to the Mesha stone from Israel's
immediate vicinity [72, cf. Albrektson, 7, 100f.]). There are sometimes astonishing parallels between Israelite and non-Israelite texts.
Albrektson's critics (Bleeker and Lambert) have accused him of
failing to note in his arguments the special character (monotheistic)
of Old Testament belief in God and its influence on the understanding of history (cf. also Speiser); Lambert in particular has
pointed above all to the deeper significance of the Word of God in
the Old Testament as disclosing a far-reaching plan for history, for
which there are no real parallels in the ancient Near East. In the
Old Testament there are two goals of divine action, maintaining
order and achieving a historical goal, whereas in the ancient Near
East on each occasion the order which has been destroyed is restored
only for a short time. However, despite these individual doubts by
a scholar with intimate knowledge of the Mesopotamian texts,
Albrektson's general thesis remains convincing. And Lambert has
already been contradicted. J.J.M.Roberts doubts whether he gives
a complete picture of the situation in the ancient Near East (1 n.3),
and adduces impressive evidence from Mesopotamia to challenge
the usual view (put forward by Hanson) that Israelite historiography
is unique. His evidence largely relativizes the difference between
what is supposed to be the first 'genuine' history-writing in Israel
and the allegedly 'mythical' view of the world in the ancient Near
East (cf. recently also the overall survey by Krecher and Müller,
though this also demonstrates the fragmentary nature of the historiography and the very different genres and interests which govern a
concern with the past in Mesopotamia [and in Israel!]. Cf. also below
117f.). It is important to note that Old Testament historiography, too,
takes account of direct 'cosmic' interventions on the part of Yahweh
in the course of history, whereas on the other hand the relationship

between human guilt and historical events is not unknown in Mesopotamia either. Roberts does not want to deny that there is any difference between historiography in Israel and that in the ancient Near East (9,12), but he rightly points out that as yet there is no adequate exegetical demonstration of this from the sources.

The comments by the Semitic scholar H.W.F.Saggs (above 114) are also valuable. He has investigated the comparison between Mesopotamian and Israelite religion over a still wider spectrum. There are virtually no differences between the Mesopotamian and the Israelite conceptions of the divine action in history (64-92). In both religions the divine intervention in events also includes the realm of nature. Significantly, Saggs sees the only essential difference between Israel and Assyria/Babylonia in the being of Yahweh himself: by being transcendent over nature he stands apart from the immanentism of the Mesopotamian conception of God (which is polytheistic, 90ff.).

The investigation by H.Cancik ('Wahrheit') takes us one step further. It emerges from a comparison of Greek, Hittite and Old Testament historiography and its concept of truth that in all three cultures we already find the beginnings of historical criticism alongside the formation and transmission of mythical tradition and the representation of the past in the cult. Here, in the view of the author, the Israelite historians are less advanced in such criticism than the Hittite historians (who were working at an earlier period). He pays particular attention to II Maccabees (108f.), which presents a kind of synthesis of Hellenistic (Jason of Cyrene) and Old Testament historiography.

One conclusion drawn by Cancik about the narrower sphere of historiography might be noticed more widely in connection with the whole of Old Testament theology. He writes at the end of his investigation: 'It is inadvisable, then, to construct a distinctive biblical or Semitic concept of truth and compare this with a fictitious Greek or European concept of truth which is supposed to be of a different kind' (129). He sees the difference between history built up on mythical foundations, handed down and made present in the cult, and a historical consciousness with a critical view more on the borderline between ancient and modern thought; here the ancient East and the ancient West, interlinked by a great many influences, hardly differ in essentials in the structure of their thought (cf. also Cancik, *Grundzüge*).

James Barr must again be acknowledged to be right here: already in *Old and New in Interpretation* (Ch.II, 'Athens or Jerusalem', 34ff.), and above all in *The Semantics of Biblical Language* (Oxford 1961, cf. also id., *Biblical Words for Time*, [above 76]) he questioned the assumption of a fundamental difference between Hebrew and Greek (Western) thought, which had long been taken for granted.

For this cf. especially Boman, T., *Das hebräische Denken im Vergleich mit dem griechischen*, Göttingen 1952 = ET *Hebrew Thought Compared with Greek*, London 1960; Hessen, J., *Platonismus und Prophetismus*, Munich 1939 ([2]1955); id., *Griechische oder Biblische Theologie?*, Leipzig 1956, Munich/Basle [2]1962; Lauer, Q., 'The Genius of Biblical Thought', in J.M.Oesterreicher (ed.), *The Bridge*, Vol.2, New York 1956, 191-211; McKenzie, J.L., *Geist und Welt des Alten Testamentes*, Lucerne 1962; id., 'Aspects of Old Testament Thought', *JBC* 2, 1968, 736-67; Patterson, C.H., *The Philosophy of the Old Testament*, New York 1953; Pedersen, J., *Israel. Its Life and Culture*, I-II, III-IV, London and Copenhagen (Danish 1920/1934) 1926/1940, [2]1959; Snaith, N.H., *The Distinctive Ideas of the Old Testament*, London 1944 ([5]1983); Tresmontant, C., *Essai sur la pensée hebraïque*, Paris 1953 = *A Study of Hebrew Thought*, New York 1960. Cf. also the works by Leist, F., *Zeugnis des lebendigen Gottes*, Donauwörth 1948, second edition entitled *Der grössere Gott*, Munich 1960; id., *Moses-Sokrates-Jesus*, Frankfurt 1959; id., *Nicht der Gott der Philosophen*, Freiburg, Basle and Vienna 1966; id., *Die biblische Sage von Himmel und Erde*, Freiburg, Basle and Vienna 1967.

A few brief comments must suffice on this theme (leaving aside the perspective from semantics, from which Barr prefers to argue).

As is now clear (see also 178f. below), most of the studies mentioned here, which (at the prompting of J.Pedersen) argue that Semitic/Hebrew/biblical thought cannot be reconciled with Greek/philosophical/Western thought and therefore end up with contrasting pairs like dynamic-static, contemplative-active, intellectual-voluntative, dualistic-monistic, speculation-direct experience of God, begin by choosing the wrong levels to compare: they compare the world-view of the Bible with the world view of the developed systems of classical Greek philosophy or even Hellenism (Neoplatonism) and then come to the conclusion that these are irreconcilable. In fact, however, there are far-reaching parallels between the thought-structure which is recognizable as the world-view of Old Testament wisdom and ancient Greek cosmology. By contrast, the narrative structures of the Bible (and corresponding genres outside the Bible) which reflect a living event are fundamentally different from the ontology of being in Greek philosophical speculation, not because one belongs to the Hebrew thought-world and the other to the Greek, but because these are two completely different kinds of intellectual activity, which are fundamentally different in aim, form and setting. A direct comparison of the two thus fails to notice the ground rules of method in the history of genres and therefore cannot lead to any usable results.

Can Israelite and Judaean religion then be regarded as completely independent in its origins from the religions and cultures of its environment? Is it not, at least genetically, to be explained from a multiplicity of roots within the religious history of the ancient Near East? K.Koch has put forward the latter view in his provocative theory 'Der Tod des Religionsstifters'; here, following Noth, he seeks to rule out Moses as having a role as the 'founder'. This theory has been challenged on theological grounds above all by Baumgärtel (*KuD* 1963, *ZTK* 1967 – Hempel also accords a central place to the 'experience of the founder', *TLZ* 1956) and also by S.Herrmann, in connection with the historical role of Moses ('Mose', *EvTh* 28, 1968, 301-28; cf. also id., *Geschichte Israels in alttestamentlicher Zeit*, Munich 1973, ²1980, 91ff. = ET *History of Israel in Old Testament Times*, London and Philadelphia 1975, ²1981, 61ff.). By contrast it is supported by R.Rendtorff ('Mose als Religionsstifter?', above 113, cf. also id., 'Die Entstehung der israelitischen Religion als religionsgeschichtliches und theologisches Problem', *TLZ* 88, 1963, 735-46 = *Gesammelte Studien* [above 46], 119-36; similarly also Stolz, *Monotheismus*, especially n.76). While it is true that excessive scepticism over the history of the tradition has led to what seems to be an underestimation of the significance of Moses, which has probably been faithfully preserved by the tradition, Koch must be granted that various religions in the area (cf. also Rendtorff) lay behind the origin of the religion of Israel (cf. also Stolz, *Monotheismus*), just as in later periods (conquest, early monarchy), too, many kinds of external influences affected its development. Similarly, J.J.M.Roberts – arguing against Wright – has recently (1975) also relativized the difference in attitudes over cultic prayer and sacrifice between Mesopotamian polytheism and Israelite belief in Yahweh (both want to get something from their God). Thus the question of the specific claims of Yahwistic belief has not been decided either way, whether negatively (as Baumgärtel thinks, under the spell of the dogma of incomparability) or positively.

Quite a long time ago Morton Smith (*JBL* 1952) claimed a common structure for religions in the ancient Near East (including the religion of Israel; N.K.Gottwald, *The Tribes of Yahweh*, Maryknoll and London 1979, 676-8, follows Smith) in which the worship of the supreme God shows corresponding features. These include his activity in history, nature and morality, and the direct connection which exists between following his commandments and the conduct of the people. It is an idealistic error to look for the special character of belief in Yahweh in the sphere of its content (cf. also above 86f.).

In most recent times the problem of 'history', including history in the Old Testament, has been raised again through the concept of 'narrative' (story) and the programme of narrative theology. Here again J.Barr has played an important role.

Barr, J., *Old and New* (above 110), 80-82; id., 'Story and History in Biblical Theology', *JR* 56, 1976, 1-17 = *The Scope and Authority of the Bible*, London 1980, 1-17; Brown, R.M., 'Story and Theology', in *Philosophy of Religion and Theology. Proceedings of the American Academy of Religion*, ed. J.W.McClennon Jr, Missoula, Mont. 1974, 55-72; id., 'My Story and "The Story"', *ThT* 32, 1975, 166-73; Clements, R.E., 'History and Theology in Biblical Narrative', *HBT* 4-5, 1982/3, 45-60; Coggins, R.J., 'History and Story in Old Testament Study', *JSOT* 11, 1979, 36-46; Crites, S., 'The Narrative Quality of Experience', *JAAR* 39, 1971, 291-311; Danto, A.C., *Analytical Philosophy of History*, Cambridge ²1968; Harvey, J., 'Symbolique et théologie biblique', *ScEc* 9, 1957, 141-57; Jüngel, E., 'Metaphorische Wahrheit. Erwägungen zur theologischen Relevanz der Metapher als Beitrag zur Hermeneutik einer narrativen Theologie', in *Metapher*, Sonderheft to *EvTh* 1974, 71-122; Metz, J.B., 'A Short Apology of Narrative', *Conc* 5/9, 1973, 84-96; Rice, C., 'The Preacher as Storyteller', *USQR* 31, 1976, 182-97; Ritschl, D., and Jones, H.O., *'Story' als Rohmaterial der Theologie*, TEH 192, Munich 1976 (which contains: Jones, H.O., 'Das Story-Konzept in der Theologie', 42-68; Ritschl, D., 'Die "Story" als Rohmaterial der Theologie', 7-41); Sanders, J.A., *Torah and Canon*, Philadelphia 1972, ²1974; id., 'Torah and Christ', *Int* 29, 1975, 372-90; Simon, U., *Story and Faith in the Biblical Narrative*, London 1975; Steimle, E., 'Preaching and the Biblical Story of Good and Evil',

USQR 31, 1976, 198-211; Stroup, G.W., 'III. A Bibliographical Critique', *ThTo* 32, 1975, 133-43 (full bibliography); id, *The Promise of Narrative Theology*, Atlanta, Ga 1983 and London 1984; te Selle, S., *Speaking in Parables. A Study in Metaphor and Theology*, London and Philadelphia 1975, esp. 119ff.; Wacker, B., *Narrative Theologie?*, Munich 1977; Weinrich, H., 'Narrative Theology', *Conc* 5/9, 1973, 46-56; Wharton, J.A., 'The Occasion of the Word of God: An Unguarded Essay on the Character of the Old Testament as the Memory of God's Story with Israel', *Austin Presbyterian Seminary Bulletin (Faculty ed.)* 84, 1968, 5-54; Zahrnt, H., 'Religiöse Aspekte gegenwärtiger Welt- und Lebenserfahrung. Reflexionen über die Notwendigkeit einer neuen Erfahrungstheologie', *ZTK* 71, 1974, 94-122.

As early as *Old and New*, above 110, Barr had pointed out that a considerable part of the Old Testament is narrative, but that only some of it is historiography in the modern sense. He has recently (*JR* 1976) taken his reflections further. In English different terms are used for the two genres, 'history' and 'story', whereas in German 'Geschichte' can mean both. Barr finds this basically a good thing (*JR* 1976,6 = 'Scope', 5f.): even so, the differentiation is not very helpful in the case of the Old Testament (Ritschl, on the other hand, would want to introduce the term 'story' into German as a technical term [6], since 'Geschichte' has too many connotations). At any rate the concept of history in the sense of universal history is a creation of the nineteenth century and alien to the Old Testament. However, certain features which are claimed for history also characterize story in the Old Testament: a distinctive literary form, the thrust at the beginning, the account of experiences which Israel had had of its God Yahweh. Barr finds a true insight in the old view that the Old Testament is a history book and in this way differs from the religious testimonies of its environment in that narrative is central to it. However, this narrative lacks central features of history: above all the ongoing context, the chronological framework, the possibility of evaluation as a reliable source for the time in which it came into being. These last two characteristics are represented relatively rarely in the Old Testament. Rather, many accounts mix historical, mythical and legendary material. Barr thinks that von Rad had a keen sense of this situation; on the other hand, his association of the narratives with credal formulations in terms of tradition history was an error of judgment. Rather, these 'creeds' are a relatively late development; by contrast the origins of Israelite religion largely

depend on influences from the environment which have also affected
the story material. So the stories, too, are sometimes aetiological
and sometimes 'paradigmatic'; above all they are 'cumulative' (*JR*
1976, 8/ 'Scope', 8): however, they do not provide any ongoing
'historical' context, but report Israel's ever new experiences of God.
J.A.Sanders has a stronger interest in an overall view when he claims
in connection with his functional view of the origin and theological
significance of the canon that story is the underlying structure in the
Torah (cf. my *Problems of Biblical Theology*, II, 7). For him, the
salvation-historical story which was recited on festal occasions (e.g.
in Shechem, Josh.24; here Sanders follows von Rad more closely),
is the basic framework of the Old Testament (and originally extended
to the time of David – P was the first, after D, to introduce the break
between the Pentateuch and the 'Former Prophets' and thus to limit
the story to the Torah in the narrower sense, cf. *Torah and Canon*,
47). The recitation of the canon as the salvation-historical story (into
which the legal parts are incorporated functionally) served as the
centre of the quest for identity by the believing community of Israel
and Judah in times of crisis after the destruction of the first and
second temples and in the exile. Sanders can also describe the
situation to which he refers as the 'myth' or 'haggada' aspect of the
Bible (*Int.* 1975, 373f., cf. 378).

The standpoints of Sanders and Barr need not be mutually
exclusive: Barr notes more closely the fine structure of the material
and thus arrives at observations which do more justice to the
relationships of traditions within the Old Testament, its lack of
unity, the breaks and new beginnings, of which von Rad had already
spoken. Ritschl, who reflects systematically on this phenomenon,
considers the possible interconnection of the individual stories, 'the
conception of an overarching, summarizing story which interprets
the various individual stories' (20). The possibility of such a story,
which points to a reality common to the detailed stories (24),
indicates the function of stories generally: these cannot always be
summarized, nor can their theoretical significance be defined (25ff.);
rather, precisely through their narrative form they can be 'the most
suitable form for expressing the identity of a person (or a group)'
(15, cf.19; for the epistemological background cf. esp. Crites, *JAAR*
1971). According to Ritschl, here Israel with its stories is a paramount
example. We should also reflect on the fact that a story not only
reproduces reality but also creates reality; what would be envisaged
here is the very entity 'Israel', which cannot be derived directly from

its origins in the people and the history of religion. For there is also such a thing as 'promised identity', 'the fact that we are dealing with the most central statements of the Bible when we hear that Israel *will* become what is said to it, namely the people of Yahweh'(33). The 'meta-story', composed of the various individual stories, would then be the comprehensive expression of the identity of Israel, which cannot be 'told statically but only in connection with history, in a wealth of individual stories'. (For criticism of the model of an overarching general-story in Barr and Wharton [see below], cf. Jones, 61ff.) However, we must remember that Ritschl firmly stresses the possibility, indeed the necessity, of summaries, and therefore of abstract theology (15ff.), thus explicitly rejecting the view that theology can only be the retelling of stories (cf. 40; Ritschl defends himself against the watchword 'narrative theology', though he welcomes the legitimate concern behind it [38-41]; cf. also above 63, on von Rad's concept).

Following Barr, J.Wharton also concerns himself with the category of story (above 121; for this article, which is so difficult to obtain, cf. the account in Jones, 45ff. and passim). For Wharton 'story' is even a comprehensive term for everything that happened to Israel according to the Old Testament account, not only the report of events but also 'lyrics and heroic narratives, autumn songs and law book' (18, cf. Jones 46). The Old Testament does not contain anything which 'is not ultimately handed on from the perspective that Israel recalls to memory its story with its Lord' (Jones,46; cf. Wharton, 27 – not a literal quotation). In this overall-story Israel becomes aware of its existence; for Wharton the category of recollection is central (cf., independently of Wharton, also Crites, *JAAR* 1971); therefore in the Old Testament we do not encounter the words and deeds of God directly, but they are 'already moulded in the idiom of story or recollection' (29, cf. Jones 47). However, this recollection does not seek to preserve what happened as something past; the recitation of it calls on the reader or hearer 'through this remembrance to recognize a present action of a present God'(30, cf. Jones 48). The inner consistency of the recollection of Israel lies in the ongoing relationship of all individual stories to Israel's God himself (40f.); the fact that this is the same God with whom Israel had all its different experiences binds together all the stories in God's own story (cf. 26f.).

While these reflections by Wharton take us a good way further, other arguments have developed, concerned with the relationship between what is reported in the stories and 'what happened', rooted in the old question of fact in history (see above III, 2, 65ff. – for criticism cf. also Coggins, *JSOT* 1979); these arguments have rightly been criticized, for this and for other reasons, by H.O.Jones (49ff.). However, we can leave them aside here.

In addition, the simple attempt to present the various individual narratives of the Old Testament one after the other and compare their narrative structures with modern narrative technique (as Simon does, using Kafka as an illustration) already contributes to the understanding of narrative theology, which could be deepened still further by systematic reflection.

Ultimately, these problems lead to the sphere of hermeneutics. Here we should remember how far Christianity down to the present is understood as a 'community of recollection and story-telling' (Wacker, 36) even in the light of the story which provides the basis for Christian identity, and thus remember how far the biblical stories and the personal story of anyone who reads the Bible or listens to a sermon (cf. the literature on preaching cited above) lead to a common identification with the biblical narrators (cf. e.g. R.Brown). But that is again a theme to be dealt with separately.

In the light of these considerations one can also object to R.Smend, who sees 'theology' in the Old Testament only in late, reflecting passages which develop a 'theoretical' theological thinking ('Theologie im Alten Testament', in *Verifikationen*, Festschrift G.Ebeling, Tübingen 1982, 11-26). Of course there are differences between, for instance, Deuteronomy or the books of wisdom on one side and the historical books or the prophetic literature on the other. There are different ways of expressing one's faith; several are to be found in the Old Testament. But neither the way of story nor the way of instruction is 'theoretical'; the teachers as well as the story-tellers or the prophets want to give notice to the audience of their creed. Cf. also the objections of H.Seebass, 'Geschichtliche Vorläufigkeit und eschatologische Endgültigkeit des biblischen Monotheismus', in A.Falaturi et al. (eds.), *Zukunftshoffnung und Heilserwartung in den monotheistischen Religionen*, Freiburg im Breisgau 1983, (49-80) 62ff.

IV

The 'Centre' of the Old Testament

Ackroyd, P.R., *Continuity. A Contribution to the Study of the Old Testament Religious Tradition*, Oxford 1962; Baker, D.L., *Two Testaments* (above 1), 377-86; Barr, J., *JTS* 1974 (above 110), 270-2; Fohrer, G., 'Der Mittelpunkt einer Theologie des Alten Testaments', *TZ* 24, 1968, 161-72 = id., 'The Centre of a Theology of the Old Testament', *NGTT* 7, 1966, 198-206; id., *Theologische Grundstrukturen des Alten Testaments*, Berlin 1972, 95ff.; id., 'Das Alte Testament und das Thema "Christologie"', *EvTh* 30, 1970, 281-98; Hasel, G.F., 'The Problem of the Center in the Old Testament', *ZAW* 86, 1974, 65-82; id., *Old Testament Theology*[2] (above 1), 77-103; Herrmann, S., 'Die konstruktive Restauration. Das Deuteronomium als Mitte biblischer Theologie', *Festschrift von Rad*, 1971 (above 60), 155-70; Hessler, B., *Anton* 1950 (above 1), 419ff.; id., 'Vom Offenbarungsgut des Alten Testaments', *WiWei* 14, 1951, 190-9; id., *WiWei* 1952 (above 1); Jepsen, A., 'Theologie des Alten Testaments' (above 45); Klein, G., ' "Reich Gottes" als biblischer Zentralbegriff', *EvTh* 30, 1970, 642-70; Martin-Achard, R., *Approche de l'Ancien Testament*, Neuchâtel 1962, 70ff.; id., 'A propos de la Théologie de l'Ancien Testament. Une hypothèse de travail', *TZ* 35, 1979, 63-71; Osswald, E., 'Das Problem der "Mitte" des Alten Testaments', *Amtsblatt d.Ev.-Luth.Kirche in Thüringen* 30, 1977 (no.20, 25.10.1977), 192-201; Prussner, F.C., 'The Covenant of David and the Problem of Unity in Old Testament Theology', in *Transitions in Biblical Scholarship*, ed. J.C.Rylaarsdam, Chicago and London 1968, 17-41; von Rad, G., *Theology* I (above 59); id., 'Offene Fragen/Postscript' (above 59); Roscam Abbing, *Inleiding* (above 72), 67ff.; Schmid, H.H., 'Ich will euer Gott sein, und ihr sollt mein Volk sein. Die sogenannte Bundesformel und die Frage nach der Mitte des Alten Testaments', in *Kirche*.

Festschrift G. Bornkamm, Tübingen 1980, 1-25; Schmidt, W., *Das erste Gebot*, TEH 165, Munich 1970; id., 'Vielfalt und Einheit alttestamentlichen Glaubens', in *'Wenn nicht jetzt, wann dann?' Festschrift H.-J. Kraus*, Neukirchen-Vluyn 1983, 13-22; Seierstad, I.P., *Bibelteologie* I (above 54); Smend, R., *Die Mitte des Alten Testaments*, TS 101, Zurich 1970 (cf. also id., *Die Bundesformel*, TS 68, Zurich 1963); Stoebe, H.J., 'Überlegungen' (above 72); Wagner, S., ' "Biblische Theologien" und "Biblische Theologie"', *TLZ* 103, 1978, 786-98; Zenger, E., 'Die Mitte der alttestamentlichen Glaubensgeschichte', *KatBl* 101, 1976, 3-16; Zimmerli, W., *VT* 1963 (above 64); id., 'Zum Problem der "Mitte des Alten Testaments"', *EvTh* 35, 1975, 97-118 (cf. also id., 'Alttestamentliche Traditionsgeschichte' [above 60], and id., 'Erwägungen' [above 46]).

Understanding the 'theology of the Old Testament' as a systematic task is not the limited province of the proponents of a systematic form of representation in the strict sense. However, they above all were the ones who felt it inadequate only to present a collection of 'those ideas, thoughts and concepts of the Old Testament which are or can be theologically significant', arranged in a proper connection (cf. above 48; for the prehistory of such attempts in the nineteenth century cf. Smend, passim), unless this construction could also culminate in a concept which, by virtue of being the basic idea, the central concept or the 'centre' of the Old Testament was capable of summarizing to some extent its entire theological content. Various proposals were made for such a concept, e.g.: the idea of the holiness of God (J. Hänel, *Die Religion der Heiligkeit*, Gütersloh 1931, passim; E.Sellin, *Theologie* [above 47], 20); 'that God is the Lord who commands' (Köhler, *Theologie* [above 48], 12,17 = ET 30, 35), 'God is the Lord who imposes his will' (J.Heller, *Festschrift Cullmann* [above 89], 5f.); the 'kingdom of God' (G.Klein, *EvTh* 1970; B.Hessler, *Anton*, 1950, 421; *WiWei* 1951, 194ff.; *WiWei* 1952, 41); the notion of election (H.Wildberger, *EvTh* 1959 [above 115], 77f.; cf. also R.de Vaux, *Conc* 1969 [above 73], 8); or the communion between God and man (Vriezen, *Outline* [above 52], 8, 157f.). A new stage of awareness was reached through Eichrodt's *Theology*. As we saw (above 52), Eichrodt deliberately rejected all patterns derived from Christian dogmatics for the systematic form of his overall presentation and instead sought to 'plot our course ... along the lines of the OT's own dialectic' (I^5, 7 = ET 33). For him the idea of the covenant is the central concept (I[5], VII = ET 13) or the 'centre which determines everything' (II[4], XII) which as the 'point of convergence for all the important lines of knowledge of God in Israel' (II[4], XII) is capable of demonstrating 'the structural unity and the unchanging basic tendency of the message of the OT' (I[5], VI = ET 13).

Cf also 51 above; in more recent times G.E.Wright (*The Old Testament and Theology* [above 73], 62; cf. also id., 'The Theological Study of the Bible', in *The Interpreter's One Volume Commentary of the Bible*, ed. C.M.Laymon, New York 1971, 986) has abandoned his former position and followed Eichrodt. Cf. also R.E.Clements, *Old Testament Theology* (above 55), esp. 119. P.Beauchamp ('Propositions sur l'alliance de l'Ancien Testament, comme structure centrale', *RSR* 58, 1970, 161-94) begins from the covenant formula (cf. K.Baltzer, *Das Bundesformular*, WMANT 4, Neukirchen 1960 = ET *The Covenant Formulary*, Philadelphia and Oxford 1971; there is criticism e.g. from Fohrer, see below) and sees it as the structural centre. F.C.Fensham ('The Covenant as Giving Expression to the Relationship between Old Testament and New Testament', *TynB* 22, 1971, 82-94) sees the 'covenant' as the binding link between the Testaments.

The discussion remained at a provisional stage while the only question under discussion was whether the 'covenant' was in fact an appropriate concept to embrace all the material in the Old Testament and whether or not Eichrodt's account had demonstrated this. There was also the doubt, which has been expressed widely since then, whether 'covenant' is in fact an old concept at all (expressed above all by G.Fohrer, 'Altes Testament – "Amphiktyonie" und "Bund"?', *TLZ* 91, 1966, 801-16, 893-904 = id., *Studien zur alttestamentlichen Theologie und Geschichte* [above 71], 84-119, and L.Perlitt, *Bundestheologie im Alten Testament*, WMANT 36, Neukirchen-Vluyn 1969. Those who nevertheless believed that there was early evidence for the concept include W.Zimmerli, 'Erwägungen zum "Bund"', *Festschrift W.Eichrodt*, ATANT 59, Zurich 1970, 171-90; W.Eichrodt, 'Prophet and Covenant', *Festschrift G.Henton Davies*, London and Richmond, Va 1970, 167-88; T.C.Vriezen, 'The Exegesis of Exodus XXIV 9-11', *OS* 17, 1972, 100-33, and above all J.Halbe, *Das Privilegrecht Jahwes. Ex 34, 10-26*, FRLANT 114, Göttingen 1975, cf. also D.J.McCarthy, *Treaty and Covenant*, AnBib 21/A, Rome [2]1978). There was the view that it was perhaps better to render the term b*ᵉrit* as 'obligation' rather than 'covenant' (E.Kutsch, especially in *Verheissung und Gesetz*, BZAW 131, Berlin 1973; but cf. the criticism by W.Eichrodt, 'Darf man heute noch von einem Gottesbund mit Israel reden?', *TZ* 30, 1974, 193-206). However, these discussions do not touch on the basic question whether it is legitimate to postulate any concept at all as the 'centre' of the Old Testament. Some authors choose a bipolar designation for the 'centre' of the Old Testament; thus R.Smend takes the so-called 'covenant formula' (cf. TS 68): 'Yahweh the God of Israel, Israel the people of Yahweh' (*Die Mitte*, 49, 55 - the idea goes back to J.Wellhausen, 'Israelitische Religion', in *Die Kultur der Gegenwart*, ed. P.Hinneberg, I, 4, Berlin/Leipzig 1905, 1-38 = *Grundrisse zum Alten Testament*, ed. R.Smend, TB 27, Munich 1965, 65-109, 8f./73f. There is criticism of the designation 'covenant formula' and its usefulness as the 'centre' of the Old Testament in H.H.Schmid, *Festschrift G.Bornkamm*), or G.Fohrer (basic structures: the combination of the rule of God and communion with God in order to indicate better the living relationship between God and people as it is reflected in the Old Testament – for Fohrer's account cf. the literature mentioned above). For Seierstad (*Bibelteologie* I [above 54], 44) the *telos* (and thus the centre) of the Old Testament is the full religious and ethical communion between God and humanity. His division (above 54) develops out of that. Similarly, N.W.Porteous ('Towards a Theology', above 2, 141/19) sees God and people as the two axes around which the theology of the Old Testament revolves.

G. von Rad in particular has spoken out against all these attempts to find a 'centre' of the Old Testament. An analysis of the Old Testament in terms of the history of traditions shows that 'the revelation of Jahweh in the Old Testament is divided up over a long series of separate acts of revelation which are very different in content. It seems to be without a centre which defines everything and which could give to the various separate acts both an interpretation and their proper theological connexion with one another. We can only describe the Old Testament's revelation of Jahweh as a number of distinct and heterogeneous revelatory acts' (*Theology* I[4], 128 = ET 115, cf. already in 'Theologie und Liturgie' [above 59], 30). The requirements of any theological systematization are alien to Hebrew thought (here again we have the supposed difference from Greek thought); instead it confirmed itself in constantly new interpretations and actualizations of the traditions of its salvation history. Now the spiritual contribution of each of these new interpretations consists in the fact that their results demonstrate an intrinsic unity and a constant reference to the one entity 'Israel', towards which all the specific individual traditions are directed. 'Here at last we come upon one unifying principle towards which Israel's theological thinking strove, and with reference to which it ordered its material and thought; this was "Israel", the people of God, which always acts as a unit, and with which God always deals as a unit' (I^4, 132 = ET 118 – for 'Israel' as a point of reference cf. also M.Noth, *The Laws in the Pentateuch* [above 114f.). However, according to von Rad the idea of a 'centre' cannot be based on the concept of 'Israel' since 'this Israel is the object of faith, and the object of a history constructed by faith' (ibid., cf. 'Offene Fragen/ Postscript' [above 59], 406/295 = ET 415. – By contrast Hasel sees 'history' as the hidden 'centre' in von Rad's *Theology* [*Old Testament Theology*^{2}, 85ff.] – though that probably goes beyond the framework of what is meant by the term). Even after von Rad had been asked whether a 'theology' must not 'to a greater degree make the venture of synthetic thinking' (W.Zimmerli, review, *VT* 1963, 105), he continued to be sceptical about the possibility of speaking of a unity of the Old Testament, 'because the Old Testament contains not just one but a number of theologies'; indeed, he finds it doubtful 'whether and in what sense we may still claim to use the title "Old Testament theology" in the singular.' Hence the question remains, 'Where is its focal point?' (quotation, 'Offene Fragen/Postscript', 405f./294 = ET 415).

Despite this objection from von Rad (similarly also Ackroyd [above 125], 30, and P.Fannon, 'A Theology of the Old Testament – Is it Possible?', *Script* 19/46, 1967, 46-53 – Westermann, *Theologie* [above 56], 5, also follows von Rad), the theme of the 'centre' of the Old Testament still remains very much on the agenda. Even in his 1963 review, W.Zimmerli asserts that 'The Old Testament has a centre' (105). R.Smend thinks that the question of the 'centre' of the Old Testament continues to be legitimate even after von Rad, since it serves the indispensable function of expressing the search for a *valid* element in an understanding of the Old Testament which can help to proclaim it ('Mitte', 23. For Smend cf. also Seebass, *Hermeneutik* [above 19], 112-23). Developing the concept which is used by von Rad of what is 'typical' of Yahwistic faith in which the true unity of the Old Testament can be found ('Offene Fragen/

Postscript', 406/295: 416/310f. = ET 415, 427), Smend looks for a 'centre' which is not static, but relevant at all times ('Mitte', 24), and thinks that he has found it in the 'covenant formula'.

Even after von Rad, there have been a whole series of attempts to determine the 'centre' of the Old Testament in terms of content. H.Seebass ('Der Beitrag des Alten Testaments zum Entwurf einer biblischen Theologie', *WuD* 8, 1965, 20-49) is impressed by von Rad's arguments (34), but sees the rule of God as a theme which also links the Old Testament to the New (but cf. his recent expression of agreement with Smend, *Hermeneutik*, 122; id., 'Über den Beitrag des Alten Testaments zu einer theologischen Anthropologie', *KuD* 22, 1976, [41-63] 47; id., 'Ein alttestamentlicher Beitrag zur heutigen Rezeption von Barmen III', in *Kirche als 'Gemeinde von Brüdern'*, *Barmen III*, I, Gütersloh 1980, [73-92] 73). For W.C.Kaiser it is the theme of 'promise' ('The Centre of Old Testament Theology; The Promise', *Themelios* 10, 1974, 1-10; id., 'The Promise Theme and the Theology of Rest', *BS* 130, 1973, 135-50). The attempts by Fohrer and Smend to find a bipolar solution similarly try to take account of von Rad's objection to any 'centre' which does not do justice to the inner dynamics of the Old Testament. Mention should also be made of F.C.Prussner's proposal ('Covenant') to make the juxtaposition of the covenant on Sinai and the covenant with David the centre (cf. also A.H.J.Gunneweg, 'Sinaibund und Davidsbund', *VT*10, 1960, 335-41; H.Gese, 'Der Davidsbund und die Zionserwäh-lung', *ZTK* 61, 1964, 10-26 = id., *Vom Sinai zum Zion* [above 113], 113-29; similarly also J.Bourke, 'The Unity of the Old Testament', *Bl.* 40, 1959, 299-312: Sinai and Zion). Recently (*TZ* 1979) R.Mar-tin-Achard has even proposed a threefold 'axis' or three 'guidelines' which could hold together the theological material in the Old Testament: the doxological, the polemical and the soteriological. However, there is no prospect of a real 'centre' (but cf. 132f. below).

Two proposals occupy a special place; they introduce a literary unit rather than a concept or a formula as the 'centre' of the Old Testament. The first derives from W.H.Schmidt, who postulates the first commandment of the Decalogue as a guideline which runs through the whole history of the Old Testament understanding of God (*Gebot* [above 126] 11). This proposal is related to that of W.Zimmerli, that the 'I, Yahweh...' of Ex.20.2 (and in reponse to that the 'You, Yahweh' of Deut 26.10) should be regarded as a 'centre' which proves to be a constant to which the faith of Israel is related, even if one recognizes the flux of history and the changing traditions in it ('Alttestamentliche Traditionsgeschichte', above 60). In 'Erwägungen' (above 46), Zimmerli varies his definition of the 'centre' and now wants to see it in the name of Yahweh as it is at the same time both concealed and revealed in Ex.3.14f.; the name proclaimed in the 'full figure of speech, ' "I am who I am"'. He has repeated the same view in *EvTh* 1975, esp. 109ff., and in *TRE* VI, 445ff.

S.Herrmann takes quite a different view; he puts the book of Deuteronomy at the 'centre' of the Old Testament (*Restauration*), because there 'the basic questions of Old Testament theology are concentrated in a nutshell and a theology of the Old Testament truly has to have its centre there if it is to be an appropriate one' (156). This comment is correct in that Deuteronomy is in fact the most 'theological' book in the Old Testament, since it contains the most thought-out theoretical conceptuality and is both the culmination of the tradition of a particular school and the beginning of a wide history of influence. However, there are other significant areas of tradition within the Old Testament which are far removed from those of Deuteronomy and the Deuteronomists, like the Priestly tradition or, in the prophetic sphere, the school of Isaiah. Moreover, Hasel (*ZAW* 1974, 78f. = *Old Testament Theology*[2] [above 1], 96) has already pointed out that a particular stress on Deuteronomy perhaps corresponds to an already outdated formation of a focal point in the Old Testament (connected with the names of von Rad, Zimmerli and Smend).

However, there is still scepticism as to whether there can be a 'centre' in the Old Testament at all, and whether we should not expect there to be several 'centres', just as there are several 'theologies' (thus e.g. Barr, *JTS* 1974, 272; cf. also Gunneweg, *Understanding* [above 89], 79f., 119f. = ET 89f., 140; id., ' "Theologie" des Alten Testaments oder "Biblische Theologie"?', *Würthwein Festschrift* [above 25], 39-46; J.Goldingay, 'Diversity and Unity in Old Testament Theology', *VT* 34, 1984, 153-68). Baker (*Two Testaments*, above 1, 386) proposes an elliptical cylinder as an image of the multiform unity of the Old Testament, with Christ as the centre, God and people as the two focal points and the various concepts like 'election', 'promise', 'covenant', and so on as concentric layers of the cylinder.

Since all the earlier attempts either to define a concept or a formula as the 'centre' of the Old Testament have proved to have very limited application, it has been increasingly recognized in recent discussion that the only 'centre' there can be in the Old Testament is the God of Israel himself (in view of the fact that all perspectives from history, literature, the history of traditions and world-view are subject to the great variations in human life and the changes of historical period). When I argued this in 1960 (*TZ* 1961 [above 2], 96), von Rad replied with some irritation: 'Of course, it can be said that Jahweh is the focal point of the Old Testament. This is, however, simply the beginning of the whole question: what kind of a Jahweh is he? Does he not, in the course of his self-revelation, conceal himself more and more deeply from his people?' ('Offene Fragen/Postscript' [above 59], 406/294f. = ET 415). So von Rad concedes the possibility of defining the centre of the Old Testament in this way, but at the same time he is concerned that here again there is a 'speculative philosophical principle which is at work as an unconscious premise' ('Offene Fragen/Postscript', 405/294, n.3a, not in ET) which must certainly be taken seriously (cf. also Hasel, *Old Testament Theology*[2], 89f; W.H.Schmidt, *VuF* 1972 [above 2], 16f.). At all events, the concept of the 'centre' may not be used in a static and constructive way.

Furthermore, an increasing number of interpreters finds the real 'centre' of the Old Testament in the God who acts dynamically, who is free and not at man's disposal, yet is constant in his faithfulness, keeping his promises despite all the unfaithfulness and apostasy of Israel. The stress on the first commandment by W.H.Schmidt (Hasel, *ZAW* 1974, 71 = *Old Testament Theology*[2], 92, makes the criticism: 'Why should it be the first commandment and not the second or another?') or on the 'name' or the 'I' of Yahweh by W.Zimmerli (cf. also F.Leist, *Nicht der Gott der Philosophen* [above 118], 9ff.) basically amounts to the same thing (cf. especially id., *EvTh* 1975 [above 126], 117f.).

Among those who see Yahweh as the real 'centre' of the Old Testament, mention should be made of: North, C.R., 'Old Testament Theology and the History of Hebrew Religion', *SJT* 2, 1949, (113-26) 122f.; Ackroyd, P.R., *Continuity* (above 125), 31; Baumgärtel, F., *TLZ* 1961(above 59), 896; Jacob, E., *ETL* 1968, 427f.; id., *Grundfragen* (above 89), 18; Martin-Achard, R., 'Approche', 73ff.; Heschel, A., *Man is not Alone*, New York 1951, 129; Lindblom, J., 'Vad innebär en "teologisk" syn pa Gamla Testamentet?', *SvTK* 37, 1961, (73-91) 85; Deissler, A., *Grundbotschaft* (above 55), passim (cf. id., 'Der Gott des Alten

Testaments', in *Die Frage nach Gott*, ed. J.Ratzinger, Freiburg im Breisgau ²1973, 45-58); Jepsen, A., 'Theologie' (above 45), esp. 24ff.; Hasel, G., *ZAW* 1974, 79ff.; id., *Old Testament Theology*², 99ff.; Stoebe, H.J., *Hertzberg Festschrift* (above 72), 208; Westermann, C., *Theologie* (above 56), 25ff. (the 'oneness of God'); Wagner, S., *TLZ* 1978 (above 126), who speaks of the 'identity of function' of God in the Bible (794); Zenger, E., *KatBl* 1976 (above 126); Roscam Abbing, *Inleiding* (above 72), 67f.

The sovereignty and freedom of God, whose 'centrality' is not to be wrongly understood as a 'principle', must be taken account of here. At the same time it is also clear that God's selfhood has a significance for a theology of the whole of the Bible, for all the differences in the history of tradition and redaction (cf. my *Problems of Biblical Theology*, III). E.Osswald (*TLZ* 1974, 646) objects to the view of God as the centre of the Old Testament because it does not express sufficiently clearly the specific character of the Old Testament over against other religious literature, where the deity is also the 'centre'. This suspicion is unfounded if this God is confessed as Yahweh and the faith of Israel is a matter of opting for this Yahweh, and if in addition (as Jepsen stresses) this God is the one of whom Jesus Christ spoke. This is the only way of avoiding the danger that as 'centre' of the Old Testament God could become an 'empty formula' (thus A.H.J.Gunneweg, 'Religion oder Offenbarung', *ZTK* 74, 1977, (151-78) 176; id., *Understanding* [above 89], 119f. = ET 140).

V

The World Horizon of Old Testament Theology

1. Creation

Albertz, R., *Weltschöpfung und Menschenschöpfung*, CThM 3, Stuttgart 1974; Anderson, B.W., *Creation Versus Chaos. The Reinterpretation of Mythical Symbolism in the Bible*, New York 1967; Bauer, J.B., 'Israels Schau in die Vorgeschichte', in *Wort und Botschaft*, ed. J.Schreiner, Würzburg 1967 ([3]1975), 74-87; Beaucamp, E., *La Bible et le sens religieux de l'universe*, Paris 1959 (= *The Bible and the Universe. Israel and the Theology of History*, London 1963); Bernhardt, K.H., 'Zur Bedeutung der Schöpfungsvorstellung für die Religion Israels in vorexilischer Zeit', *TLZ* 85, 1960, 821-4; Boman, T., 'The Biblical Doctrine of Creation', *CQR* 165, 1964, 140-51; Craigie, P.C., 'Hebrew Thought about God and Nature and its Contemporary Significance', *CJT* 16, 1970, 3-11; Crüsemann, F., 'Die Eigenständigkeit der Urgeschichte. Ein Beitrag zur Diskussion um den "Jahwisten"', *Die Botschaft und die Boten. Festschrift H.W.Wolff*, Neukirchen-Vluyn 1981, 11-29; Davidson, R., 'The Old Testament – A Question of Theological Relevance', *Biblical Studies*, ed. J.R.McKay and J.F.Miller [above 65], 43-56; Drewermann, E., *Strukturen des Bösen 1. Die jahwistische Urgeschichte in exegetischer Sicht*, Paderborn [4]1982; Evdokimov, P., 'La nature', *VC* 73, 1965, 49-69 = 'Die Natur', *KuD* 11, 1965, 1-20; Festorazzi, F., 'La creazione nella storia della salvezza', *ScC* 90, 1962, 3-27; Fischer, L.R., 'Creation at Ugarit and in the Old Testament', *VT* 15, 1965, 313-24; Foerster, W., '*ktizo*', *TDNT* 3, 1000-1034, esp.1001-15; Galling, K., 'Jahwe der Weltenschöpfer', *ThBl* 4, 1925, 257-61; Gunkel, H., *Schöpfung und Chaos in Urzeit und Endzeit*, Göttingen 1895 ([2]1921); Haag, E., *Der Mensch am*

Anfang, TTS 24, Trier 1970; id., 'Gott als Schöpfer und Erlöser in der Prophetie des Deuterojesaja', *TTZ* 85, 1976, 193-213; de Haes, P., *De schepping als heilsmysterie*, Tielt/Den Haag 1962 = *Die Schöpfung als Heilsmysterium*, Mainz 1964; Harner, P.B., 'Creation-Faith in Deutero-Isaiah', *VT* 17, 1967, 298-306; Haspecker, J., 'Religiöse Naturbetrachtung im Alten Testament', *BiLe* 5, 1964, 116-30; id., 'Natur und Heilserfahrung in Alt-Israel', *BiLe* 7, 1966, 83-98; Hoguth, A., 'Probleme der Schöpfungstheologie', *BiLe* 7, 1966, 161-4; Humphreys, W.L., 'Pitfalls and Promises of Biblical Texts as a Basis for a Theology of Nature', in G.C.Stone (ed.), *A New Ethic for a New Earth*, New York 1971, 99-118; Hyatt, J.P., 'Was Yahweh Originally a Creator Deity?', *JBL* 86, 1967, 369-77; Kapelrud, A.S., 'Die Theologie der Schöpfung im Alten Testament', *ZAW* 91, 1979, 159-70; Koch, K., 'Wort und Einheit des Schöpfergottes in Memphis und Jerusalem', *ZTK* 62, 1965, 251-93; Kraus, H.J., 'Schöpfung und Weltvollendung', *EvTh* 24, 1964, 462-85 = id., *Biblisch-theologische Aufsätze*, Neukirchen 1972, 151-78; Lambert, G., 'La création dans la Bible', *NRT* 75, 1953, 252-81; Landes, G.M., 'Creation and Liberation', *USQR* 33, 1978, 79-89; Legrand, L., 'La création, triomphe cosmique de Yahwé', *NRT* 83, 1961, 449-70 = *TD* 11, 1963, 154-8 (shorter version); Liedke, G., *Schöpfung und Erfahrung. Zum interdisziplinären Beitrag der neueren Arbeit am Alten Testamentes*, epd-Dokumentation 31, 1975, 8-24; Lindeskog, G., 'The Theology of the Creation in the Old and New Testaments', in *The Root of the Vine. Essays in Biblical Theology*, ed. A.Fridrichsen, Westminster 1953, 1-22; Loretz, O., *Schöpfung und Mythos*, SBS 32, Stuttgart 1968; Luck, U., *Welterfahrung und Glaube als Grundproblem biblischer Theologie*, TEH 191, Munich 1976; Ludwig, T.M., 'The Traditions of the Establishing of the Earth in Deutero-Isaiah', *JBL* 92, 1973, 345-57; Lux, R., 'Schöpfungstheologie im Alten Testament', *ZdZ* 31, 1977, 416-31; Macquarrie, J., 'Creation and Environment', *ExpT* 83, 1971, 4-9; Martin-Achard, R., 'Remarques sur la signification théologique de la création selon l'Ancien Testament', *RHPR* 52, 1972, 3-11; McCarthy, D.J., ' "Creation" Motifs in Ancient Hebrew Poetry', *CBQ* 29, 1967, 393-406; McKenzie, J.L., 'God and Nature in the Old Testament', *CBQ* 14, 1952, 18-39, 124-45 = id., *Myths and Realities: Studies in Biblical Theology*, Milwaukee 1963, 85-132; Napier, B.D., 'On Creation-Faith in the Old Testament: A Survey', *Int* 16, 1962, 21-42; Otto, E.,

'Schöpfung als Kategorie der Vermittlung von Gott und Welt in Biblischer Theologie', in *Festschrift H.J.Kraus* (above 46), 53-68; von Rad, G., 'Das theologische Problem des alttestamentlichen Schöpfungsglaubens', *Werden und Wesen des Alten Testaments*, BZAW 66, Giessen 1936, 138-47 = id., *Gesammelte Studien* I (above 59), 136-47 = 'The Theological Problem of the Old Testament Doctrine of Creation', in *The Problem of the Hexateuch and Other Essays*, Edinburgh 1965, reissued London 1984, 131-43; id., 'The Problem of the Hexateuch' (above 59); id., *Genesis*, ATD 2/4, Göttingen 1949 = ET, OTL, London and Philadelphia (1961), revised ed. 1972, ⁵1981; id., 'Glaube und Welterkenntnis' (above 72), 255-66; id., 'Aspekte alttestamentlichen Weltverständnisses' (above 63); Rendtorff, R., 'Die theologische Stellung des Schöpfungsglaubens bei Deuterojesaja', *ZTK* 51, 1954, 3-13 = id., *Gesammelte Studien* (above 46), 209-19; id., 'Genesis 8,21 und die Urgeschichte des Yahwisten', *KuD* 7, 1961, 69-78 = *Gesammelte Studien*, 188-97; id., 'Hermeneutische Probleme der biblischen Urgeschichte', *Festschrift F.Smend*, Berlin 1963, 19-29 = *Gesammelte Studien*, 198-208; Saebø, M., 'Creator et Redemptor. Om skapelsens teologiske plass og funksjon i Det gamle testamente', *Deus Creator. Festschrift I.P.Seierstad*, Oslo 1971, 1-28 = *Ordene og Ordet* (above 2), 138-65; Scheffczyk, L., *Einführung in die Schöpfungslehre*, Darmstadt 1975; Schmid, H.H., *Gerechtigkeit als Weltordnung*, Tübingen 1968; id., 'Rechtfertigung als Schöpfungsgeschehen', *Käsemann Festschrift*, (above 90), 403-14; id., 'Schöpfung, Gerechtigkeit und Heil. Schöpfungstheologie als Gesamthorizont biblischer Theologie', *ZTK* 70, 1973, 1-19 = id., *Altorientalische Welt in der alttestamentlichen Theologie*, Zurich 1974, 9-30; Schmidt, W.H., *Die Schöpfungsgeschichte der Priesterschrift*, WMANT 17, Neukirchen-Vluyn 1964 (³1974); id., 'Schöpfungsgeschichte – Mythos und Glaube', *KiZ* 21, 1966, 258-61; id., *Alttestamentlicher Glaube in seiner Geschichte*, Neukirchen ²1975, 166-76; id., 'Schöpfung durch das Wort im Alten Testament', in *Schöpfung und Sprache*, ed. W.Strolz, Freiburg im Breisgau 1979, 15-43; Schunk, K.-D., 'Die Auffassung des Alten Testaments von der Natur', *TLZ* 104, 1979, 401-12; Steck, O.H., 'Deuterojesaja als theologischer Denker', *KuD* 15, 1969, 280-93 = id., *Wahrnehmungen Gottes im Alten Testament*, TB 70, Munich 1982, 204-20; id., 'Genesis 12,1-3 und die Urgeschichte des Jahwisten', *Festschrift von Rad*, 1971 (60 above), 525-54 = id., *Wahrnehmungen*, 117-48; id., *Der*

Schöpfungsbericht der Priesterschrift, FRLANT 115, Göttingen 1975; id., *Friedensvorstellungen im alten Jerusalem*, TS 111, Zurich 1972; id., 'Zwanzig Thesen als alttestamentlicher Beitrag zum Thema: "Die jüdisch-christliche Lehre von der Schöpfung in Beziehung zu Wissenschaft und Technik"', *KuD* 23, 1977, 277-99; id., 'Alttestamentliche Impulse für eine Theologie der Natur', *TZ* 34, 1978, 202-11; id., *Welt und Umwelt*, Biblische Konfrontationen, Stuttgart 1978; Stolz, F., *Strukturen und Figuren im Kult von Jerusalem*, BZAW 118, Berlin 1970; id., *Monotheismus* (above 114); Stuhlmueller, C., 'The Theology of Creation in Second Isaiah', *CBQ* 21, 1959, 429-67; id., ' "First and Last" and "Yahwe Creator" in Deutero-Isaiah', *CBQ* 29, 1967, 495-511; id., 'Yahwe-King and Deutero-Isaiah', *BR* 15, 1970, 32-45; id., *Creative Redemption in Deutero-Isaiah*, AnBib 41, Rome 1970; Vischer, W., 'Quand et pourquoi Dieu a-t-il révélé à Israël qu'il est le "Créateur"?', *FV* 58, 1959, 3-27; Vosberg, L., *Studien zum Reden vom Schöpfer in den Psalmen*, BEvTh 69, Munich 1975; Weippert, H., *Schöpfer des Himmels und der Erde. Ein Beitrag zur Theologie des Jeremiabuches*, SBS 102, Stuttgart 1981; Westermann, C., 'Das Reden von Schöpfer und Schöpfung im Alten Testament', in *'Das ferne und nahe Wort'*, Festschrift *L.Rost*, BZAW 105, Berlin 1967, 238-44 (short version also in *TLZ* 92, 1967, 243-6); id., 'Der Mensch im Urgeschehen', *KuD* 13, 1967, 231-46; id., 'Neuere Arbeiten zur Schöpfung (Eliade, Brandon)', *VF* 14, 1969, 11-28; id., *Der Segen in der Bibel und im Handeln der Kirche*, Munich 1968, reprinted GTB Siebenstern, Gütersloh 1981 = ET *Blessing in the Bible and the Life of the Church*, Philadelphia 1978; id., *Schöpfung*, ThTh 12, Stuttgart 1971 = ET *Creation*, London 1974; id., 'Einleitung zur Urgeschichte Genesis 1-11', *Genesis* BK I/1, Neukirchen-Vluyn 1974, 1-103; Würthwein, E., 'Chaos und Schöpfung im mythischen Denken und in der biblischen Urgeschichte', in *Zeit und Geschichte. Dankesgabe für R.Bultmann*, ed. E.Dinkler, Tübingen 1964, 317-27 = id., *Wort und Existenz* (above 40), 28-38; Young, N., *Creator, Creation and Faith*, Philadelphia 1976, 25-82; Zimmerli, W., *Die Weltlichkeit des Alten Testaments*, Göttingen 1971 = ET *The Old Testament and the World*, Atlanta, Ga and London 1976 (cf. also id., *TRE* VI, 448f.).

Ancient Near Eastern Sources

> Bottéro, Jean, et al., *La Naissance du Monde*, Paris nd. = *Quellen des Alten Orients* I. *Die Schöpfungsmythen*, with an introduction by M.Eliade, Zürich/Cologne 1964, reprinted Darmstadt 1977; Brandon, S.G.F., *Creation Legends of the Ancient Near East*, London 1963.

For a long time, judgments about the significance of the theme of creation for Old Testament theology were governed in advance by the predominant role which was assigned to the theme of history in the Old Testament. An approach by way of the history of traditions made this almost mandatory; along with this approach G. von Rad had established the direction for any assessment of the theology of creation. The apodictic character of this assessment is already expressed in the first sentences of his 1936 article: 'The Yahwistic faith of the Old Testament is a faith based on the notion of election, and therefore primarily concerned with redemption. This statement, *which requires no justification here* (my italics) poses simply and precisely the problem with which we are here concerned' ('The Theological Problem', 138/136 = ET 131). Towards the end of 'The Problem of the Hexateuch', where von Rad traces the changes in the 'small historical creed' through the Hexateuch and elsewhere (see above 60f.), he also speaks of the 'pre-structure of the primal history' (58ff./71ff. = ET 63ff. [here the ET is too vague to reproduce the original meaning]); according to this view, at a later stage the Yahwist used his creation narratives (for some features of which there were probably already models in the Canaanite world) as a preface to the history of salvation which began with Gen.12.1-3. However, he did not do this to provide a superfluous completion taking the story further back into the past; he had a deep theological concern: in accordance with Gen.12.1-3 the promise of the blessing for Israel ultimately aims at the blessing for all peoples: 'In thus welding together the early history of the world and the history of redemption, the J writer submits his account of the meaning and purpose of the redemptive relationship which Yahweh has vouchsafed to Israel. He provides *the aetiology of all Israelite aetiologies*.... He proclaims in a manner which is neither rationally justifiable nor yet capable of detailed explanation, that the ultimate purpose of the redemption which God will bring about in Israel is that of bridging the gulf between God and the entire human race' (60f./73 = ET 65f.). Von Rad sees this linking of salvation history and primal history as the Yahwist's specific theological contribution; he argues that it is very improbable that the Yahwist had predecessors here: 'His presentation of the data is too clearly stamped with his own purpose, and one cannot avoid the feeling that the looseness of the composition as a whole stems from the fact that this is the first trial of a new venture' (61/74 = ET 67). Later, however, he abandoned this view (under the impact of the comment by H.Gese that an outline of world history embracing creation, primal period, flood and a new foundation for history could already be found in Sumeria ['Geschichtliches Denken im alten Orient und im Alten Testament', *ZTK* 55, 1958 (127-45) = id., *Vom Sinai zum Zion* (above 113), (81-98) 142f./96] – cf. the letter mentioned in Napier, 21 n.). However, even according to the *Theology* (I⁴, 168 = ET 155), the connecting of the individual narratives, which were originally independent, to their theological framework was the work of the Yahwist.

Evidently what is said about the primal history generally applies also to the Yahwistic creation narrative in particular; here von Rad draws no distinctions (thus he says in *Theology* I⁴, 152 = ET 139, that the beginning of the salvation history is predated to the creation in J and also in P, and then deals with the accounts in Gen2.4bff. and Gen.1 in detail). One important point is that 'Creation is regarded as a work of Jahweh in history, a work within time' (ibid.). From a theological perspective, a decisive feature of creation faith is that it has to be incorporated into faith in salvation. In his early article ('The Theological Problem', 139ff./138ff. = ET 133ff.) von Rad refers in this connection to psalms like 136; 148; 33, and above all to Deutero-Isaiah. It is in Deutero-Isaiah that he finds what is theologically the most mature function of creation faith; while what formerly was the usual reference to divine election is replaced by a reference to the creation of Israel, which keeps occurring in Deutero-Isaiah, precisely as a result of this the idea of creation is incorporated into a soteriological understanding which puts creation at the service of redemption. Statements like Isa.43.1; 44.21,24; 46.3; 54.5, in which the keywords 'create' ('form') and 'redeem' are associated, are evidence for this. Von Rad's pupil R.Rendtorff pursued the role of creation faith in Deutero-Isaiah further (*ZTK* 1954) and came to the conclusion that in this prophet creation and election are closely related concepts (for the theme of creation in Deutero-Isaiah cf. also B.J. van der Merve, *Pentateuchtradisies in die Prediking van Deuterojesaja*, Groningen/Djakarta 1956, 1ff.; W.Kirchschläger,

'Die Schöpfungstheologie bei Deuterojesaja'', *BiLi* 49, 1976, 407-22). This confirms the soteriological understanding of creation which was von Rad's perspective. The works of e.g. Stuhlmueller point in the same direction; only Harner (with the same basic approach) wants to assign the theme of creation in Deutero-Isaiah a rather greater weight.

Only Psalms 19; 104; 8 do not fit in with this classification. In them von Rad also finds the affirmation that the cosmos bears witness to the power of God by its ordering, and to this degree sees them as 'real evidence for an unadulterated doctrine of creation which stands on its own ground' ('The Theological Problem', 144/144 = ET 140). However, these Psalms are very much on the periphery of the Old Testament; their alien origin, which is particularly recognized in the case of Pss.19; 104, puts them at one remove from what is characteristic of Yahwistic belief. Von Rad would find them characterized by a markedly rational interest in the divine economy in the world and thinks that they derive ultimately from wisdom. So he does not propose to consider them further.

In the *Theology* von Rad goes one stage further: in the section 'Israel before Yahweh (Israel's Answer)' (I⁴, 366f. = ET 355ff.) the hymn ('The Praises of Israel') comes first, and in this context the theme of the creation of the world as the subject of the praises has an important place. However, quite apart from the subordination of this section to the main theme of the salvation-historical traditions of Israel (see 63f. above) – von Rad here again begins from the sequence 'history – creation', since in his view, in the hymn Israel first and foremost praised God's actions in history (I⁴, 368ff. = ET 357ff.), and Yahweh's rule over nature is only 'the other great theme in the hymns of the Old Testament' (I⁴, 371 = ET 360). However, most of these creation hymns are relatively late compositions. That also applies to Job 38ff., which von Rad cites. Here he comes to speak of the third sphere within which the theme of creation plays a role within the Old Testament. It has been frequently noted that wisdom has only an extremely peripheral place in von Rad's work. It is far removed from the centre because, as von Rad notes, it is not very interested in the phenomenon of history (I⁴, 153, 459f., 463 = ET 151, 445f., 450). Moreover, it is striking that he assigns the book of Job to another sphere: it is included with the psalms of lamentation under the heading 'Israel's trials' (it is well known that the forms of lament play an important role in Job, cf. esp. C.Westermann, *Der Aufbau des Buches Hiob*, BHT 23, Tübingen

1956, [2]1977). However, these poems belong in a 'marginal theological situation' (I[4], 430 = ET 417). That is completely true of the sphere of theological wisdom proper, which, as in Job 28; Prov.8, raises the rational question of the meaning of nature as a whole: 'Here the faith of Israel saw itself really confronted with a new phenomenon, and new insights and experiences, with which it had to reckon' (I[4], 460 = ET 446). As the fruit of a late period in which 'interest in the traditions of the saving history had grown weak' (I[4], 463 = ET 449) in wisdom circles, there was now a growing concern to relate the mysteries of creation to the revelation of salvation. The original situation which was still to be found in Genesis 1 was now reversed: whereas there the problem lay 'in linking the saving history with Creation, in drawing Creation towards the saving history', it was the task of wisdom to find a connection between creation, with which it was confronted, and salvation history or the revelation of the will of Yahweh (I[4], 464 = ET 450). Cf. also the summary of his standpoint in 'Glaube und Welterkenntnis' (above 72)

Von Rad's classification of creation faith within the central belief in salvation history has been followed by a large number of Old Testament scholars, and in addition by a wide range of theologians in other branches of the subject (among systematic theologians e.g. recently by J.Moltmann, 'Schöpfung als offenes System', *Creation, Christ and Culture. Studies...T.F.Torrance*, ed. R.McKinney, Edinburgh 1976, 119-34 = 'Creation as an Open System', in *The Future of Creation*, London 1979, 115-30; W.Kasper, 'Die Schöpfungslehre in der gegenwärtigen Diskussion', in G.Bitter/G.Miller (eds.), *Konturen heutiger Theologie*, Munich 1976 [92-107] could already declare: 'This salvation-historical approach has widely gained acceptance in more recent systematic theology' (94). The extent of its influence can hardly be overestimated. Of the writings mentioned above the following present it in a pure form : Anderson (cf. esp. 'Creation and History', in id., *Creation Versus Chaos*, above 134, 11-42), Bauer, Beaucamp, Bernhardt, Boman, Festorazzi, Foerster, de Haes, Hoguth, Humphreys, Lambert, Martin-Achard, Napier (summarizes von Rad), Saebø, Vischer and Zimmerli. Thus e.g. J.Muilenburg writes (*HTR* 1961 [above 76], 242): 'The biblical doctrine of creation is a derivative of history, the sacred history of the chosen people. The creation account in Genesis 1 is not only prologue to the history which follows it – but is also a development of the election-historical life, of the redemptive history which has the Exodus as its centre.' And W.H.Schmidt enthusiastically exclaims (*Schöpfungsgeschichte*, 187; cf. also H.D.Preuss, *Jahwe-glaube und Zukunftserwartung* [above 64], 96ff.): 'Is not to speak of creation to speak of nature, the world and history?' The same basic view also found a place in the official study document 'God in Nature and History' (*New Directions* [above 110], 7-31) at the 1967 Bristol Faith and Order Conference; there, too, the Old Testament notion of creation is said to be subordinate to the faith of Israel in history, and a line is extended to what the commission believes to be a Christian conception of creation and history which can be reconciled with modern evolutionary thought. Only the Scandinavian school has developed a critical and independent view; thus e.g. G. Lindeskog (*Theology*) sees the exodus theme, which comes from Israel's earliest belief in election, and the creation theme, which derived from Canaanite origins, as two elements of equal standing in Hebrew religion. Monotheism, universalism and human worth give the idea of creation in Israel its specific dignity. 'It cannot reasonably be relegated to a subordinate place' (4). However, this has hardly affected opinion on the continent generally.

It is illuminating to see how this view finds a striking parallel in the dogmatic assessment of creation as developed by Karl Barth in his *Kirchliche Dogmatik* III/1, Zollikon-Zurich 1945 = ET *Church Dogmatics* III/1, *The Doctrine of Creation*, Edinburgh 1958 (cf. E.Haible, *Schöpfung und Heil*, Mainz 1964, 89ff.; C.Link, *Die Welt als Gleichnis. Studien zum Problem der natürlichen Theologie*, BEvTh 73, Munich 1976, 115ff.). Barth connects creation closely with covenant: 'The purpose and therefore also the meaning of creation is to make possible the history of God's covenant with man which has its beginning, its centre and its culmination in Jesus Christ. The history of this covenant is as much the goal of creation as creation itself is the beginning of this history' (III/1, 44 = ET 42). Here, according to Barth, creation is not only the external basis of the covenant (its presupposition) (ibid., 103ff. = ET 94ff.); the covenant is also the internal basis of creation (ibid., 258ff. =ET 228ff.). 'If creation was the formal presupposition of the covenant, the latter was the material presupposition of the former. If creation takes precedence historically, the covenant does so in substance' (ibid., 262 = ET 232). Barth thinks that he can also locate these two sides exegetically in the juxtaposition of Gen.1. and Gen.2.4b-25. Without doubt, at this point, too, von Rad's position fits into the broader framework of a time conditioned by the climate of a dialectical theology. Moreover, in his outline, E.Jacob (*Théologie*[2], above 00f., 110ff. = ET 136ff.) expressly follows Barth (cf. also Legrand, *NRT* 1961, 465), as above all does K.H.Miskotte (cf. esp. *Zur biblischen Hermeneutik*, TS 55, Zollikon 1959, 24ff., on the agreement between Barth and von Rad). Cf. also my *Problems of Biblical Theology*, II, 5.

We may note how this subordination of the biblical idea of creation to the idea of history went on to influence theological thought and even political thinking generally in a particular period: here it is worth recalling the theory of secularization (which derives from F.Gogarten and is recognizable as a sideline of dialectical theology). Above all, representatives of political theology like H. Cox in his book *The Secular City*, London and New York 1965, or J.B.Metz, *Zur Theologie der Welt*, Mainz/Munich 1958 = ET *Theology of the World*, New York 1969, refer specifically precisely to Gen. 1 in so far as the biblical (Priestly) account of creation sees the world as wholly at the disposal of human beings who, on their own responsibility (though as representatives of God or Jesus Christ) can shape it in the political sphere and control it through scientific research and economic exploitation. (Cf. also F.Elder, *Crisis in Eden: A Religious Study of Man and Environment*, Nashville and New York 1970, 74ff. – For a criticism of the secularization theory cf. most recently W.Jaeschke, *Die Suche nach den eschatologischen Wurzeln der Geschichtsphilosophie*, BEvTh 76, Munich 1976).

Conversely, this is where the criticism by the ecological movement began. It made the Christian doctrine of creation beginning from Gen.1.26-28 responsible for the exploitation of nature and the ecological world crisis which arose as a result and thus indirectly regarded the Old Testament idea of creation as the ultimate root of the present disastrous situations (for what follows cf. also S.M.Daecke, 'Auf dem Weg zu einer Praktischen Theologie der Natur', in *Frieden mit der Natur*, ed.K.M.Meyer-Abich, Freiburg, Basle and Vienna 1979, 262-86).

The American, L.White Jr, popularized this charge in 1966 ('The Historical Roots of our Ecological Crisis', *Science* 155, 1967, 1203 = G.de Bell [ed.], *The Environmental Handbook*, New York 1970, 12-26; I.G.Barbour [ed.], *Western Man and Environmental Ethics*, Reading, Mass 1973, 18-30; cf. also id., 'Continuing the Conversation', in I.G.Barbour [ed.], op.cit., 55-65.) This has been put most acutely by C.Amery (*Das Ende der Vorsehung. Die gnadenlosen Folgen des Christentums*, Reinbek 1972, cf. also id., *Natur als Politik. Die ökologische Chance des Menschen*, Reinbek 1976). Cf.

also I. McHarg, 'Man: Planetary Disease', *Vital Speeches of the Day* 37, 1971, (634-40) 636; J.B.Cobb Jr, *Is it too late?*, New York 1972; D.L.Meadows, *The Limits to Growth. A Report for the Club of Rome's Project on the Predicament of Mankind*, London and New York 1972; G.Kade, 'Ökonomische und gesellschaftspolitische Aspekte des Umweltschutzes', *Gewerkschaftliche Monatshefte* 22, 1971, (257-69) 259f.; J.W.Forrester, 'Churches at the Transition between Growth and World Equilibrium', in D.L. and H.D. Meadows (ed.), *Toward Global Equilibrium*, Cambridge, Mass. 1973, 337-53, esp.350).

Although it must be conceded that the effect of the influence of Gen.1.28 in a secularized atmosphere has favoured such lines of thought in modern times (cf. G.Liedke, 'Von der Ausbeutung zur Kooperation', in E.von Weizsäcker (ed.), *Humanökologie und Umweltschutz*, SFF 8, Stuttgart and Munich 1972, 36-65 – Evidently that is still not the case for the church's understanding before modern times, cf. D.K.Jobling, *'And have Dominion...'*, Union Theological Seminary Dissertation, New York 1972; G.M.Treutsch, 'Die Schöpfungsethik im Verlauf der Theologiegeschichte', *Beitr.päd.Arb.* 22, 1978, 41-9; U.Krolzik, *Umweltkrise-Folge des Christentums?*, Stuttgart 1979, esp. 70ff.; id., ' "Machet Euch die Erde untertan...!" und das christliche Arbeitsethos', in Meyer-Abich (ed.), *Frieden* [above 143], 174-95) it has been increasingly recognized in recent years (thus J.Passmore, *Man's Responsibility for Nature. Ecological Problems and Western Traditions*, London 1974, 8-27, makes a clear distinction between the Old Testament, indeed the genuine Christian understanding, and what Greek Stoic and humanistic influence has made of it in modern times. Only the latter reduces nature to an object of human exploitation. For the limited significance of the Christian tradition for the problem see also R.Dubos, *A God Within*, London 1973, 157ff.; D.W.Moncrief, 'The Cultural Basis of our Environmental Crisis', in I.G.Barbour (ed.), *Western Man*, 31-42; A.R.Peacocke, 'On "The Historical Roots of our Ecological Crisis"', in H.Montefiore (ed.), *Man and Nature*, London 1975, 155-8), that it derives from a mistaken interpretation of the verse. In accord with its connection with vv.26f., the focal point of the verse is rather the idea of the responsibility of mankind for creation. On several occasions, Gen.2.15 has been recognized as adequate help towards interpretation. Rightly understood, the biblical accounts of creation do not support the exploitation of nature by mankind, but rather remind us of our task in accordance with creation. On the other hand, it should not be forgotten that the biblical primal history does not present the utopia of a healed world but begins from the deep gulf which runs through creation because of man (cf. esp. Drewermann, *Strukturen*, above 134).

Cf. e.g. Henry, M.L., *Das Tier im religiösen Bewusstsein des alttestamentlichen Menschen*, Tübingen 1958, 12-25; Elder, *Crisis* (above 145), 81ff.; Sittler, I., 'Ecological Commitment as Theological Responsibility', *Zygon* 5, 1970, 172-81; Barr, J., 'Man and Nature – The Ecological Controversy and the Old Testament', *BJRL* 55, 1972, 9-32; Derr, T.S., *Ecology and Human Liberation*, WSCFB III, 1, Geneva 1973; Liedke, G., 'Ausbeutung', op.cit., 42ff.; id., 'Die Verheissung gilt aller Kreatur', *LM* 18, 1979, 469-73; Altner, G., *Schöpfung am Abgrund. Die Theologie vor der Umweltfrage*, Neukirchen-Vluyn 1974, 55ff.; Lohfink, N., ' "Macht euch die Erde untertan?"', *Orient* 38, 1974, 137-42; id., 'Die Priesterschrift und die Grenzen des Wachstums', *StZ* 192, 1974, 435-50; id.,' "Seid fruchtbar und füllt die Erde an!" Zwingt die priesterliche Schöpfungsdarstellung in Gen 1 die Christen zum Wachstumsmythos?', *BiKi* 30, 1975, 77-82; id., 'Wachstum', in *Unsere grossen Wörter*, above 61, 156-71; Baker, J.A., 'Biblical Attitudes to Nature', in Montefiore (ed.), *Man and Nature*, 87-109; Scheffczyk, L., *Einführung*, above 136, 85ff.; Schüngel-Straumann, H., 'Macht euch die Erde untertan?', *KatBl* 101, 1976, 319-32; Jensen, O., *I vaekstens vold. Økologie og Religion*, Kopenhagen 1976 = id., *Unter dem Zwang des Wachstums*, Munich 1977, esp. 49ff., 144ff.; Rendtorff, R., 'Machet euch die Erde untertan. Mensch und Natur im Alten Testament', *EK* 10, 1977, 659-61; Wilms, F.-E., 'Der Mensch als Mitgeschöpf. Alttestamentliche Vorgaben zu einer Schöpfungsethik', *Beitr.päd.Arb.* 22, 1978, 1-28; Lehmann, K., 'Kreatürlichkeit des Menschen als Verantwortung für die Erde', in Altner, G. (ed.), *Sind wir noch zu retten?*, Regensburg 1978, 41-64; Steck, O.H., *Welt und Umwelt* (above 137), esp.143ff.; Liedke, G., *Im Bauch des Fisches. Ökologische Theologie*, Stuttgart 1979; Zimmerli, W., 'Der Mensch im Rahmen der Natur nach den Aussagen des ersten biblischen Schöpfungsberichtes', *ZTK* 76, 1969, 139-58; Schunck, K.-D., *TLZ* 1979 (above 136); Westermann, C., 'Bebauen und Bewahren', in H. Aichelin and G. Liedke, *Naturwissenschaft und Theologie. Texte und Kommentare*, Neukirchen 1974, 203-13; Wiebering, J., *Die Natur als Partner des Menschen*,

Theologische Versuche XI, Berlin 1979, 165-76, esp. 168ff.; Houston, W.J., ' "And let them have dominion..." ' Biblical Views of Man in Relation to the Environmental Crisis', in E.A.Livingstone (ed.), *Studia Biblica* , 1978, I, *Papers on Old Testament and Related Themes*, JSOT Suppl. 11, Sheffield 1979, 161-84; Beauchamp, A., 'Reflexions théologiques à propos d'une éthique de l'environnement', *ScE* 32, 1980, 217-33 = *ThD* 29, 1981, 127-31; Wilms, F.-E., *Mitgeschöpflichkeit als Verantwortung für die Erde*, Karlsruher pädagogische Beiträge, 1980, 75-85, esp. 81ff.; Treutsch, G.M., 'Umwelt oder Schöpfung?', in *Energie, Umwelt, Ernährung*, Politische Studien Sonderheft I, 1980, (119-29) 124ff.; Zenger, E., 'Hoffnung für die Erde. Der Mensch als Sachwalter des Lebens', *Christ in der Gegenwart* 33, 1981, 213f.; Splett, J., ' "Macht euch die Erde untertan?" ' Zur ethisch-religiösen Begrenzung technischen Zugriffs', *ThPh* 57, 1982, 260-74; Friedrich, G., *Ökologie und Bibel: Neuer Mensch und alter Kosmos*, Stuttgart 1982; Preuss, H.D., 'Biblisch-theologische Erwägungen eines Alttestamentlers zum Problemkreis Ökologie', *TZ* 39, 1983, 68-101; Koch, K., 'Gestaltet die Erde, doch heget das Leben! Einige Klarstellungen zum *dominum terrae* in Genesis 1', in *Festschrift H.J.Kraus* (above 136), 23-36; also Strohm, T., 'Die Gottesebenbildlichkeit und die Ursprünge der Entfremdung', *TP* 12, 1977, 296-308.

From the New Testament side see Moule, C.F.D., *Man and Nature in the New Testament*, London 1964 and Philadelphia 1967; Grässer, E., 'Neutestamentliche Erwägungen zu einer Schöpfungsethik', *Beitr.päd.Arb.* 22, 1978, 29-40 = *WPKG* 68, 1979, 98-114; id., 'Die falsche Anthropozentrik. Plädoyer für eine Theologie der Schöpfung', *DtPfrBl* 78, 1978, 263-6; cf. also id., 'Ehrfurcht vor allem Lebendigen. Zur Aktualität der Ethik Albert Schweitzers', *DtPfrBl* 80, 1980, 274-7; Hegermann, H., 'Biblisch-theologische Erwägungen eines Neutestamentlers zum Problemkreis Ökologie', *TZ* 39, 1983, 103-18. Hendry, G.S., *Theology of Nature*, Philadelphia 1980, treats the whole problem from a systematic standpoint. Dembowski, H., 'Ansatz und Umrisse einer Theologie der Natur', *EvTh* 37, 1977, 33-49, considers the matter from a completely one-sided soteriological understanding of theology ('theology is soteriology', 33,37,46) focussed on christology and the New Testament. Of course this does not take in all the dimensions of the message of the Bible.

Meanwhile the situation in the theological assessment of the theme of creation has shifted over the last ten years in various directions and for various reasons. Reference must be made first here to the works of C.Westermann. While his programmatic writing, *Der Segen in der Bibel und im Handeln der Kirche*, is not a change from von Rad's position, it is a noticeable modification, in that Westermann contrasts God's act of blessing with his redemptive action as a form of approach which must be distinguished from it in principle. Whereas the redemptive action takes place in contemporary acts of God in history, with salvation as its aim, blessing (of which above all the books of Genesis and Deuteronomy speak) is a constant action; it is 'the power that furthers life, growth and increase, and preserves creation from danger and damage' (44). Originally the blessing was conceived in completely unhistorical or prehistorical terms within the sphere of the family (just as it forms the sociological background in the patriarchal narratives, where the continuity of blessing is depicted in the genealogies). It is the Yahwist, in Gen.12.1-3 (and the Balaam pericope Num.22-24) who introduces the transition from the pre-historical existence of the family to the historical mode of existence of the people. The Yahwist broke the originally magical character of the blessing and made it a historical concept (60); the people now becomes the recipient of the blessing (this is the presupposition above all in Deuteronomy). With this distinction (cf. also D. Vetter, *Jahwes Mit-Sein ein Ausdruck des Segens*, AzT 45, Stuttgart 1971, who follows Westermann) the approach oriented on history is not yet abandoned, but a perspective is opened up which indicates another theological approach. (J.Macquarrie's proposal of an 'organic model' [6] points in the same direction. He too derives this from the priestly theology, which he feels to be unjustly neglected: God and the world are not as strictly separated here as they are in prophetic theology.) It also provides one of the two aspects under which, according to Westermann, biblical primal history sees man's creatureliness: created man is man blessed by God – and on the other hand also man limited by sin and death (cf. *KuD* 1967, 236ff.). Westermann finds the division between saving and blessing so important that he also adopts it as a scheme for the divisions in *Theologie des Alten Testaments* (above 56). Under 'blessing' (88ff.) there is nothing essentially new there in comparison to the earlier book. We may note that the theory that the Yahwist incorporated the concept of blessing into historical action is by no means sharply defined; other interpretations are possible here. Westermann himself has made a major contribution to them. In his view, the use of 'blessing' in the story of creation (where it takes place in narrative form, not conceptually) is to be distinguished from the one mentioned above (cf. *Genesis*, I, 192f.). However, this observation, too, does not take us much further.

In his contribution to the Rost Festschrift, Westermann (241) attacks the attempt to give a soteriological relevance to all statements about creation in the light of Deutero-Isaiah. The tradition of the creation is rather different from the tradition of the saving acts of God (240, cf. *TLZ* 1967, 245); whereas this begins from an experience for which there are witnesses, the same cannot be said of the creation tradition (*KuD* 1967, 236). Indeed, it also has a fundamentally different character: 'Every event in primal history or every primal event relates to the present, excluding what we call history.' 'The primal period is beyond the temporal sequence, beyond history' (*KuD* 1967, 235f.). At another point (*Genesis*, I, 89ff.; cf. also *Schöpfung* [above 137], 29ff.), Westermann stresses the weight of the primal event, that these *traditions of humanity* take up from the beginning and seek to hand on (hence also the adoption of traditions from communities in the ancient Near East). Nor is the primal event the object of a confession or of faith (*Schöpfung*, 14); rather, to some extent it is a presupposition behind which we may not inquire (cf. also – following Westermann – G.Liedke, 'Die Selbstoffenbarung der Schöpfung', *EK* 8, 1975, 398-400; cf. also id., *epd-Dokumentation*, 31/75 [above 135], 19: 'Going a little beyond von Rad and Westermann I would propose the formula: *in the primal event the conditioning of every event is depicted...*'),for it was taken for granted in the ancient Near East that man is a creature. On the other hand Westermann asserts that this primal history has a twofold aspect in the Old Testament: through its connection with the history of the people in Gen.11/12 and the totality conception in J and P it has also become the prelude to the history of God with Israel. By virtue of the fact that the events are put in a fixed sequence within *primal history* (as opposed to the free association of the themes of the *primal event* in the world of the ancient Near East), they have also taken on a specific character (*Genesis* I, 88 – similarly Drewermann, *Strukturen* [above 134], esp.319, who, taking up von Rad's interpretation, that the key to the Yahwistic primal history lies in Gen.12.1-3, sees the culmination of primal history in the development of evil as a deliberate construction on the part of the Yahwist which is only comprehensible in the light of the counterpart provided by the new start beginning with the promise to Abraham). So in one sense, in his new approach to the role of creation, Westermann is still at the half-way stage (cf. also 164 below). F.Crüsemann, 'Eigenständigkeit' (above 134) goes an important step further: he stresses the independent character of the primeval history in Gen.1-11 in terms of literary form and tradition history. Genesis 12.1-3 is just a secondary bridge between originally independent traditions. The primeval history has its own origin and its own theology; it belongs to a settled, rural society of Yahweh-believers who experience the acting of their God in the living world of the land far off from history. So it can claim a place of its own in Old Testament theology. E. Zenger, 'Beobachtungen zur Komposition und Theologie der jahwistischen Urgeschichte', in *Dynamik im Wort; Lehre von der Bibel; Leben aus der Bibel*, FS des Katholischen Bibelwerks in Deutschland, Stuttgart 1983, 35-54, restricts the primeval history of J to Gen 2.4b-9.19 and sees in Gen.8.21f. the clue for understanding its theme: its main topic is the life of man on the earth, the continuing existence of the creation through God's forbearance in spite of human guilt, but with all the restrictions in the conditions of life which are the result of that guilt. So it has its own message to give.

Westermann has advanced the understanding of creation further at two other points. First, his distinction between two different forms of creation account, the creation of the world and the creation of humanity, is important (cf. *KuD* 1967, 233f.; *Festschrift Rost*, 243; *Genesis* I, 31ff.). His pupil R.Albertz pursued this distinction (in which from a history-of-religions perspective the creation of man is older) further, outside Genesis. Another important observation by Westermann (though it is no more than a hint) relates to the history of tradition: the tradition about creator and creation takes three forms: narrative (myth), hymn and wisdom (*VuF* 1969, 17).

In fact, in the context of tradition history the greatest progress has been achieved in defining the position of the theme of creation within the Old Testament. The difficulties in arriving at an appropriate classification of the theme within the Old Testament lay above all in the fact that it was taken as a matter of course that the starting point was a single context within the tradition, so that e.g. von Rad could find only a peripheral place for creation alongside the traditions of salvation history, which formed the focal point of his interest. In the meantime, a clearer picture has been formed of the significance of the world of Canaan, too, for the development of the general structure of expressions of faith in the Old Testament. Here (rightly or wrongly? – Albertz, *Weltschöpfung*, 159, doubts whether so exclusive an orientation is correct) Jerusalem and its traditions have come to form the centre of interest. Since Herbert Schmid collected the material for the first time in his article 'Jahwe und die Kulttraditionen von Jerusalem' (*ZAW* 67, 1955, 168-97), those elements of the Old Testament tradition which do not fit in with an approach in terms of salvation history but point to another origin and another *Sitz im Leben* have become increasingly clear. In particular, the parallels from Ugarit made the derivation from Canaanite religion obvious, as in the idea of the kingdom of God (cf. W.H.Schmidt, *Königtum Gottes in Ugarit und Israel*, BZAW 80, Berlin 1961, ²1966; also J.Schreiner, *Sion-Jerusalem. Jahwes Königssitz*, SANT VII, Munich 1963); the theme of the struggle with chaos (O.Kaiser, *Die mythische Bedeutung des Meeres in Ugarit und Israel*, BZAW 78, Berlin 1958, ²1962; Stolz, *Strukturen*, 12-71); and that of the mountain of God which in Jerusalem is identified with Zion (R.J.Clifford, *The Cosmic Mountain in Canaan and the Old Testament*, Cambridge, Mass. 1972; Steck, *Friedensvorstellungen*, 13ff.; J.J.M.Roberts, 'Zion in the Theology of the Davidic-Salomonic Empire', in *Studies in the Period of David and Solomon and Other Essays*, ed. T.Ishida [International Symposium for Biblical Studies, Tokyo, 5-7 December 1979], Tokyo 1982, 93-108). As a result of this we can see to what a great extent Israel incorporated conceptions from Canaanite religion into Yahwistic belief after the conquest and obviously above all after the rise of the Canaanite city of Jerusalem to be David's capital and the rededication of the Temple there as a sanctuary of Yahweh (for this cf. e.g. J.A.Soggin, 'Der offiziell geförderte Synkretismus in Israel während des 10.Jahrhunderts', *ZAW* 78, 1966, 179-204; G.Fohrer, 'Israels Haltung gegenüber den Kanaanäern und anderen Völkern', *JSS* 13, 1968, 64-75; E.Otto, 'El und JHWH in Jerusalem', *VT* 30, 1980, 316-29, uses other arguments. - F.Stolz, *Monotheismus* [above 114f.] wants to see monotheistic belief in Yahweh primarily as the final phase in the development of an Israelite religion which originally had a polytheistic Canaanite stamp, but H.P.Müller, 'Gott und die Götter in den Anfängen der biblischen Religion', ibid., 99-142, differs. – On the topic cf. also B.Lang [ed.], *Der einzige Gott. Die Geburt des biblischen Monotheismus*, Munich 1981; id., 'Persönlicher Gott und Ortsgott. Über Elementarformen der Frömmigkeit im Alten Testament', in *Fontes atque Pontes. Festgabe für Hellmut*

Brunner, Wiesbaden 1983, 271-301; N.Lohfink, 'Polytheistisches und monotheistisches Sprechen von Gott im Alten Testament', in *Unsere grossen Wörter* [above 61], 126-44; H.Seebass, 'Geschichtliche Vorläufigkeit und eschatologische Endgültigkeit des biblischen Monotheismus', in A.Falaturi/W.Strolz/S.Talmon [eds.], *Zukunftshoffnung und Heilserwartung in den monotheistischen Religionen*, Freiburg/Basle/Vienna 1983, 49-80). Above all, a considerable part of the theme of creation seems to be of Canaanite or specifically Jerusalemite origin. Several of the themes of the Jerusalem tradition mentioned above are connected with it, e.g. the mountain of God, which already appears in Sumerian mythology as a dam against the primal waters and as the 'bond between heaven and earth' (Stolz, *Strukturen*, 110ff.,144ff.), and has the same function in Jerusalem (W.H.Schmidt, *Königtum Gottes*, 32ff.; Stolz, *Strukturen*, 163ff.; cf. also R.Hillmann, *Wasser und Berg. Kosmische Verbindungen zwischen dem kanaanäischen Wettergott und Jahwe*, Diss theol. Halle 1965 [microfilm], 10ff., 158ff.), and the struggle with chaos which is part of the theme of creation in the form of binding the primal waters (thus recently again Steck, *KuD* 1977, 286 n.19 – against W.H.Schmidt, *Alttestamentlicher Glaube*, 166-70 = ET *The Faith of the Old Testament*, Oxford 1983, 166-70; Albertz, *Weltschöpfung*, 112ff.; Vosberg, 10f., 46f.). Functions of El and also Baal (cf. Fisher) were transferred to Yahweh in the process. Both Schmidt (*Königtum Gottes*, 58ff.; cf. already H.Schmid, *ZAW* 1955, 179-83) and Stolz (*Strukturen*, esp.167ff.) have discussed the evidence in detail; this bears witness to the adoption of originally Canaanite conceptions of creation, associated with El and Baal, into Yahwistic belief. Here a particularly important passage is Gen.14.18-20, which Stolz has called 'virtually a compendium of Jebusite religion' (151; bibliography, ibid., 149 n.1; cf. further N.C.Habel, 'Jahwe, Maker of Heaven and Earth', *JBL* 91, 1972, 321-37; Albertz, *Weltschöpfung*, 159). The divine predicate of El Elyon there as 'creator of heaven and earth' is later transferred to Yahweh. For G.Lindeskog, Hebrew religion came into being from the fusion of two relatively independent elements, the creation myth and the exodus story (5).

The Psalter is the main place in which remarks about creation are to be found, which originally came from the Canaanite sphere. As Albertz (taking further Westermann's similar position and also his terminology – cf. C.Westermann, *Das Loben Gottes in den Psalmen*, Göttingen 1954 = ET *The Praise of God in the Psalms*, Richmond,

Va 1965, fifth German edition entitled *Lob und Klage in den Psalmen*, 1977; cf. id., *Der Psalter*, Stuttgart 1967, ³1975) has shown (*Weltschöpfung*, 91ff.), the theme of the creation of the world has a place in descriptive psalms of praise (Gunkel's term is 'hymn'), usually to describe the majesty of God; in special cases (Ps.104.10ff. – cf. also O.H.Steck, 'Der Wein unter den Schöpfungsgaben: Überlegungen zu Ps.104', *TTZ* 87, 1978, 173-91 = id., *Wahrnehmungen* (above 136f.), 240-61 – 136.25; 145.15; 147.8f; Job 5.10; 38.39ff.) also in the sense of *creatio continua*, the preservation of creation by grace. From the hymn the theme of the creation of the world then also reached Deutero-Isaiah in the form of the 'dispute'; here the exiles, too, are to be shown the superiority of Yahweh as creator (Albertz, *Weltschöpfung*, 7ff.). Alongside this in Deutero-Isaiah is quite a different theme (above 149f.), that of the creation of mankind, which originally had its place in the individual lament (*Weltschöpfung*, 118ff.; on this cf. id., *Persönliche Frömmigkeit und offizielle Religion*, CThM A, 9, Stuttgart 1978, 23ff.), from where it also found a way into the oracle of salvation (*Weltschöpfung*, 26ff.). It is important that Deutero-Isaiah was by no means the first to give the statements about creation the function that they have there; he merely continues to give them the role which they originally had in the tradition, shaped by long cultic usage, and applies them to the specific situation of the exile. H.Haag (*TTZ* 1976) has recently taken these comments one stage further by pointing out that both areas of tradition, the creation of mankind and the creation of the world, no longer appear in isolation in Deutero-Isaiah (and there are already the beginnings of this in the Yahwistic creation narrative), but are related to the theme of Yahweh's lordship (kingly rule) over the world and history and his action as redeemer of his people. It is also possible to note mixed forms between the two spheres. H.Weippert, *Schöpfer*, distinguishes between two traditions of creation: the first originates with the conquest of the land and means that Yahweh inherits the duties of the Ba'al of the land in keeping the covenant by caring for the harvest, sending the rain, etc. When in the time of Jeremiah the loss of the land seems to be imminent, the prophet comes upon the idea of Yahweh as the creator of the whole world and lord of world history. The distinction would then be older than Deutero-Isaiah – but is H.Weippert right in attributing it to the invention of Jeremiah?

Unfortunately the study by Vosberg, which regards all the psalms discussed as exilic or post-exilic, is of little use on the theme because its questions are one-sided and it has severe methodological weaknesses; cf. also the review by R.Albertz, *TLZ* 103, 1978, 645-7; similarly one cannot accept the view of G.Wanke, *Die Zionstheologie der Korachiten*, BZAW 97, Berlin 1966, that all the material is post-exilic.

In the light of the new definition of the theological relevance of the primal event introduced by Westermann and a corresponding exegesis of individual passages like Gen.1.26-28, a new actualizing of the biblical idea of creation may also be possible, particularly also in conversation with modern science (cf. also the reflections by E.Otto, 'Schöpfung', above 136). The attempt at a total theology which includes God's relationship to the world (Elder, *Crisis* [above 143], calls the representatives of this view 'Inclusionists') has long been undertaken by American process theology.

Cf. esp. Whitehead, A.N., *Process and Reality*, Gifford Lectures 1927/28, London 1929, New York 1969; Hartshorne, C., *A Natural Theology for Our Time*, Chicago 1967; Cobb, J.B., *A Christian Natural Theology: Based on the Thought of Alfred North Whitehead*, Philadelphia 1965/London 1966; id., *God and the World*, Philadelphia 1969 (but cf. the criticism by T.S.Derr, *Ecology and Human Liberation*, above 145 and the discussion: T.S.Derr, J.B.Cobb Jr, D.R.Griffin, C.Birch and P.Verghese, 'Rights for Both Man and Nature?', *Antic.* 16, 1974, 20-36). Introductions: Peters, E.H., *The Creative Advance. An Introduction to Process Philosophy as a Context for Christian Faith*, St Louis 1966; Cobb, J.B. and Griffin, D.R., *Process Theology. An Introductory Exposition*, Brescia 1976, esp. ch.4, 62ff.; 9, 142ff. Cf. also Williams, D.D., 'Prozess-Theologie. Eine neue Möglichkeit für die Kirche', *EvTh* 30, 1970, 571-82 = K.M.Beckmann (ed.), *Protestantische Theologie*, Düsseldorf and Vienna 1973, 304-14; Birch, C., *Nature and God*, London 1965; id., 'What does God do in the World?', *USQR* 30, 1975, 76-84; Brown, D., 'Gott verändert sich. Konzepte und Entwicklungen der Prozesstheologie in den Vereinigten Staaten', *EK* 10, 1977, 595-7; Cobb, J.B., Jr, 'Der Mensch ist ein Teil der Schöpfung: Ein neuer Ansatz der Prozesstheologie', *EK* 13, 1980, 701-4; Welker, M., 'Relativität der wirklichen Welt. Prozessdenken und Prozesstheologie' (on Whitehead, Cobb/Griffin and the collection ed E.Wolf-Gazo, *Whitehead. Einführung in seine Kosmologie*, Freiburg and

Munich 1980), *EK* 13, 1980, 595-7; id., *Universalität Gottes und Relativität der Welt. Theologische Kosmologie im Dialog mit dem amerikanischen Prozessdenken nach Whitehead*, Neukirchen 1981; also *Semeia* 24, 1982: 'Old Testament Interpretation from a Process Perspective', ed. W.A.Beardslee/D.J.Lull. Cf. also Daecke,S.M., 'Schöpfungsglaube als Gotteserkenntnis, Selbstverständnis, Weltverantwortung, Naturerfahrung und Umweltbewusstsein', *WPKG* 7, 1978, 398-411, 588-94 (this also shows the breadth of more recent dogmatic approaches in the understanding of creation. Cf. also below 162f.).

Evidently limitations of the traditional historical-critical view still have to be overcome here (cf. e.g. the criticism of W.Herrmann and R.Bultmann in O.Jensen, *Theologie zwischen Illusion und Restriktion*, BEvTh 71, Munich 1975). This discussion has recently begun to be carried on in connection with the problem of ecology by G.Liedke (*Im Bauch des Fisches*, above 145). The fact that Liedke expressly incorporates a reference to New Testament eschatology (cf. also above 145f.) makes a specifically Christian approach to the Old Testament particularly promising in this sphere, too, and therefore also in connection with the pressing problems of the present. One interesting attempt is the essay by E.Otto, 'Schöpfung als Kategorie der Vermittlung von Gott und Welt in Biblischer Theologie', *FS Kraus* (above 136), 53-68, who sees in the creation traditions of the Old Testament the struggle of biblical faith with the dialectics between the experience of man in the ultimate world and the divine transcendence. However, these are only the first steps.

2. Myth

If we recognize that the connection between the theme of creation and the historical traditions is largely conditioned by the history of tradition (cf. also the works by V.Maag on the nomadic and sedentary elements in the picture of God in the Old Testament: 'Der Hirte Israels', *STU* 28, 1958, 2-28 = id., *Kultur, Kulturkontakt und Religion* [above 67], 111-44; id., 'Malkuth JHWH', *Congress Volume Oxford 1959*, SVT VII, Leiden 1960, 129-53 = id., *Kultur*, 145-69; id., *NedThT* 1966/67 [above 67] = id., *Kultur*, 256-99), we can see much more clearly its independent significance for the theology of the Old Testament. Recently it has also been necessary to accord independent significance to the Yahwistic and Priestly creation narratives, since there has been a revolution in the assessment of myth.

This re-evaluation has come about on the one hand as a result of research into religion (cf. J.Henninger, 'Le mythe en ethnologie', *DBS* VI, 225-46). However, it must be said that Old Testament scholarship has hardly taken any account of this development, but is still governed largely by earlier definitions of myth (as 'history of the gods' [H.Gunkel, *Genesis* HK I/1, ⁹1977, xiv – this is still one of the points in the definition of 'myth' in C.Petersen, *Mythos im Alten Testament*, BZAW 157, Berlin 1982, 31], or as an outdated 'three-storey' view of the world [R.Bultmann, 'New Testament and Mythology', see below]). The concept of myth deriving from the Enlightenment (cf. J.Pepin, *Mythe et allégorie*, Paris 1958, 34ff.) and mostly drawn from C.G.Heyne (cf. C.Hartlich and W.Sachs, *Der Ursprung des Mythosbegriffes in der modernen Bibelwissenschaft*, Tübingen 1952, 14ff.; P.Barthel, *Interprétation du langage mythique et théologie biblique*, Leiden 1963, 15ff.; J.W.Rogerson, *Myth in Old Testament Interpretation*, BZAW 134, Berlin 1974, 1ff.; for the whole problem see also H.J.Jensen, 'Mytebegrebet i den historisk-kritiske og i den structuralistiske forskning', *DTT* 47, 1984, 1-19), which differentiates myth, as an original and primitive thought-form, from modern, rational thinking (thus esp. E.Nestle, *Vom Mythos zum Logos*, Stuttgart 1940, ²1942; cf. also H.Weinrich, 'Structures narratives du mythe', *Poétique*, 1, 1970, 25-34 = 'Erzählstrukturen des Mythos', in id., *Literatur für Leser. Essays und Aufsätze zur Literaturwissenschaft*, Stuttgart 1971, 137-49) and has been taken up by Bultmann in his well-known article on demythologization ('Neues Testament und Mythologie', in *Offenbarung und Heilsgeschehen*, BEvTh 7, Munich 1941, 27-69 = *Kerygma und Mythos* I, Hamburg 1948, 15-48 = ET 'New Testament and Mythology', in *Kerygma and Myth* [I], London 1953, 1-44; for further discussion see later volumes in the *Kerygma und Mythos* series and *Kerygma and Myth* 2, London 1962) has also had an effect on Old Testament scholarship (cf. e.g. the markedly rationalistic examples in E.L.Allen, 'On Demythologizing the Old Testament', *JBR* 22, 1954, 236-41). As a consequence, even in more recent statements by experts there has been considerable obscurity about the meaning of the term and its content (Rogerson, op.cit., gives a good survey of the history of research; cf. also the brief survey of the various definitions in W.Herberg, 'Some Variant Meanings of the Word "Myth"', in id., *Faith* [above 89], 139-48). The partly Anglo-Saxon (in the 'Myth and Ritual' school around S.H.Hooke, cf. Rogerson, 66ff.) and partly Scandinavian (especially in the so-called Uppsala school and in S.Mowinckel, cf. esp. *Religion und Kultus*, Göttingen 1953, 94ff.) theories which brought the relationship between myth and ritual into the centre of the discussion (cf. recently B.Otzen, H.Gottlieb and K.Jeppesen, *Myths in the Old Testament*, London 1980 = ET of Danish, Copenhagen [2]1976) have not helped to clarify matters, since by assuming a cultic pattern spanning the whole of the Ancient Near East and determining Old Testament conceptions, they apply in far too sweeping a way insights into the connection between myth and cult though they are intrinsically apt (cf. e.g. K.H.Bernhardt, *Das Problem der altorientalischen Königsideologie im Alten Testament*, SVT VIII, Leiden 1961, esp. 51-66).

The technical religious concept of myth, especially as arrived at by B.Malinowski (*Myth in Primitive Psychology*, London 1926) and deepened among others by K.T.Preuss (*Der religiöse Gehalt der Mythen*, SGV 162, Tübingen 1933) and H.Baumann (*Schöpfung und Urzeit des Menschen im Mythus der afrikanischen Völker*, Berlin 1936, reprinted 1964; cf. id., 'Mythos in ethnologischer Sicht', *StGen* 12, 1959, 1-17, 583-97; cf. also F.Medicus, *Das Mythologische in der Religion*, Zurich 1944; R.Pettazoni, 'The Truth of Myth' in id., *Essays on the History of Religions*, Leiden 1954, 1967, 11-23; A.E.Jensen, *Mythos und Kult bei Naturvölkern*, Wiesbaden 1951), defines myth as the reality on which the present order is founded, or – thus M.Eliade, (*Le sacré et le profane*, Paris 1956 = ET *The Sacred and the Profane*, New York 1968; cf. also id., *Images et symboles*', Paris 1952; id., 'Les mythes du monde moderne', *NRF* 9, 1953, 440-58) – as an 'exemplary model' (cf. further K.Kerenyi, 'Über Ursprung und Gründung in der Mythologie', in C.G. Jung and K.Kerenyi, *Einführung in das Wesen der Mythologie*, Amsterdam and Leipzig 1941, 9-37 = K.Kerenyi, *Humanistische Seelenforschung*, Darmstadt 1966, 150-75; id., *Wesen und Gegenwärtigkeit des Mythos*, Munich and Zurich 1965; [see the new version of 128-44 , 'Die Eröffnung des Zugangs', 234-52; K.Beth, 'Mythologie und Mythos', *HWDA* VI, 720-52]; for myth in classical life and art cf. e.g. H.Marwitz, 'Mythos-Dichtung-Sage', *Jahreshefte d. Österr.Arch.Inst.Wien*, 1981/2, 1-17). W.Pannenberg, who begins from this concept in his work 'Christentum und Mythos' (in *Terror und Spiel. Probleme der Mythenrezeption*, ed. M.Fuhrmann,

Munich 1971, 473-525, printed separately Gütersloh 1972 = ET
'The Later Dimensions of Myth in Biblical and Christian Tradition',
in *Basic Questions in Theology* III, London 1973, 1-79 [American
volume entitled *The Idea of God and Human Freedom*, Philadelphia
1973]), rightly observes that it is too little noted in the philosophical
and theological discussion on myth and 'demythologizing' (13 = ET
7). That is particularly true of Old Testament scholarship (27ff. =
ET 23ff.) Here we can see the effect of a climate strongly marked
by kerygma theology. 'Myth' is then understood *a priori* in terms of
non-Israelite mythology with its polytheistic stamp, and on the basis
of precise exegesis it is noted that (apart from a few exceptions) this
seems to have been eliminated from the biblical primal history.
C.Westermann's more qualified judgment (*Genesis* II, BK I, 2,
Neukirchen 1977ff., 45,; cf. also H.P.Müller, 'Gott und die Götter'
[above 150], 102) is to be preferred to the classification of this
discovery as a 'process of demythologizing' which e.g. W.Zimmerli
once thought could not be praised highly enough. Westermann
distinguishes between the polytheistic myths of the high cultures
'and the "myths" of the early cultures in which there is usually only
one god or supernatural being and the other partner in the event is
human'. The biblical primal history also fits into the second category.
B.Uffenheimer, 'Biblical Theology and Monotheistic Myth', *Imm.*
14, 1982, 7-24, openly speaks of 'monotheistic myth', though he
stresses the strict ontological detachment between God and his
world in biblical faith. 'Monotheistic myth' is opposed to pagan
myth and tries to uproot it. By doing so it does not evade picturing
God as 'the king, the judge, the man of war and the loving God who
is both bridegroom and husband' (24).

However, the limitation of mythical discourse to the ancient
high cultures and 'early cultures' and the designation of myth as
polytheistic is obviously too narrow. More recently it has been
recognized that mythical thought and language represents, rather,
a way in which human beings deal with the world which cannot be
limited to any particular stage of culture or religion but extends right
down to the present. Alongside the scientific investigation of the
origin of myth, a contribution has been made by the recognition of
its significance as a symbolic form of expression, which goes back
especially to E.Cassirer (*Die Begriffsform im mythischen Denken*,
SBW 1, 1922 = id., *Wesen und Wirkung des Symbolbegriffs*,
Darmstadt 1956, reprinted 1965, 1-70; id., *Sprache und Mythos. Ein
Beitrag zum Problem der Götternamen*, SBW 6, 1925 = *Wesen und*

Wirkung, 71-158 [159-67]; id., 'Der Begriff der symbolischen Form im Aufbau der Geisteswissenschaften', *VBW* 1921/22, 11-39 = *Wesen und Wirkung*, 169-200; id., 'Zur Logik des Symbolbegriffs' = *Theoria* 4, 1938, 145-75 = *Wesen und Wirkung*, 201-30; id, *Philosophie der symbolischen Formen 2. Das mythische Denken*, Berlin 1925, Darmstadt ²1953, reprinted 1977; cf. also S.K.Langer, *Philosophy in a New Key. A Study in the Symbolism of Reason, Rite and Art*, Cambridge, Mass. 1942, ³1957, reprinted 1974; E.Buess, *Die Geschichte des mythischen Erkennens*, Munich 1958, and the contributions in the collected volume ed. E.Castelli, *Mythe et foi*, Paris 1966. There is an application to the Old Testament in J.L.McKenzie, 'Myth and the Old Testament', *CBQ* 21, 1959, 265-82 = id., *Myths and Realities* [above 135], 182-200); E.Leach, 'Genesis as Myth', *Discovery* 23, 1972, 30-35 = id., *Genesis as Myth and Other Essays*, London 1969, 7-24, and with D.A.Aycock, *Structuralist Interpretation of Biblical Myth*, Cambridge 1983, and adopting the insights of depth psychology (cf. on this, following C.G.Jung, M.T.Kelsey, *Myth, History and Faith*, New York, Paranus and Toronto 1974) and the use of the concept of myth in the French school of semiology (cf. R.Barthes, *Mythologies*, Paris 1957) by P.Ricoeur in his attempts at a biblical hermeneutic which begin from the symbolic content of language and are specifically directed to the Old Testament.

For this see the supplement to *EvTh*, *Metapher*, 1974, with the introduction to Ricoeur by P.Gisel, 5-23 (= French *ETR* 49, 1974, 31-52) and the contributions by Ricoeur, 'Philosophische und theologische Hermeneutik', 24-45; 'Stellung und Funktion der Metapher in der biblischen Sprache', 45-70; *Semeia* 4, 1975, with the introduction to Ricoeur's work by L.Dornisch, 1-22, and a short hermeneutical study by Ricoeur himself, 29-148. Cf. also L.Dornisch, *A Theological Interpretation of the Meaning of Symbol in the Theory of Paul Ricoeur*, PhD Dissertation Milwaukee, Wisconsin 1973 (Ann Arbor Microfilm) and the composite volume ed. C.E.Reagan, *Studies in the Philosophy of Paul Ricoeur*, Athens, Ohio 1979 (bibliography of Ricoeur to 1976, 179-94). In similar terms already J.P.Manigne, *Pour une poétique de la foi. Essai sur le mystère symbolique*, CFl 43, Paris 1969; cf. especially the distinction between ontology and 'ontophany', 45, 62ff.

A series of Old Testament scholars has also appropriated the scientific concept of myth, or at least believes that it can be applied to Old Testament evidence. J.Hempel ('Glaube, Mythos und Geschichte im Alten Testament', *ZAW* 65, 1953, [109-67] 110 – also separate, Berlin 1953) wants myth to be regarded as a possible form of the expression of belief, and B.S.Childs, *Myth and Reality in the Old Testament*, SBT 27, London 1960, ²1962, reprinted 1968, accepts the function of myth as providing a basis for structure, following Jensen, above 156. Cf. also S.B.Frost, 'Eschatology and Myth', *VT* 2, 1952, 70-80; E.L.Allen, *JBR* 1954 [above 155]; G.Henton Davies, 'An Approach to the Problem of Old Testament Mythology', *PEQ* 88, 1956, 83-91; A.Strobel, 'Wort Gottes und Mythen im Alten Testament', *Cath(M)* 17, 1963, 180-96. K.H.Bernhardt, 'Bemerkungen zum Problem der "Entmythologisierung" aus alttestamentlicher Sicht', *KuD* 15, 1969, 193-209, is more obscure in his talk of a 'mythical world-view' (for criticism cf. Pannenberg, 'Later Dimensions' [above 156f.], 30 n.54 = ET 26 n.54), though he regards it as an indispensable presupposition for faith (209). On the other side are figures like W.H.Schmidt, who, under the spell of Gunkel's definition, thinks that faith and myth are 'alien' to each other (*Schöpfungsgeschichte* [above 136], 108; cf. id., 'Mythos im Alten Testament', *EvTh* 27, 1967, 237-54; id., *Alttestamentlicher Glaube* (above 151), 176-80 = ET 177-81), so that demythologizing is also appropriate in connection with the Old Testament, or was already practised by the Old Testament when it took over pagan mythology (thus already M.Noth, 'Die Historisierung des Mythos im Alten Testament', *CuW* 4, 1928, 265-72, 301-9 = id., *Gesammelte Studien zum Alten Testament II* [above 76], 29-47, and also e.g. A.Ohler, *Mythologische Elemente im Alten Testament*, Düsseldorf 1969, 1ff.).

Over against this Pannenberg very rightly observes: 'If myths cannot occur in Israel in the polytheistic form found elsewhere in the ancient Near East, this does not mean that the idea of a primal age on which the present world order is based is not a living element in Israel, and is not represented in certain traditions' ('Later Dimensions' [above 156f.], 31 = ET 28). For the function of myth is more general: 'For the myth is concerned with the order which overcomes the terrifying chaos, and order which is thought of as rooted in the events of the primal age' (22 n.36 = ET 17 n.36). Pannenberg, however, is then reluctant to apply the designation 'mythical' to this way of thinking which he finds indispensable, and therefore cautiously chooses the term 'religious world view' (29 = ET 26). J.L.McKenzie (above 158, 199) also has hesitations about a possible misunderstanding of the term 'mythical' in circles less familiar with academic discussion. Conversely, for Morton Smith (*JBL* 1969, above 114 32) the assertion by 'pseudo-orthodoxy' that there are no myths in the Old Testament is 'absurd' and part of its apologetic obscurantism (cf. my *Problems of Biblical Theology*, ch.I).

These suspicions seem less justified in most recent times since (especially under the influence of K.Jaspers, cf. 'Wahrheit und Unheil der Bultmannschen Entmythologisierung', in K.Jaspers and R.Bultmann, *Die Frage der Entmythologisierung*, Munich 1954, 7-55) in a situation 'beyond demythologizing', an understanding of the profundity of mythical discourse begins to grow and it seems indispensable (in changing forms but as a principal constant of the human understanding of self and the world) as a form of expression for an existence related to transcendence.

According to M.Knevels, 'Wesen und Sinn des Mythos', *StGen* 15, 1962, 668-86, 687-705, myth is 'the account of the encounter with a transcendent power in the form of images and stories' (668); it has a relationship to the totality of the world. W.Stählin (*Auch darin hat die Bibel recht. Sage, Legende, Märchen und Mythos in der Bibel überhaupt*, Stuttgart 1964, 29ff.) stresses the understanding of reality as a totality in the thought-form of myth which at the same time expresses the ultimate background of being in a way which cannot be resolved rationally. As an atheist, L.Kolakowsky sees an abiding basic component of human existence in the mythical order alongside the rational one (*Die Gegenwärtigkeit des Mythos*, Munich 1973). H.Halbfas (*Fundamentalkatechetik*, Stuttgart 1968, 196ff., esp. 252ff.; id., *Religion*, ThTh ErgB, Stuttgart 1976), recognizes in myth (which unfolds in narrative form, cf. also id., 'Erfahrung und Sprache. Plädoyer für eine narrative Unterrichtskultur', in H.Halbfas, F.Maurer and W.Popp (eds.), *Sprache, Umgang und Erziehung*, Stuttgart 1975, [170-87] 177ff.): myth is a complementary category to that of the Logos: 'So myth is the true word, the self-attesting, unconditionally valid narrative which interprets the existence against which the Logos stands out as structure and function' (*Religion*, 51). He thinks that myth is also indispensable in the context of academic work: mythical awareness remains indispensable to the dimension of human existence which is oriented on transcendence ('trust, hope and love can only be related to the mythical world', ibid., 82): 'Demythologizing can at best mean interpreting the myth as myth, that is, bringing it to itself' (ibid., 64). 'The real task is therefore not to demythologize, but again to stress the human capacity for language so that man can again accept the religious dimension of existence with his newly won language' (*Fundamentalkatechetik*, 253). Cf. also the volume *Thought and Mythic Images*, ErJb 14, 1979 (with numerous contributions).

The observations by T.Roszak, *Where the Wasteland Ends*, New York 1972/London 1973, esp. ch.4, 109ff., are important. They relate to what in his view are the detrimental results which the Jewish Christian tradition has had in reducing a symbolic and mythical understanding of the world which in reality cannot be abandoned (for criticism cf. however, D.M.Ryan, 'The New Romanticism and Biblical Faith', in E.Fleischner (ed.), *Auschwitz: Beginning of a New Era? Reflections on the Holocaust*, New York 1977, [277-305] 292ff.- Cf. also E.Wyschogrod, 'Romantic Consciousness and Biblical Faith', ibid., 331-42). He pleads, albeit at a critical distance from the Christian tradition, whose nadir he finds in respect of what he is talking about in Protestantism (but also in the scientific revolution at the beginning of the seventeenth century, cf. ch.5, 142ff.), for a rediscovery of the transcendental symbolic character of creation: 'Why, one wonders, should it be crude or rudimentary to find divinity brightly present in the world where others find only dead matter or an inferior order of being?' (117). Also important is his reference to the eucharist as the last resort of the 'ever-renewed experience of God's miraculous embodiment in the natural world' (121). In this notion he is in agreement with an awareness of the symbolic content of all matter as a mirror for the divine transcendence which has recently become very lively in Anglican sacramental piety, above all in connection with William Temple; here the sacrament takes its place as the focal point and the incarnation as a culmination of divine action in creation.

On this cf. e.g. Raven, C.E., *Natural Religion and Christian Theology*, Cambridge 1953; Peacocke, A.R., *Science and the Christian Experiment*, London 1971; id., 'Matter in Theological and Scientific Perspectives – A Sacramental View', in I.T.Ramsey (ed.), *Thinking about the Eucharist*, London 1972, 14-37 = (shortened version) 'A Sacramental View of Nature', in H.Montefiore (ed.), *Man and Nature* (above 114), 132-42; id., *Creation and the World of Science*, Bampton Lectures 1978, Oxford 1979;

Birch, C., 'Creation, Technology and Human Survival: Called to Replenish the Earth', *ER* 28, 1976, (66-79) 77 (for this lecture see also Daecke, S.M., 'Neue Beiträge zu einer Theologie der Natur und der Umwelt', *Anstösse*, Hofgeismar, 5, 1976 [123-33], 125ff.).

The Orthodox view, which was already presented in 1974 in a much-noted ecumenical lecture by P.Verghese, 'Mastery and Mystery', World Council of Churches Conference on Science and Technology for Human Development, Bucharest 1974, paper no.10 (cf. also Daecke, ibid., 123ff.), is also similar. Cf. recently id. (Gregorius, P.), *The Human Presence. An Orthodox View of Nature*, Geneva 1978. Cf. also above 153f. One may well join M.Knevels in saying: 'Myth only seemed to be dead. It revived.'

A series of definitions of myth which still influence Old Testament discussion needs to be rejected: these are the aetiological definition (which similarly goes back to Gunkel, *Genesis*, XVf., and plays a role e.g. in Bernhardt, *KuD* 1969, above 159, 194ff.) or the 'magical' definition (e.g. H.P.Müller: myth arises in an encounter with 'power': 'Mythische Elemente in der jahwistischen Schöpfungser-zählung', *ZTK* 69, 1972, (259-89) 260ff.; id., 'Mythos und Transzen-denz', *EvTh* 32, 1972, [97-118] = *Eschatologie im Alten Testament*, ed. H.D.Preuss, Darmstadt 1978 [415-43] 98/416ff.; id., *Mythos, Tradition, Revolution. Phänomenologische Untersuchungen zum Alten Testament*, Neukirchen 1973, 9ff., reprinted under the title *Jenseits der Entmythologisierung*, 1979; cf. also id., 'Mythos, Ironie und der Standpunkt des Glaubens', *TZ* 31, 1975, [1-13] 2 – however, for the new perspective in Müller's understanding of myth in Krecher/Müller and in 'Religiöse Grunderfahrungen' cf. below 165f.).

Finally, reference should also be made to the summary investi-gation by G.S.Kirk, (*Myth. Its Meaning and Functions in Ancient and Other Cultures*, Cambridge 1970). After a discussion of the structuralist approach of Levi-Strauss, which he argues is only relatively right, *among other* approaches (cf. 78), Kirk gives exten-sive surveys of the nature of myths in Ancient Mesopotamia (84ff.) and Greece (172ff.) and gains from them an essentially more differentiated typology of myth and its functions than has been produced by previous schools which are often one-sided in treating certain elements and forms of myth as absolutes (cf. esp. the final chapter, 252ff.). Most important of all is the basic principle: 'There is no invariable connexion between myths and gods or rituals' (252).

Instead of this, Kirk stresses the narrative and speculative aspects of myth and thus comes to divide them into three types, which often overlap: 1. a primarily narrative, discursive type; 2. a type determined by action and repetition to preserve the validity and effectiveness of certain forms of order (natural and social); 3. a speculative and explanatory type, which is concerned with the obscure and mysterious aspects of the world and human existence.

This recognition of the function of myth as describing an underlying order should have been applied more obviously than hitherto to the understanding of the biblical creation narratives. Here both Childs and, above all, Pannenberg (who is dependent for the details of his account [27ff. = ET 23ff.] on the view shaped by the von Rad school) assume that the Old Testament myth has been basically historicized, even within the creation narratives.

Childs (83, 93) stresses the eschatological character of Yahweh's action in history, as does Pannenberg (59ff. = ET 55ff.). Cf. also O.Cullmann, 'The Connection of Primal Events and End Events with the New Testament Redemptive History', in B.W.Anderson (ed.), *The Old Testament and Christian Faith* (above 38), 115-23, who thinks that the biblical authors had incorporated the mythical events of beginning and end into salvation history and therefore that they must be interpreted as 'ontic' historical events.

Over against this Steck (*KuD*, 1977 [above 137], 283) asserts: 'The main interest of the creation texts is... the effort to express in the modes of description mentioned above the depth-dimension of the present world of experience and to bring out those basic data and determinations which are *a priori* valid for the world and man as a whole.'

Cf. also Steck's comments on the Yahwistic primeval history, 'Genesis 12,1-3 und die Urgeschichte des Jahwisten', *Festschrift von Rad*, 1971 (above 60), 525-54, esp.549: 'In the understanding of the Yahwist, Gen.2-11 is a totality intended to embrace the typical situation of humanity which at the same time is shaped by the possibility of life and the diminution of life.' Cf. also id., *TZ* 1978 (above 137); id., *Welt und Umwelt* (above 137), 55ff. Also J.J.Kim, 'Hierophany and History', *JAAR* 40, 1972, 334-48; Liedke, epd-Documentation 31/75 (above 135).

C.Westermann similarly indicates the character of the primeval history as narratives (*Creation* [above 137], 9), in which universal human *experiences* are expressed in man's being and being-in-the-world (*Genesis* [above 137], 91f.).

However, Westermann immediately tones down these ideas by speaking in one breath of the connection between Gen.1-11 and Gen.12ff., though they ought to be kept separate. In terms of method a distinction would need to be made between the redaction-critical assessment, where moreover the 'Yahwist' has recently become a problematical factor (cf. R.Rendtorff, *Das überlieferungsgeschichtliche Problem des Pentateuch*, BZAW 147, 1977; H.H.Schmid, *Der sogenannte Jahwist*, Zürich 1976), and the independent significance of the creation narratives. – In this connection cf. also H.Werner, *Uraspekte menschlichen Lebens nach Texten aus Gen 2-11*, ExBib V, Göttingen 1971; A.H.J.Gunneweg, 'Schuld ohne Vergebung?', *EvTh* 36, 1976, 2-14 (the pre-Yahwistic polytheistic stage of creation narratives saw human destiny as an irrational doom, whereas the Yahwistic stage sees 'wanting to be like God' as human guilt); J.Illies, *Der Mensch in der Schöpfung*, Zurich 1977.

The primeval history expresses the fact that Israel, too, used the forms of expression of an ancient Near Eastern culture to tell of the origins and thus of the permanent ordering of the world, humanity and the peoples in it, at the same time assuring itself of their permanence. In contrast to its environment, it did not do this in the light of a polytheistic view of the world but in terms of one which laid great stress on the contrast between world and creator (cf. esp. Craigie, *CJT* 1970, above 134). Thus the biblical creation narratives in no way fall outside the category of mythical discourse (*pace* Gunneweg, *EvTh*, 1976, who identifies 'myth' with the pre-Yahwistic strata of the creation narratives).

We may rightly be sceptical about O.H.Steck's view (*KuD* 1977 [above 137], 281, cf. *Welt und Umwelt* [above 137], 53, 86ff.) that a total perspective on the world as nature was not yet grasped in Israel before it became a state. That would be an excessive conclusion to draw from what is in fact later evidence and is therefore also stamped by Canaanite thought-forms. In this point, as in many respects, a verdict of not-proven is more appropriate towards the thinking of an earlier period.

In connection with the function of myth in primal history reference should also be made to the notable contribution from the school of British linguistic philosophy which has been formulated by D.D.Evans, *The Logic of Self-Involvement. A Philosophical Study of Everyday Language about God as Creator*, London 1963, starting from the theory of 'performative' language put forward by J.L.Austin, *How to Do Things with Words*, ed. J.O.Urmsson, Oxford 1962. According to this, the language used in the Bible to speak of creation and God as creator is a language of self-implication, in two ways: when God speaks the creative word, at the same time he expresses his own obligation to preserve creation (157), just as conversely the human word about creation as an answer implies an acknowledgement of an obligation too (158). Or again, God's creative word is expressive in respect of God in that God reveals his glory and majesty in the work of creation (174ff.); in respect of man it is impressive, calling forth the human answer in praise and reverence (for Evans' theory cf. also J.Ladrière, *L'articulation du sens. Discours scientifique et parole de foi*, Paris/Neuchâtel/Brussels 1970, 99-150).

In the transition from performative to reflexive language these considerations also lead back to the function of myth which Ladrière describes from his cosmological perspective in the light of its pedagogical and ground-laying function: myth is pedagogical in the way in which it transcends the visible world in the direction of a unity of the cosmos (which is already presupposed). At the same time, it is a way of thinking about the constitution of the world: it answers the question of meaning by taking men back to the dimension of the original by telling stories about origins.

Ladrière's demonstration that in this sense (as a conceptual *a priori*) a myth underlies any intellectual theory (even Newtonian mechanics or relativistic physics) is impressive. However, it falls outside our theme.

Finally, reference should be made to the possibility that the dimension of myth also had a far greater significance for the Old Testament understanding of history than has hitherto been thought conceivable under the influence of the demythologizing debate and the well-known contrast between myth and history which arose from it (cf. e.g. Wright, *The Old Testament against its Environment* [above 73], 20ff.). The dilemma which emerged here as a result of the schematic approaches leading to it was evident e.g. in H.P.Müller, who (in Krecher/Müller [above 113]) on the one hand follows Gunkel's definition of myth as 'narratives about the gods' (31 and n.59) and on the other hand detects a mythical depth-dimension in the historical accounts of the Old Testament itself which is formed by the reference of all historical interpretation to God. He therefore coins the term 'salvation historico-myth' (32, etc.). F.M.Cross, Jr ('The Divine Warrior in Israel's Early Cult', in *Biblical Motifs*, ed. A.Altmann, Cambridge, Mass 1966, 11-30) had noted that in the Israelite presentation of salvation history (bound up as it was with the cult), the mythical element keeps breaking through. L.Clapham ('Mythopoeic Antecedents of the Biblical World-View and Their Transformation in Early Israelite Thought', *Magnalia Dei. The Mighty Acts of God... G.E.Wright*, Garden City, NY 1976, 108-19) continues Cross's observations and asserts that the earliest salvation-historical traditions in the Pentateuch already build on the mythical conception of Yahweh as the warrior king with the use of mythical imagery and that in the time of the monarchy the cosmic-universal dimensions of this group of notions again comes to the fore. Here Clapham sees an indisputably strong influence from mythical conceptions outside Israel. We could add that N.K.Gottwald (*The Tribes of Yahweh* [above 120], 679ff.) derives the specific character of Yahwistic belief, various aspects of which he describes, solely from the distinctive feature of its exclusive reference to a single 'high God', Yahweh (for the sociological basis of his arguments cf. my *Problems of Biblical Theology*, I). What is said about the only possible 'centre' of the Old Testament (above 131-3) should be compared with this. What we have already ascertained about attempts to define the character of Yahwistic belief in the light of its unique understanding of history is also confirmed from this side: 'The usual contrast between "myth" and "history" seems to be a too simple manner of juxtaposing the two world-views in question' (*Magnalia Dei*, 111). Clapham sees the decisive peculiarity of Old Testament faith only in the transcendence of Yahweh over against the gods of the polytheistic system, who in the last resort remain embodiments of aspects of nature (116). From here we get an exactly opposed view of the relationship between the dimension of creation and that of the historical action of Yahweh in the faith of Israel to that presented by von Rad: that Yahweh was the creator was the presupposition for Israel in its acts of liberation, and not vice versa (thus recently G.M.Landes, *USQR* 1978 [above 135]).

Clearly Old Testament theology so far has also been far too simplistic over the question of a possible mythical dimension to history and has fallen victim to a false dogmatic dialectic. So far, it has yet to take up the promptings towards a new approach which can already be found in modern research into the history of religions. Thus W.C.Smith ('The Study of Religion and the Study of the Bible', *JAAR* 39, 1971, [131-49] 138f.) speaks of the high price which our culture has to pay for its inability to remythologize (!) and comments: 'Myth and history can be re-integrated by the modern intellect, perhaps, by pondering the role of myth in human history... The mythical, far from contrasting any longer with the historical, can nowadays be seen as what has made human history human.' The predominant functions of myth in narrative and as a basic foundation demonstrated by Kirk (above 162) also assign it a prominent place, particularly in historical tradition (even that of the Old Testament).

Similarly, the historian of religion W.Beltz can give the sub-title 'Biblische Mythologie' to his book *Gott und die Götter*, Berlin/Weimar 1975, Düsseldorf 1977, Munich 1980 (dtv 1523) =ET *God and the Gods*, Harmondsworth 1983, in which he discusses all the texts of the Old Testament which 'provide information about the miraculous action of a god towards the world and man' (33). Here not only the creation narratives of Genesis but the whole salvation-historical and miraculous account of the Bible down to the New Testament are classified as 'myth' in the positive sense.

H.P.Müller (*TZ* 1975 [above 162]; id., 'Zum alttestamentlichen Gebrauch mythischer Rede', *Religiöse Grunderfahrungen*, ed. W.Strolz, Freiburg 1977, 67-93) has recently argued in a similar way. Of course his programme for a 'post-critical recovery of the mythical' (*TZ* 1975, 10; *Grunderfahrungen*, 88) considers with critical detachment ('irony of faith') its continued rationalistic acceptance in structuralism and hermeneutics (faithful to Bultmann's warning against 'objectification', cf. *TZ* 1975, 10); however, he sees in the mythical the possibility of a return to an order which shows itself in a 'transparency of transcendence in the objective' which cannot be ascertained and confirmed rationally, but is perceived aesthetically.

3. Wisdom

This brings us very close, in a modern context, to the third sphere in which the theme of creation can be found in the Old Testament: Israelite wisdom.

Alt, A., 'Die Weisheit Salomos', *TLZ* 76, 1951, 139-44 = *Kleine Schriften* II, Munich (1953) ²1959, 90-99 = ET 'Solomonic Wisdom', in *Studies in Ancient Israelite Wisdom*, ed. J.L.Crenshaw, New York 1976, 102-12; Bauer-Kayatz, C., *Einführung in die alttestamentliche Weisheit*, BS 55, Stuttgart 1969; Baumgartner, W., *Israelitische und Altorientalische Weisheit*, Tübingen 1933; id., 'The Wisdom Literature', in *The Old Testament and Modern Study*, ed. H.H.Rowley, Oxford 1951, reprinted 1961, 210-37; Blenkinsopp, J., *Wisdom and Law in the Old Testament*, Oxford 1983; Brueggemann, W., 'The Triumphalist Tendency in Exegetical History', *JAAR* 38, 1970, 367-80, esp. 375f.; id., *In Man We Trust: The Neglected Side of Biblical Faith*, Richmond, Va 1972 (cf. also the review by M.Fishbane, *JBL* 93, 1974, 457-9); id., 'Scripture and an Ecumenical Life-Style. A Study in Wisdom Literature', *Int* 24, 1970, 3-19; Brunner, H., 'Gerechtigkeit als Fundament des Throns', *VT* 8, 1958, 426-8; id., 'Die Weisheitsliteratur', *HO* 1, 1952, 90-110; Bryce, G.E., 'Omen-Wisdom in Ancient Israel', *JBL* 94, 1975, 19-37; Cazelles, H., 'Bible, sagesse, science', *RSR* 48, 1960, 40-54; Collins, J., 'The Biblical Precedent for Natural Theology', *JAAR Suppl.* 45, 1977, 35-62 (abstract *JAAR* 45, 1977, 70); Crenshaw, J.L., 'Method in Determining Wisdom Influence upon "Historical" Literature', *JBL* 88, 1969, 129-42 = *Studies*, ed. Crenshaw, 481-94; id., 'Prolegomenon', ibid., 1-60, with bibliography; id., *Prophetic Conflict*, BZAW 124, Berlin 1971 (excursus B: '*esa* and *dabar*: The Problem of Authority/Certitude in Wisdom and Prophetic Literature', 116-23); id., 'Wisdom', in J.H.Hayes (ed.), *Old Testament Form Criticism*, San Antonio 1974, 225-64; id., 'In Search of Divine Presence: Some Remarks Preliminary to a Theology of Wisdom', *RExp* 74, 1977, 353-69; id., *Old Testament Wisdom*, Atlanta, Ga and London 1983; Duesberg, H., *Les scribes inspirés*, Maredsous 1966; Fichtner, J., *Die altorientalische Weisheit in ihrer israelitisch-jüdischen Ausprägung*, Giessen 1933; id., 'Zum Problem Glaube und Geschichte in der israelitischen Weisheitsliteratur', *TLZ* 76, 1951, 145-50 = *Gottes Weisheit*, AzT II, 3, Stuttgart 1965, 9-17; Fohrer, G., *sophia*, *TWNT* VII, 476-

96 = *TDNT* VII, 476-96 = *Studies*, ed. Crenshaw, 63-83; Galling, K., *Die Krise der Aufklärung in Israel*, Mainz 1952; Gemser, B., 'The Spiritual Structure of Biblical Aphoristic Wisdom', *HeB* 21, 1962, 3-10 = id., *Adhuc loquitur*, ed. A.van Selms and A.S.van der Woude, Leiden 1968, 138-49; Gerstenberger, E., *Wesen und Herkunft des 'apodiktischen Rechts'*, WMANT 20, Neukirchen 1965; id., 'Zur alttestamentlichen Weisheit', *VF* 14, 1969, 28-44; id., 'Die Krisis der Weisheit bei Kohelet', in *Les Sagesses du Proche-Orient ancien. Colloque de Strasbourg 17-19 mai 1962*, Paris 1963, 139-51 = 'The Crisis of Wisdom in Koheleth', in J.L.Crenshaw (ed.), *Theodicy in the Old Testament*, Philadelphia and London 1983, 141-53; Gese, H., *Lehre und Wirklichkeit in der alten Weisheit*, Tübingen 1958; Gilbert, M. (ed.), *La Sagesse de l'Ancien Testament*, BETL 51, Paris/Gembloux/Louvain 1979; Golka, F.W., 'Die israelitische Weisheitsschule oder "des Kaisers neue Kleider"', *VT* 33, 1983, 257-70; Hermisson, H.-J., *Studien zur israelitischen Spruchweisheit*, WMANT 28, Neukirchen 1969; id., 'Observations on the Creation Theology in Wisdom', in *Israelite Wisdom... Essays in Honor of S.Terrien*, Missoula 1978, 43-57; id., 'Weisheit und Geschichte', *Festschrift von Rad*, 1971 (above 60), 136-54; Hoppe, L.J., 'Biblical Wisdom: A Theology of Creation', *Listening* 14, 1979, 196-203; Humbert, P., *Recherches sur les sources égyptiennes de la littérature sapientale d'Israël*, Neuchâtel 1929; Jacob, E., 'Wisdom and Religion in Sirach', *Essays... Terrien*, 247-60; Kaiser, O., *Der Mensch unter dem Schicksal. Studien zur Geschichte, Theologie und Gegenwartsbedeutung der Weisheit*, BZAW, Berlin 1984; Kidner, D., 'Wisdom Literature of the Old Testament', in *New Perspectives on the Old Testament*, ed. J.B.Payne, Waco, Tex. 1970, 117-31; Lang, B., *Die weisheitliche Lehrrede*, SBS 54, Stuttgart 1972; id., *Frau Weisheit*, Düsseldorf 1975; id., *Schule und Unterricht im alten Israel*, in *La Sagesse...*, ed. Gilbert (see above), 186-201 = id., *Wie wird man Prophet in Israel?*, Düsseldorf 1980, 104-19; Leveque, J., 'Le contrepoint théologique apporté par la réflexion sapientelle', in *Questions disputées de l'Ancien Testament*, BETL 33, Louvain 1974, 183-202; Mack, B.L., 'Wisdom, Myth and Mythology', *Int* 24, 1970, 46-60; McKane, W., *Prophets and Wise Men*, SBT 44, London 1965, reprinted 1983; McKenzie, J.L., 'Reflections on Wisdom', *JBL* 86, 1967, 1-9; Maillot, A., 'La sagesse dans l'Ancien Testament', *ETR* 51, 1976, 333-49; Marböck, J., *Weisheit im Wandel*, BBB 37, Bonn 1971; id.,

'Gesetz und Weisheit', *BZ* 20, 1976, 1-21; Martin-Achard, R., 'Remarques sur la tradition sapientale d'Israël', *Bulletin du Centre Prot. d'Etudes* 25, 1973, 14-24; Meinhold, H., *Die Weisheit Israels in Spruch, Sage und Dichtung*, Leipzig 1908; Morgan, D.F., 'Wisdom and Prophets', in *Studia Biblica* 1978 (see above), 209-44; id., *Wisdom in the Old Testament Traditions*, Atlanta, Ga./ Oxford 1981; Murphy, R.E., 'Assumptions and Problems in Old Testament Wisdom Research', *CBQ* 29, 1967, 407-18; id., 'The Hebrew Sage and Openness to the World', in *Christian Action and Openness to the World*, Villanova Univ. Symposium II, III 1970, 219-44; id., 'The Interpretation of Old Testament Wisdom Literature', *Int* 23, 1969, 289-301; id., 'The Wisdom Literature of the Old Testament', *Conc* 20, 1965, 126-40; id., 'Wisdom and Yahwism', in *No Famine in the Land... Studies J.L.McKenzie*, Claremont 1975, 117-26; id., 'Wisdom Theses', in *Wisdom and Knowledge. Festschrift J.Papin* II, Philadelphia 1976, 187-200; id., 'Wisdom -Theses and Hypotheses', *Essays... Terrien*, 35-42; id., 'Israel's Wisdom: A Biblical Model of Salvation', *StMiss* 30, 1981, 1-43; id., 'Hebrew Wisdom', *JAOS* 101, 1981, 21-34; Perdue, L.G., *Wisdom and Cult*, SBL.DS 30, Missoula 1977; Preuss, H.D., 'Alttestamentliche Weisheit in christlicher Theologie?', *Questions disputées*, 165-81; id., 'Erwägungen zum theologischen Ort alttestamentlicher Weisheitsliteratur', *EvTh* 30, 1970, 393-417; id., 'Das Gottesbild der älteren Weisheit Israels', in *Studies in the Religion of Ancient Israel*, SVT XXIII, Leiden 1972, 117-45; Priest, J.F., 'Humanism, Skepticism, and Pessimism in Israel', *JAAR* 36, 1968, 311-26; de Pury, A., 'Sagesse et révélation dans l'Ancien Testament', *RTP* III, 27, 1977, 1-50; von Rad, G., 'Josephsgeschichte und ältere Chokma', SVT I, 1953, 120-7 = id., *Gesammelte Studien* I (above 59), 272-80 = ET 'The Joseph Narrative...', in *The Problem of the Hexateuch* (above 00), 292-300; id., 'Die ältere Weisheit Israels', *KuD* 2, 1956, 54-72; id., 'Glaube und Welterkenntnis' (above 110); id., 'Christliche Weisheit?', *EvTh* 31, 1971, 150-4 = id., *Gesammelte Studien* II (above 59), 267-71; id., 'Natur- und Welterkenntnis im Alten Testament', in id., *Gottes Wirken in Israel*, ed. O.H.Steck, Neukirchen-Vluyn 1974, 119-40; id., 'Weisheit in Israel', ibid., 230-7; id., *Weisheit in Israel*, Neukirchen 1970 = ET *Wisdom in Israel*, Nashville and London 1972 (cf. also Crenshaw J.L., *RSR* 2, 1976, 6-12; Timm, H., ' "Das weite Herz". Religiöses Philosophieren in Israel', *ZTK* 74, 1977, 224-37; Zimmerli, W.,

EvTh 31, 1971, 680-95); Rendtorff, R., *EK* 1976 (above 110); id., *Festschrift W. Zimmerli* (above 72), 344-53; Richter, W., *Recht und Ethos. Versuch einer Ortung des weisheitlichen Mahnspruches*, SANT 15, Munich 1966; Ringgren, H., *Word and Wisdom*, Diss.Lund 1947; Rylaarsdam, J.C., *Revelation in Jewish Wisdom Literature*, Chicago 1946; M.Saebø, 'Israels visdomsdiktning – et aktuelt forskningstema', in *Ordene og Ordet* (above 136), 166-79; Schmid, H.H., *Wesen und Geschichte der Weisheit*, BZAW 101, Berlin 1966 (cf. also Harvey, J., 'Wisdom Literature and Biblical Theology, I', *BTB* 1, 1971, 308-19); id., *Gerechtigkeit* (above 136); id., *šalom. 'Frieden' im Alten Orient und im Alten Testament*, SBS 51, Stuttgart 1971; id., *ZTK* 1973 (above 136) = *Altorientalische Welt* (above 136), 9-30; id., 'Jahweglaube und altorientalisches Weltordnungsdenken', ibid., 31-63; id., 'Altorientalisch-alttestamentliche Weisheit und ihr Verhältnis zur Geschichte', ibid., 64-90; id., 'Heiliger Krieg und Gottesfrieden im Alten Testament', ibid., 91-120; id., 'Altorientalische Welt in der alttestamentlichen Theologie', ibid., 145-64; Scott, R.B.Y., *The Way of Wisdom in the Old Testament*, London 1971; id., 'The Study of Wisdom Literature', *Int* 24, 1970, 20-45; id., 'Wise and Fool, Righteous and Wicked', *Studies in the Religion*, SVT XXIII, 146-65; Sheppard, G.T., *Wisdom as a Hermeneutical Construct. A Study in the Sapientializing of the Old Testament*, BZAW 151, Berlin 1980; Toombs, L.E., 'Old Testament Theology and the Wisdom Literature', *JBR* 23, 1955, 193-96; Towner, W.S., 'The Renewed Authority of Old Testament Wisdom for Contemporary Faith', in G.W.Coats and B.O.Long (eds.), *Canon and Authority*, Philadelphia 1977, 132-47; Whybray, R.N., *The Intellectual Tradition in the Old Testament*, BZAW 135, Berlin 1974; id., *Wisdom in Proverbs*, SBT 45, London 1965; id., 'Wisdom Literature in the Reigns of David and Solomon', in *Studies in the Period of David and Solomon...*, ed. Ishida (above 150), 13-26; Wood, J., *Wisdom Literature. An Introduction*, London 1967; Ziener, G., 'Die altorientalische Weisheit als Lebenskunde. Israels neues Verständnis und Kritik der Weisheit', in *Wort und Botschaft*, ed. J.Schreiner (above), 258-71; Zimmerli, W., 'Zur Struktur der alttestamentlichen Weisheit', *ZAW* 51, 1933, 177-204 = 'Concerning the Structure of Old Testament Wisdom', in *Studies*, ed. Crenshaw (see above 168), 175-207; id., 'Ort und Grenzen der Weisheit im Rahmen der alttestamentlichen Theologie', in *Les sagesses du Proche-*

Orient ancien. Colloque de Strasbourg, Paris 1963, 121-37 =
'The Place and Limit of Wisdom in the Framework of the
Old Testament Theology', *SJT* 17, 1964, 146-58 = *Studies*, ed.
Crenshaw, 314-26; id., *Grundriss* (above 54f.), ch.18, 136-46 =
ET 155-66; id., *TRE* VI (above 2), 450f.; '*ḥakam*', *TWAT* II, 920-
44 = *TDOT* IV, 364-85 (H.P.Müller and M.Krause); '*ḥkm* be
wise', *THAT* I, 557-67 (M. Saebø).

For a long time the sphere of 'wisdom' in the Old Testament was
completely in the shade as far as exegetes and, even more, Old
Testament theologies, were concerned. Apart from the treatment
of introductory questions to the Old Testament writings which
are usually counted as 'wisdom' (the 'wisdom literature'), hardly
anything is to be found in the earlier secondary literature on these
parts of the Old Testament, even if the earlier view, that this is all
very late material within the Old Testament, had been abandoned
(cf. e.g. the extremely brief contribution by W.Baumgartner to the
collected volume *The Old Testament and Modern Study* [above
168]). It was hardly supposed that the wisdom writings could have
any possible theological significance. In addition to the general
theological climate, which was not disposed to accept any other
perspective, a contributory factor was the affinity of Old Testament
wisdom to Egyptian wisdom, a view already put forward in the 1920s
by Gunkel ('Ägyptische Parallelen zum Alten Testament', *ZDMG*
63, 1909, 531-9), which was confirmed above all by the sensational
publication of the *Teaching of Amenemope* in 1923 (E.A.W.Budge,
Facsimiles of Hieratic Papyri in the British Museum, second series,
London 1923, plates 1-14).

The theory that Prov.22.17-24.22 is dependent on the *Teaching
of Amenemope*, first put forward by A.Erman ('Eine ägyptische
Quelle der Sprüche Salomos', SPAW.PH 15, 1924, 86-93), and
widely discussed (for the literature cf. B.Gemser, *Sprüche
Salomos*, HAT 16, Tübingen 1937, ²1963, 13f.) was given a
foundation which takes in the whole wisdom literature of both
areas above all by P.Humbert – cf. also W.O.E.Oesterley, *The
Wisdom of Egypt and the Old Testament*, London 1927;
Baumgartner, *Israelitische und altorientalische Weisheit*;
E.Würthwein, *Die Weisheit Ägyptens und das Alte Testament*,
Marburg 1960 = id., *Wort und Existenz* (above 40), 197-216;
Gese, 'Lehre'; G.E.Bryce, *A Legacy of Wisdom: The Egyptian*

Contribution to the Wisdom of Israel, Lewisburg/Cranbury, NJ/ London 1979.

A development which was so obviously not a special feature of the Old Testament – and since then it has become increasingly evident that ancient Near Eastern wisdom was an international phenomenon (cf. e.g. *Les Sagesses du Proche-Orient Ancient* [above 171f.]; J.J.A. van Dijk, *La sagesse Suméro-Accadienne*, Leiden 1953; E.I.Gordon, *Sumerian Proverbs*, Philadelphia 1959; W.G.Lambert, *Babylonian Wisdom Literature*, Oxford 1960, reprinted 1967, etc.) seemed to be almost irrelevant to the specific interests of Old Testament theology, especially since so much stress was laid on the distinctive character of the Old Testament (cf. above 113–15, 118–20 and esp. on Wisdom, de Pury, *RTP* 1977).

W.Zimmerli (*ZAW* 1933) has given classical expression to a view which has long been typical of the assessment of wisdom (though see now the preface to *Gottes Offenbarung*, 88). According to this the central concerns of wisdom have an exclusively anthropocentric and eudaemonistic orientation (178, 203): like the old experiential wisdom of the Egyptian court from which it derives, it is solely concerned with the question how one can get on best in the world. Its admonitions are not supported by any kind of authority other than impersonal experience (187), 'it retains its focal point in the individual, unhistorical man, whose happiness it seeks' (178). Nor does it know of any ordering in which man has been placed: 'It is the autonomous man, not controlled by any previous ordinances and made to hear, who means to shape and control the world freely and in his own right' (179), whereas the people of the Old Testament immediately know themselves to be members of the covenant people. Just as the precepts of wisdom are not really binding commandments but advice which appeals to the reason of the hearer (188), so too wisdom sees man's relationship to God (in those passages in which there is mention of Yahweh, the fear of Yahweh and the blessing of Yahweh) from a human perspective even when the creative power of Yahweh is not infringed (191); here too, 'human interest is expressed in veiled form as being finally normative' (192). Of course Ecclesiastes, too, knows the existence of a divinely given order, but the fact that he accedes to it of necessity is a carefully considered calculation: 'But because Ecclesiastes does not want to die, of necessity he goes the way of the fear of Yahweh' (203). This conflict does not exist for earlier wisdom, with its harmonizing thought: its view is 'that man's real claim to happiness is fully satisfied by his readiness to fit in with the divine ordering of the world' (ibid.).

This estimation of earlier wisdom as being purely utilitarian and secular (which is to be found similarly in G.E.Wright, *God who Acts* [above 73], 102-5, and above all in W.McKane, 1965, 48ff. – cf. also his commentary *Proverbs*, OTL, London and Philadelphia 1970; W.Brueggemann in particular claimed it in this sense during the period of the secular gospel movement in the USA [cf. above 143f., especially in *In Man we Trust*, cf. above 168 and below 175]) and as 'universally human' (a negative evaluation) – without reference to the specific elements of the faith of Israel (Fichtner, *Glaube und Geschichte*, 145/9; Zimmerli, *Ort und Grenze*, is more restrained) certainly contributed to the fact that wisdom occupies so small a space in accounts of Old Testament theology – even if, above all since Fichtner (1933), the view prevailed that in its later expressions in the Old Testament wisdom had been 'Yahwized' (cf. e.g. Rylaarsdam). The almost exclusive orientation on the sphere of the historical and prophetic traditions of the Old Testament, because they were judged to be 'specifically Israelite' (thus e.g. Fohrer, 'Die zeitliche und überzeitliche Bedeutung des Alten Testaments', *EvTh* 9, 1949/50, 447-60, saw the view of the world held in magic and in wisdom as being overcome by the distinctive character of Yahwistic belief, especially as put forward by the prophets), had an even more marked effect. One example of this is again the minor role accorded by G. von Rad to 'Israel's wisdom deriving from experience' (earlier wisdom) and 'theological wisdom' (later wisdom) in his *Theology* (I⁴, 430-67 = ET I, 418-452). There it is right at the periphery. Von Rad's view here is that earlier wisdom deals with theological themes only to a very limited degree when it undertakes to fix the external and internal ordinances by which human life is supported and of which human beings have to take account (I⁴, 448 = ET 434f.). This is primarily a 'wholly secular pursuit' (I⁴, 450 = ET 436), even if it cannot be disputed that for Israel Yahweh of course stood behind these ordinances (ibid.). In arguing that the direct mention of the name of Yahweh in some proverbs represents a later 'theologizing' of wisdom which took place at some indeterminate point, von Rad also repeats a frequently heard judgment, as when he thinks that 'theological' wisdom in the strict sense can be found only in post-exilic wisdom (esp.Prov.1-9), in which wisdom itself is understood as a means of revelation (I⁴, 454ff. = ET 441ff.).

However, von Rad also has a special theory about the *Sitz im Leben* of earlier Israelite wisdom, which can be pursued through various of his works, beginning with *The Problem of the Hexateuch* [above 59]). This theory has become known under the catchphrase 'Solomonic Enlightenment'; in his late work *Wisdom in Israel* von Rad has once again dealt in detail with the question. According to him the early monarchy was the time when wisdom was principally cultivated at the court (as an art form, cf. *KuD* 1956, 62ff. – there is also a popular proverbial wisdom). This was the time of a secularization which had taken the place of an earlier period of 'pan-sacralism' (M.Buber), the time of the patriarchs, Moses and the wilderness, and was characterized by an enlightened spirituality (*Wisdom*, 82ff. = ET 59ff; cf. already 'Joseph Narrative', 120/272ff., ET = 292ff.). However, even the 'enlightened' wisdom teachers will have held together the autonomy of the reality of this-worldly experience and its ordering with belief in the omnipotence of Yahweh (thus Prov.16.9; 19.16,21; 20.24; 21.30f.; cf. already *KuD* 1956, 70ff., and above all *Wisdom*, 131ff. = ET 97ff., 'The Limits of Wisdom'); indeed experiences of God, too, belonged in this context (*Wisdom* 85ff. = ET 61ff.). Von Rad thinks that he can also discover this theological attitude of enlightened wisdom in the Joseph story (Gen.45.5ff. and above all Gen.50.20); its climax is that God has all the threads in his hand, even if this interweaving of divine guidance and human action remains a complete mystery ('Joseph Narrative', 123/276f. = ET 298). Like von Rad, W.Brueggemann (*In Man We Trust*) saw a 'theological revolution' in the early period of the monarchy; indeed for him David was the embodiment of the enlightened man, taking responsibility for himself (29ff., cf. also Brueggemann's earlier articles [above 168]; for criticism cf. Fishbane [above 168]). In this sense the time of David is a period of spiritual maturity, of 'secularization'; now man receives a central place in the world (with more caution, Towner, too, seeks to use biblical wisdom to justify a modern, 'secular' view of the world in which man has the freedom to act but God remains in the background as the one who holds this order in being). In particular, the saying that the fear of the Lord is the beginning of wisdom, which occurs in different forms (Prov.1.7; 9.10; 15.33; Ps.111.10; Job.28.28), seems to von Rad to express the general attitude of earlier wisdom as well (*Wisdom*, 91ff. = ET 65ff.). 'With this astounding statement von Rad has baptized Israel's wisdom thinking', observes Crenshaw at this point (*RSR* 1976 [above 170],

7). Von Rad can put it in quite general terms, 'that the wisdom practised in Israel was a response made by a Yahwism confronted with specific experiences of the world'. He affirms quite decisively: 'This wisdom is, therefore, at all events to be regarded as a form of Yahwism, although – as a result of the unusual nature of the tasks involved – an unusual theological form and, in the structure of its statements, very different from the other forms in which Yahwism reveals itself. But Yahwism was thoroughly imbued with this specific unique quality from the very beginning' (*Wisdom*, 390 = ET 307). Evidently von Rad is here going a decisive step forward from the *Theology*, where he had followed the theory of 'secular' wisdom more closely in the case of early wisdom. Zimmerli's last remarks about the theological context of wisdom (*Grundriss* [above 54f.], ch.18; *TRE* VI [above 2], 450f.) take a similar direction. With von Rad he attaches central significance to talk of the 'fear of Yahweh', in the case of earlier wisdom as well. However, as is particularly clear in *TRE* VI, the focal point of his argument lies in Ecclesiastes and Job, whose testimony he claims for the view that wisdom is to be understood theologically in connection with the 'centre' of the Old Testament, which he sees as being Yahweh, made known to Israel through his historical action and in his 'name', whom Israel therefore also recognized as its creator.

Evidently the group of didactic poems which includes Prov.8; Job 28; Sir.28 plays an important role for von Rad's last view; in them wisdom appears as a personified entity in connection with the theme of creation. In the case of Prov.8 von Rad is not uninfluenced by the results of the work of his pupil C.Kayatz (now Bauer-Kayatz), who had drawn attention to Egyptian parallels in which Maat appears in similar personified form (C.Kayatz, *Studien zu Proverbien 1-9*, WMANT 22, Neukirchen 1966, 76ff., 93ff.; cf. von Rad, *Wisdom*, 199f. and n.8 = ET 153 and n.8 – recently also Lang, *Frau Weisheit*, 168ff.: as a personification in the context of didactic poetry). While von Rad does not want actually to challenge the usual late dating of Prov.8, he now thinks that conceptions from very much earlier in the tradition can be found there (cf. recently also Lang, *Lehrrede*, 46ff., with arguments for a possibly early date). Here and elsewhere in wisdom von Rad sees the theme of creation playing a significant role (*Wisdom*, 209ff., 377ff. = ET 157ff., 296ff.), and starting from Prov.1.24-31 and Job 12.7ff. he sees this role as the call of a self-revelation of creation which now takes on a revelatory quality of its own alongside the traditions of salvation history. It is a 'primeval revelation' (ibid., 227 = ET 175) relating to the creaturely reality of the world and man and thus referring back to the predication of creation in the hymn. Now von Rad claims that precisely here – again in the sphere of wisdom – we have a specifically Israelite characteristic, for 'the idea of a testimony emanating from creation is attested only in Israel. The doctrine of the primeval revelation with its distinctive element... stands, therefore, on a genuinely Israelite basis.' It is interesting that at this point von Rad is criticized by W.Zimmerli (*EvTh* 1971 [above 170f.], 693f. – there is also a similar basic attitude in 'Ort und Grenze der Weisheit') . Zimmerli fails to find in the talk of a 'primeval revelation' a reference to the claim of revelation in the 'law and prophets', i.e. to 'the mention of creation oriented on the history of Yahweh with Israel'; in other words he does not want to join von Rad in taking this most important step beyond von Rad's earlier view, which was oriented on history.

Von Rad (*Wisdom*, 373 and n.9 = ET 294 and n.9) resolutely rejects the view that history writing recognizes this mystery (his pupil Hermisson had claimed that the Yahwist was influenced by wisdom, *Studien*, 126ff., 133; in connection with the so-called Succession narrative Hermisson rightly thinks that he is continuing the beginning made by his teacher [*Weisheit und Geschichte*]).

However, it is questionable whether the step can in fact be taken in this direction, for von Rad pursues his way to some degree within his own system, and above all does not take seriously enough the relationship between Israelite wisdom and the ancient Near East. 'Von Rad's fundamental thesis that wisdom is a branch of Yahwism flies in the face of much sapiential scholarship' (Crenshaw, *RSR*, 1976 [above 170], 8). Crenshaw, for example, sharply criticizes the theory of a 'Solomonic enlightenment' preceded by 'pan-sacralism' (*RSR* 1976, 8ff., id., 'Prolegomenon', *Studies*, above 168, 16ff.). He is also certainly right that the collection in Prov.1-9 does not fit von Rad's system. Even if the date of its origin can no longer be put relatively late with as much confidence as before, it (along with the other passages chosen by von Rad) represents such a developed form of artistic poetry that it cannot be taken as representative of the whole gamut of wisdom statements.

Von Rad remained remarkably unaffected by the insights into the central presuppositions of wisdom thinking in the light of its international connections which were achieved during his lifetime. He even believed that he had to reject them firmly in the light of his own approach, in the interests of defending the special character of the Old Testament. As early as 1956 (*KuD* 1956, 60f.) we read: 'For Israel the world was not a stable and harmonious organic order which as it were embraced everything, whether organic or inorganic, and which was regarded so much as a whole that one could look for its ultimate determining principle. Israel never found its way to the conception of a world thus permeated by unchangeable laws. The event in which it found itself was too mysterious and too much a domain under the sway of Yahweh for that.' The same view is still expressed in *Wisdom in Israel*. Here von Rad sees the special character of Israel's knowledge, in contrast to the Ionian natural philosophers – he also makes explicit mention of the conceptions of Egyptian wisdom (with its concept of Maat) – in the fact that Israel did *not* arrive at any understanding of a cosmos and its ordering (71f.). All the ordinances of which wisdom speaks thus have only a partial character.

Basically, then, both the old eudaemonistic and extremely individualistic interpretation of wisdom, and the specifically Yahwistic interpretation of wisdom put forward by von Rad, are ruled out by the insights which have now been available for some time into the character of the order to which wisdom refers in its rules of life and admonitions. H. Gese did pioneering work here (referring back to insights in A.de Buck, 'Het religieus karakter der oudste egyptische wijsheit', *NThT* 21, 1932, 322-49, and H.Frankfort, *Ancient Egyptian Religion*, New York 1948, reprinted 1961). He made a closer investigation of the Egyptian concept of Maat as a designation for the world order and rejected the 'erroneous eudaemonistic interpretation' of Egyptian wisdom teaching (*Lehre*, 7ff.), stressing the divine character of Maat, its autonomy and validity (1ff.). His subsequent comments on the conceptions of order underlying early Israelite wisdom (Prov.10-22.16; 25-29; 22.17-24.22 [without 22.17-23.11, see above]) were decisive for the Old Testament; here it proved that Israel for the most part shared the idea of order in ancient Near Eastern wisdom. Thinking in a context of 'action and outcome' played a particular role here; in this connection Gese could refer to the preliminary work by J.Pedersen, *Israel*, above 118, I-II, 336-77; K.H.Fahlgren (*Ṣedāqā nahestehende und entgegengesetzte Begriffe im Alten Testament*, Uppsala 1932, extract also in K.Koch [ed.], *Um das Prinzip der Vergeltung in Religion und Recht des Alten Testaments*, WdF 125, Darmstadt 1972, 87-129), and K.Koch, 'Gibt es ein Vergeltungsdogma im Alten Testament?',

ZTK 52, 1955, 1-42 = id. [ed.], *Um das Prinzip der Vergeltung*, 130-80 = 'Is There a Doctrine of Retribution in the Old Testament?', in J.L.Crenshaw [ed.], *Theodicy in the Old Testament* [above 168], 57-87 – cf. also R.Knierim, *Die Hauptbegriffe für Sünde im Alten Testament*, Gütersloh 1965, 73ff.; von Rad, *Wisdom*, 165ff. = ET 128ff.). As these scholars have recognized, in wisdom thinking (and far beyond that) for a long time the predominant notion is that an action (good or evil) immediately produces consequences without the need of divine action (retribution). However, according to Gese, even in early Israelite wisdom there are references to a determinism which stresses the sovereign freedom of Yahweh who is ultimately bound to no order (*Lehre*, 45-50). An unspoilt concept of order cannot be found even in the earlier period of wisdom (cf. already Fichtner). Thinking in terms of action and outcome is then completely superseded in Job (which belongs to the late period of the Old Testament): while Job's friends put forward this orthodox teaching, the exemplary righteous man who suffers (in direct contrast to the Accadian-Sumerian paradigm of the hearing of a complaint [cf.62ff.], which is based on this order) is shown the freedom and faithfulness of the personal God who also transcends this order (70ff.).

H.H.Schmid has been most active in developing this line marked out by Gese. He began (*Wesen und Geschichte*) by attempting to understand wisdom primarily in existentialist categories (for the 'historicity' of wisdom cf. 80-2; he regarded a 'system' in wisdom as a late fossilization, 196ff.), but later oriented his understanding of wisdom on the idea of order in wisdom. In his book *Gerechtigkeit als Weltordnung* (above 136), on the basis of a number of preliminary studies (see the literature mentioned in 1.n.1) he argued that the term 'righteousness' (*ṣedeq/ṣedāqā*), with a wide range of reference (law, wisdom, nature and fertility, war, victory over enemies, cult and sacrifice, kingship) is the Hebrew designation for world order which corresponds to Egyptian Maat (and Sumerian *me*, 61ff.). Accordingly, the idea of order in the ancient Near East has to be seen as the background to righteousness in the Old Testament also. What is said of *ṣedeq/ṣedāqā* equally applies to a series of other concepts, the most important of which is *šālōm*, salvation, peace, to which H.H.Schmid has similarly devoted a monograph (SBS 51). Cf. most recently my 'Friedensverheissungen im Alten und im Neuen Testament', *FÜI* 62, 1979, 99-109, 147-53 and the further literature there.

In his collection of articles, *Altorientalische Welt in der alttesta-mentlichen Theologie* (above 136), Schmid brought together a series of contributions which draw the theological conclusions from his conceptual investigations. It is important that here the concept of creation occupies a central place; indeed Schmid can even describe the theology of creation as the overall horizon of biblical theology – this is the title of the first article (which I quote from the collected volume). For in the ancient Near East – and Israel shared fully in its thought – the ordering of creation did not just cover the sphere of the world and nature, but also that of the state and its legal ordering. In their preaching of judgment, the prophets begin from this order, which they see as having been violated by the people: the proclamation of salvation which appears particularly in post-exilic prophecy looks to the final restoration of this order. In the historical traditions, too, the connection between action and outcome which is central to this order (see above) is also a central theme. From this follows the conclusion 'that the dominant background to the thought and belief of the Old Testament is the idea of the all-embracing ordering of the world; that is, creation faith in the wider sense of the term; the creation faith which in some respects Israel shared with its environment' (11/21. J.L.Crenshaw, 'The Eternal Gospel, Eccl.3.11', in J.L.Crenshaw and J.T.Willis (eds.), *Essays in Old Testament Ethics, J.P.Hyatt in Memoriam*, New York 1974, [23-56] 32f. recognizes the idea of world order as the horizon of creation in wisdom, but he denies the significance of the *theme* of creation at least for earlier wisdom. Against the latter cf. Hoppe [above 169]). After similar comments have also been extended to the New Testament (cf. my *Problems of Biblical Theology*, ch. III), the conclusion which follows is diametrically opposed to the earlier view 'Belief in creation, that is, the belief that God has made and sustains the world with its manifold ordinances, is not a marginal theme of biblical theology but in essentials its main theme' (15/25).

The second contribution in the collected volume, 'Belief in Yahweh and the Notion of World Order in the Ancient Near East', continues the same line and seeks to defend it against objections. Of course the main objection must be that after rejecting the old view which saw revelation in history as the central, indeed almost the only, content of the Old Testament, Schmid has now fallen into a one-sided view on the opposite side. Therefore this second article seeks to loosen up the rather monolithic and rigid picture produced by the first (on this see Schmid himself, ibid., 31), depicting the historical development of the conceptions of order in Yahwistic belief from the nomadic stage, through the adaptation of Canaanite conceptions, down to the development of Israel's own specific conceptions of order. Behind this process Schmid sees above all tensions produced by the prophets, which in his view end up with a reorientation of the idea of order; this now has a theocentric stamp, in that a decisive differentiation between God and the world is introduced, giving rise to a new form of the idea of order which enabled Israel to overcome the crisis caused by the upheavals of the exile. Schmid thinks that he can discover yet another decisive reorientation at the period of pre-exilic prophecy (especially in Hosea, ibid., 50), namely in the basis of order. In Hosea the exodus from Egypt and the election of Israel in the wilderness take the place of the grounding of order on creation, which is usual elsewhere in the ancient Near East; this represents a specifically Israelite form of the conception of this order.

It is at this point, i.e. over the question of the relationship between the various areas of Old Testament thought, that the discussion will have to be continued: in other words, between the conception of order which is characteristic of wisdom (and not just wisdom) and the areas governed by the tradition of salvation history.

J.Halbe (' "Altorientalisches Weltordnungsdenken" und alttes-tamentliche Theologie', *ZTK* 76, 1979, 381-418) has criticized Schmid's approach from the perspective of system theory (following N.Luhmann et al.). However, on closer examination he is much nearer to Schmid than he thinks. Although he does not deny the presence of a conception of world order in Israel, he attacks the connection between the Israelite idea of world order and that of the rest of the Near East by distinguishing between the basic universal, anthropological phenomenon of the presence of a notion of order which can be universally established ('world order idea I') and the specific view which occurs from time to time ('world order idea II'). The idea of world order is developed specifically in Israel 'on the actual basis of experiences of the reality of Yahweh' (ibid., 403). He rejects the characterization of this order by Schmid as an order of creation, claiming that it has no foundation (410f.). However, here the semantic field of *ṣedeq, ṣ°dāqā, šālōm* and *'emet* needs to be examined more closely against its conceptual background; if that is done, one cannot simply ignore the insights into its cosmological background which have been gained not least by Schmid. Halbe does not go into that at all.

Schmid himself regards his work as a contribution to the discussion, which is why he deliberately presented it in a rather one-sided way (Preface, ibid., 7). At all events, we must recognize how he has again restored a central aspect of Old Testament thought to its due place. (For the contribution of U.Luck and H.Schmid to the question of a 'biblical theology' cf. my *Problems of Biblical Theology*, ch. III).

By contrast, Schmid's own attempts to define the relationship between thought based on order and thought based on history in the Old Testament are unsatisfactory. As a result, there will continue to be questions about his view that the decline of the old political order as a result of the exile and the crisis of the conceptions of order associated with it (going back to the promises to the patriarchs and the covenant) led to the main outlines of a theology of history (*Altorientalische Welt*, 77, cf. also 'Das alttestamentliche Verständnis von Geschichte in seinem Verhältnis zum gemeinorientalischen Denken', *WuD* 13, 1975, 9-21), because of his late dating of the Yahwist. Moreover, in terms of content, simply to arrange the thought forms one after the other is hardly a satisfactory answer to a problem to which we can probably do justice only by recognizing the juxtaposition of various different spheres of thought and tradition in the Old Testament.

In this context it is worth noting the comment by R.Rendtorff, *Festschrift Zimmerli* (above 72), that the understanding of history also begins from the notion of a continuity and that prophetic thinking is also interested in the regularity of Yahweh's action. Moreover, different spheres of life can also be found elsewhere in the Old Testament. For the problem cf. also F.E.Eakin, 'Wisdom, Creation and Covenant', *PRS* 4, 1977, 225-39. I have also made my own attempt to take both aspects into account in *Rechtfertigung im Horizont des Alten Testaments* (above 90).

Schmid's position has recently been taken up by J.L.Crenshaw ('Prolegomenon', 26ff.). He also goes back to Schmid's comments on the notion of order, central to the understanding of the world in wisdom, in which the concept of righteousness plays a central role, and to Gunkel's theories about the relationship between creation and chaos. According to Gunkel, the idea of creation in the Old

Testament is determined by the conception that the order originally instituted by the creator is constantly endangered by the powers of chaos, both human and divine (Gunkel, *Schöpfung und Chaos*, above 134). Accordingly, creation is a defence of the divine righteousness: Crenshaw bases this view e.g. on Job, where the theme of creation is closely connected with the problem of theodicy, and on Sirach.

> Sir.18.1 accurately reflects the idea of creation in Sirach: this is a defence of the righteousness of God deduced from the ordering of the world. As God has *a priori* divided the world into the spheres of good and evil, good and evil receive their appropriate place. Cf. also Marböck, *Weisheit im Wandel*, 149: the real aim of Ben Sira's comments about creation is 'to awaken trust and faith in view of the doubt and questions about a right and meaningful ordering of the world'.

However, Crenshaw's assertion at the end of his comments that in this way creation is again forced into a dependent function is evidently a misunderstanding; he claims that, instead of its being subordinated to salvation history, as in von Rad, its role is now to support belief in divine righteousness ('Prolegomenon', 34), if Schmid is right in thinking that righteousness is one of the designations for the world order itself. Crenshaw has evidently narrowed the concept again. However, in general Old Testament theology has not yet come to accord wisdom thinking a legitimate place within the Old Testament. There is still considerable fear of finding a new form of 'natural theology' here (cf. also J.Collins, 'The Biblical Precedent for Natural Theology', *JAAR* 45, 1977, 35-62). H.D.Preuss makes the clearest comments in this respect. Beginning from a deliberately dogmatic position (cf. also id., 'Das Alte Testament im Rahmen der Theologie als kirchlicher Wissenschaft', *DtPfrBl* 72, 1972, 356-60), he emphatically questions whether what is said by wisdom means anything to the contemporary Christian reader of the Old Testament. Preuss believes that to think in terms of action and outcome, which in his view is the 'central dogma' of wisdom, the 'sound world order' as the presupposition of its thought and the role assigned to Yahweh as creator and guarantor of this world order (cf. SVT XXIII) are a 'piece of natural theology' (*Questions disputées*, 174): with Job and Koheleth he sees a fatal crisis arising for this idea of order, because the sovereignty of Yahweh simply breaks the connection between action and outcome, 'and that means the failure of wisdom before Yahweh' (ibid., 175; for the whole question cf. above all *EvTh* 1970). In the light of the New Testament conception of the cross, according to which 'the cross of Christ also means that God may be believed to be near and benign even in the negative' (ibid., 174), no bridge can ever be built to the question of the connection between action and outcome.

It is impossible not to have fundamental doubts about this view. To put them in the form of a question: does not the message of the justification of the sinner which has come about through the representative suffering of Christ derive precisely from the validity of the correspondence between right action within the order willed by God and the salvation of the world, and is not the restoration of this order the eschatological goal of all divine action? The book of Job, too – which Preuss evidently does not take seriously enough – is part of the canon of wisdom: the central focus of its content is similarly on the validity of this order, in which, however, it is given a deeper answer to its problem than can happen in the popular understanding developed in the contribution of the friends to the discussion. An outward, mechanical connection between action and outcome in which human action is a direct barometer of man's moral attitude is taken to extremes by the speeches of God in Job 38ff. However, this solution, too, which preserves the sovereignty of Yahweh and incorporates the basic question contained in the paradigm of the hearing of a complaint (cf. Westermann, 'Aufbau' [above 140f.) into a reference to a hidden confirmation of order (for Job *is* a just man) gives an answer in the context of wisdom. That is also true, in a different way, of Koheleth. Precisely at this point questions are touched on which cannot be avoided in the context of a biblical theology. Preuss's recommendation that Christian theology 'must refuse to give Old Testament wisdom a place in its thinking' (ibid., 180) leads to a curtailing of the Old Testament witness, and like similar counsels of the past is to be rejected decisively.

The incorporation of wisdom into Old Testament theology remains a still unresolved task for the future to deal with.

W. Pannenberg ('Glaube und Wirklichkeit im Denken Gerhard von Rads', id. et al. (eds.), *Gerhard von Rad* [above 60], (37-54) 50, has described 'the tension between Israel's experience of a history of divine guidance and the alienation of wisdom from history' as 'the open problem' which von Rad 'has left behind not only for Old Testament scholarship but for theology generally'.

There are attempts to indicate a possible solution, like Leveque's proposal that the concern in wisdom for a structuring of the created world and the existence of humanity (as the two main themes of wisdom) are to be understood contrapuntally in relationship to the other spheres of the Old Testament – i.e. complementary, though in tension (by contrast, Maillot, who subordinates it to the Torah, oriented on salvation history, is more rooted in the old view). Mention of a 'horizontal revelation' (Gemser, HAT, above 172, 11; Ziener, 263) which appears alongside the vertical revelation in history, is an attempt to refer to this relationship of tension in which both perspectives nevertheless retain their place. However, further reflection is needed on the relationship of the different levels of thought.

The simple statement by Moltmann (*Creation* [above 141], n.8) that 'access to creation faith via wisdom' is to be seen as a complement, is not much more help. Here Pannenberg's notion (*Glaube*, 51) seems to be more promising: he argues that the openness of the reality comprehended in ordinances, which is what von Rad sees as being the nature of Yahwistic faith, 'is to be understood not only as a consequence of faith in Yahweh but at the same time also as the presupposition of faith in a divine action in history' (C.Link, *Welt* [above 142], 268ff., esp. 282ff. argues in a similar way).

By contrast, J.L.Crenshaw ('Prolegomenon', 9ff.) has rightly rejected the fashionable attempts which have often been evident recently to find forms of wisdom discourse and thought in every possible context (for a comprehensive survey cf. Morgan, *Wisdom* [above 170]), as for example in history writing (von Rad; R.N.Whybray, *The Succession Narrative*, SBT II 9, London 1968; Hermisson, *Festschrift von Rad* 1971 [above 60]); in prophecy (J.Fichtner, 'Jesaja unter den Weisen', *TLZ* 74, 1949, 75-80 = *Gottes Weisheit* [above 168], 18-26; W.Whedbee, *Isaiah and Wisdom*, Nashville and New York 1971; J.Jensen, *The Use of tōrā by Isaiah*, CBQ.MS 3, Washington 1973; S.Terrien, 'Amos and Wisdom', in *Israel's Prophetic Heritage, Muilenburg Festschrift*, New York 1962, 108-15; H.W.Wolff, *Amos' geistige Heimat*, WMANT 18, Neukirchen 1964); and in apocalyptic (von Rad). The second of

Crenshaw's objections to the unlimited extension of the sphere of 'wisdom' is important: he argues that it overlooks the existence of a common vocabulary and the universal circulation of many views about the human situation. There is a need to consider further whether, at a late stage of the Old Testament, additions from wisdom have not found their way into texts where they did not originally belong (cf. G.T.Sheppard). However, that would affect only a marginal area. Only a careful investigation of genres will bring the clarity that we need here. It is no more admissible to exclude wisdom from the sphere of the legitimate theological statements of the Old Testament than it is to see it as a key which will help towards understanding all its problems.

Postscript

We have come to the end of our survey of the various groups of problems which have been discussed in the 'theology of the Old Testament' over recent decades. However, it is evident that so far we have not been able to discuss sufficiently the central question which first makes possible a comprehensive theological under- standing of the Old Testament for Christian faith, namely the question of the relationship of the two Testaments and the unity of scripture (it appeared for the first time in the chapter on 'salvation history'). Here a further field of problems opens up, on many levels, which has been recently discussed with increasing intensity because of a realization of the need to recover a biblical theology. A second volume, under the title *Problems of Biblical Theology in the Twentieth Century*, therefore discusses the more recent history of research into the relationship between Old and New Testaments. It is an essential complement to the present work.

Index of Names